JOHN COLTER

HIS YEARS IN THE ROCKIES

By Burton Harris

Introduction to the Bison Book Edition by
David Lavender

University of Nebraska Press
Lincoln and London

First Bison Book printing: 1993

Library of Congress Cataloging-in-Publication Data
Harris, Burton.
John Colter, his years in the Rockies / by Burton Harris; introduction to the Bison book
edition by David Lavender.
p.   cm.
Originally published: New York: Scribner, 1952.
Includes bibliographical references (p.   ) and index.
ISBN 0-8032-7264-2 (pa)
1. Colter, John, ca. 1775–1813. 2. Explorers—West (U.S.)—Biography. 3. Trap-
pers—West (U.S.)—Biography. 4. Frontier and pioneer life—West (U.S.) 5. Yellow-
stone National Park. 6. United States—Exploring expeditions. 7. Wyoming—
Description and travel.
I. Title.
F592.C716   1993
978'.02'092—dc20
[B]
92-41922   CIP

Reprinted from the original 1952 edition published by Charles Scribner's Sons, New
York. The addenda appeared in a 1983 reprint by the Big Horn Book Company, Casper,
Wyoming.

∞

To
Mother and Dad

Table of Contents

List of Maps

Map 1 is reproduced on page xxxviii.
Maps 2, 3 and 4 will be found between pages 80 and 81.

Introduction to the Bison Book Edition

By David Lavender

Who came here first—first to the great sagebrush valleys, the deep mountain passes, the twilight silence of the forests? Americans like to ask those questions. Their country is still young. The exhilaration of exploration, discovery, and conquest can still be relived with a feeling of immediacy.

Such was the urge that consumed Burton Harris, author of *John Colter, His Years in the Rockies,* half a century ago. Although Harris was then living in New York City, he had grown up in Wyoming's Big Horn Basin, at a town called Basin, forty miles south of the Montana border. Because the huge, mountain-rimmed bowl was part of his identity, he began wondering. Who had been the first white person there? Where had he or she come from? How? Why?

The search led Harris to the redoubtable figure of John Colter—so redoubtable that the searcher felt the explorer deserved a fresh, scholarly biography. But soon he was faced with a lack of verifiable material about his subject. Although he worked diligently, the same dearth continued to haunt him twenty-five years later when he was preparing an addendum to the original text of this book.

John Colter probably lived no more than forty years. He was born, presumably in Virginia, sometime between 1770 and 1775. He died in Missouri Territory in November 1813. Nothing is known of his childhood or youth and very little about his final three years. He is said to have been six feet tall and marvelously coordinated, with a countenance like Daniel Boone's, but such statements are stereotypes for almost all pioneers.

He emerged from obscurity late in the summer of 1803 when he enlisted as a private in what President Jefferson called the Corps of Discovery, but which we refer to more often as the Lewis and Clark Expedition. He left the homeward-bound group on August 15, 1806, at the villages of the Mandan Indians in what is now North Dakota. The next four years produced the materials that form the basis of Harris's book. They include a dotted line drawn by William Clark on a highly conjectural map to represent the extraordinary solo journey Colter made during the winter of 1807–8. Then there are stories of four desperate Indian encounters told by three of Colter's contemporaries. Finally it is known that Colter left the beaver grounds of the high country for an edge-of-civilization farm in Missouri Territory. There he married a woman named Sally. Harris said he could not learn Sally's maiden name. Reason enough: as an Indian, Sally had no Anglo-style maiden name—one more example of how elusive Harris found Colter's trail to be.

During such time as he could spare from his office job in New York City, Harris educated himself about the early years of the fur trade as it was conducted in the watersheds of the upper Yellowstone and Missouri rivers. Using that knowledge as his mortar, he built his small blocks of information into the best story of John Colter we have. His production is also one more powerful item in what historian Richard Slotkin labels America's protean and persistent Frontier Myth— not myth as tall tales (Harris devotes his first chapter to those) but myth as a symbolic representation of the nation's view of itself and its historic directions. But let's leave myths aside for the moment while we notice how the author went about crafting the biography presented in this book and its addendum.

The Lewis and Clark material was the easiest for Harris to deal with. The author simply summarizes the long trip from the mouth of the Missouri to the mouth of the Columbia River and back in such a way as to emphasize the episodes in which Colter played a prominent part. The most critical of those events, for Colter, was the party's encounter, during its homeward journey, with two trappers, Joseph Dixon and Forest Hancock. They were following the Corps' outward route in search of unexploited beaver grounds. A guide recruited from the expedition's personnel would add strength to their prospects—or so they thought.

Eager to join them, Private John Colter asked his captains for an honorable discharge from his enlistment. They promptly gave it in recognition of his meritorious services. Colter thereupon led Dixon and Hancock . . . where? During the Corps' homeward journey, Colter had floated with part of the men down the Missouri River. (Clark meanwhile had taken the rest of the troops down the Yellowstone.) Was it wise for Colter to go with his new partners up the familiar Missouri? Meriwether Lewis had killed two Blackfeet Indians off north of that stream, and the tribe was presumably lusting for vengeance. Harris believes that Colter avoided the threat by trapping some of the tributaries of the Yellowstone. It is a logical assumption, but unprovable, although Harris uses local lore and bits of circumstantial evidence to advantage while trying to fill the gaps.

In this section of the book Harris also leans heavily on what might be called biography by association. He explains in detail how the craft of trapping was conducted and how beaver lived. After reading this, we feel we know what was going on and hence we suppose we know what Colter was like. That is to say, Harris, like many good biographers, is asking us to create Colter out of our own imaginations.

Actually our next documented sight of Colter doesn't come until the spring of 1807, when he appears floating down the Missouri—no beaver pelts, no Dixon or Hancock—in a dugout canoe hewn from a cottonwood log. Any furs he had taken during the winter he could have sold to British traders working at the Mandan villages. But we don't know that. Nor do we know with certainty what caused his partnership with Dixon and Hancock to break up. One questionable story does exist, as Harris learned after the first publication of the biography (see the addendum). The narrator of the tale was a hell-roaring Illinois circuit preacher, Peter Cartwright, who says he met Joseph Dixon shortly after Dixon's return from the mountains, bearing a gruesome story. Colter and Hancock, he told Cartwright, had abandoned him, injured and starving, in the snow-heaped Rockies. By embracing religion he survived. Thirty years later Cartwright wrote in his autobiography his memory of what he had heard. Harris is reluctant to accept the story, which he discusses in the addendum, and in the absence of corroboration—Cartwright was using the episode for religious ends—probably we, too, should be cautious.

But let's return to what we do know, thanks to Burton Harris's research. Colter's lone descent of the Missouri River in 1807 ended at the mouth of the Platte River, a dozen miles below the site of today's Omaha. There he encountered the first organized company of trappers to follow the Lewis and Clark trace toward the Rocky Mountains. Led by Manuel Lisa, a native of Spanish Louisiana, the large group contained three former members of the Corps of Discovery, George Drouillard, John Potts, and Peter Weiser. Colter was easily persuaded to become the fourth.

This time the trapper unquestionably saw the Yellowstone River. In his report to the government, William Clark had recommended the junction of the stream with the Big Horn River as a good site for a trading post. Knowing this, Lisa made the confluence his goal. After a suitable structure had been erected there, he sent George Drouillard and John Colter on separate routes into what is now the Big Horn Basin of northern Wyoming—Burton Harris's home territory. Their purpose was to let the Crow Indians know that the newly arrived whites were ready for business. The date: October, 1807, with winter just around the corner.

The only firm information we have about Colter's phenomenal journey, which was much longer than Drouillard's, comes from the dotted line, mentioned earlier, that Clark drew on his "master map" of 1810, later revised and published in 1814. Harris was obsessed by the thought of that trip, which stretched out for at least five hundred miles and supposedly was made alone and on foot, to what end we can't be sure. The author's speculations about it fill a full quarter of his book and an equal chunk of his addendum.

The first part of Colter's route is attested to by Drouillard's notes and a sketch map he handed to William Clark in 1808. There is no doubt, for instance, that both Drouillard and Colter, traveling separately, saw the geysers and hot springs (inspiring the name Colter's Hell) that gushed from the earth beside the Stinking Water (now the Shoshone) River in what became northern Wyoming. But after Colter turned west and southwest, the line marking his route wanders into such a mishmash of speculative geography that reconstructing it becomes impossible, in spite of Harris's valiant efforts, which continued long after the book's publication.

Some of Clark's troubles in mapping Colter's route arose from trying to delineate landforms he had never seen. A far more damaging problem is suggested by his notation on the final map that one could go from the junction of the North and South Forks of the Shoshone to "the Spanish settlement" in twenty-two days. Or so Crow Indians had told Drouillard—assuming always that Drouillard understood them properly. He might not have. He had no fluency in the Crow tongue, or they in English. Nevertheless, he felt he had to pass on to Clark his concept of what the Indians had said.

American frontiersmen of that time were very curious about the fabled Spanish city of Santa Fe. Shadowy contacts between the New Mexican capital and St. Louis had been made as early as 1792–93. Interest soared when the Louisiana Purchase of 1803 expanded U.S. boundaries to the edges of the Southwest. Concurrently, notions sprang up about developing water transport, which was cheaper than horse transport, between the upper Missouri River and Spanish New Mexico by way of a large stream in the West called variously the Collorado [sic] or the Del Norte (the Rio Grande). But where did such odd notions come from?

To oversimplify: when armchair geographers began speculating about the shape of North America, they invented a pyramidal height of land that served as the source of the West's major rivers, which were deemed to flow out from the uplift like spokes from a hub. Some of those rivers, it was argued, had to flow south. Although the conjectured location of the pyramid and its rivers changed over the years, the theory was still very much alive when the Lewis and Clark expedition was getting underway.

Accordingly, President Jefferson instructed the captains to inform themselves as thoroughly as possible about rivers running from the vicinity of the upper Missouri south toward New Mexico and the Gulf of California—all without sacrificing their main goal of reaching the Pacific. In 1804, Manuel Lisa, operating through a partner, Jacques Clamorgan, sent a party overland from St. Louis to open trade with Santa Fe. He also began speculating about linking the southwestern commerce with the upper Missouri fur trade by means of the Collorado or Del Norte, a consideration Harris seems to have missed.

Lisa may well have told both George Drouillard and John Colter that in addition to advertising the new fort on the Yellowstone they should ask the Indians about Spanish settlements to the south. The questioning must have been laborious—stumbling phrases, sign language, guesswork. But something the Indians said in response made the whites believe the Spanish settlements were only twenty-two days away—or so Drouillard reported to William Clark during a trip to St. Louis in 1808.

As for Colter, he took off toward the West and Southwest, searching for . . . what? Spaniards? Indian trade? Or was he just curious about the fur resources of the unexplored land?

Meanwhile Zebulon Pike—and Harris does note this—returned from his southwestern explorations convinced that he had actually seen the fabled height of land in what is now the state of Colorado. Clark incorporated the apparent discovery into the map of the West he was constantly revising. The consequence was an erroneous scrunching together of the central and northern Rockies. The Missouri and the Yellowstone rivers, as he drew them, extended much too far to the south, while the Rio Grande and Colorado reached too far north. His idea, of course, was to make it seem they all arose from the same compressed hump.

Straight through this mutilated geography he drew, in the form of a dotted line, a representation of Colter's presumed journey to the West. (Clark could have learned of the trip into the unknown from either Drouillard or Lisa). All things considered, Harris used his knowledge of the country effectively when reconstructing the early portions of that trip. But when he tried to determine how far west or southwest the trapper went, he came a cropper.

The cause of his error was a piece of lava rock roughly carved to resemble a human head. On it was scratched "John Colter, 1808." The stone had been found by a farmer just west of the Idaho-Wyoming border and had eventually made its way to the museum at Grand Teton National Park. Scholars there decided it had indeed been carved by Colter. That was enough for Harris. John Colter, he wrote triumphantly, had gone as far as southeastern Idaho during his great trek. Unfortunately, at the very time Harris was writing his manuscript, half a dozen similar stones bearing different dates and inscriptions popped up in the same area of Idaho without his being aware of them. It is generally believed now that the carvings had been scattered about as a hoax by young members of Ferdinand Hayden's survey party of 1872. It is the sort of disaster all biographers dread—theories honestly arrived at being destroyed by the emergence of new material. Strangely, knowledge of the purported hoax had not reached Burton Harris as late as 1977, when he was composing his addendum.

The hoax doesn't mean, of course, that Colter did not go as far as Teton Basin. Or farther south to the headwaters of the Green River, which, in fact, is a branch of the Colorado, though there were no Spanish settlements on it then or ever. It is fruitless to speculate. All we know is that the trapper did find a way into what is now Yellowstone National Park and followed another highly conjectural route north to a point labeled "Hot Springs Brimstone."

That spot, not far from today's Tower Junction, has been identified by Aubrey Haines, one-time historian of the Park, as a ford across the Yellowstone River once used by Bannock Indians during their hunting trips. In all probability the Bannock Trail led Colter east across the lofty Absaroka Range and from there down the Shoshone to Colter's Hell, which definitely is not in Yellowstone Park.

As Harris points out, the explorer could have traversed this five-hundred-mile circuit in either direction. Legend insists that he did it alone, on foot, in winter, without an Indian guide to help or an Indian horse to ride once in awhile.

More legendary conflicts with Blackfoot Indians followed his return to the Missouri. All are known to us through tales passed on by three men who heard the original versions from either Manuel Lisa or from Colter himself. The full stories need not be summarized here. But they are suggestive of the way myths take form out of facts.

The first storyteller was Henry Brackenridge. Son of a well-known novelist, Henry had literary ambitions of his own. To further them he went part-way up the Missouri with Lisa in 1811, after Colter had left the mountains. He did not see Colter in person, but he did hear of the mountain man's amazing circuit, undertaken with only his gun and a thirty-pound pack of necessaries—knife, hatchet, flint and steel, blanket, and the like. From this brief description, published in *Views of Louisiana* in 1814, emerges a stylized picture of the pioneer as a lonely trailblazer, powerful, enduring, utterly self-reliant.

Also traveling partway up the Missouri in 1811, but with a different party, was the English naturalist John Bradbury. He definitely did talk with Colter and is a primary source about the trapper's desperate race, barefooted, stripped naked, with pursuing Blackfeet. Bradbury ended his tale by saying, "These were circumstances under which almost any man but an American hunter would have despaired."

The only storyteller who actually traveled the fur grounds of the upper Missouri with Colter was Thomas James. An adventurer and something of a scalawag, James too had literary ambitions. In 1846—Colter had been dead thirty-three years—he published his tales of mountain men in *Three Years among the Indians and Mexicans*. Concerning Colter, he proclaimed, "Such men, and there are thousands of them, can only live in a state of excitement and constant action." All told, Colter furnished "a fine example of the quick and ready thoughtfulness and presence of mind in a desperate situation, and the power of endurance, that characterizes the western pioneer."

Such overstatement is symbolic as well as historic. The frontier has always excited the American imagination. Our views of ourselves and of our expanding nation have always led us to celebrate, often in hyperbole, those of our fellow citizens who dared move beyond familiar boundaries into the unknown. Even before the United States had asserted its full sovereignty over the Far West, Lewis and Clark fired the young nation's pride by physically spanning the entire continent. Following close on the Corps' heels and elaborating constantly on their discoveries came the fabled mountain men of the West. They were far roamers, those insistent beaver hunters, but none of them traveled farther, in those heady days, than did one of Lewis and Clark's principal troopers, John Colter. We can wish we knew more details about Colter's amazing career than we do. But by meticulously molding such facts about him as the author could resurrect, Burton Harris has given us a seminal interpretation of an epic figure in an epical age. Turn the pages that follow and see for yourself.

Foreword

When I was a boy in Basin, Wyoming, the two Civil War cannon in front of the County library fascinated me. The cannon were reputed to have been abandoned by the army near the town site of Basin, during a futile pursuit of an Indian tribe on the warpath. These relics were a constant reminder of one of my earliest disappointments—the realization that, apparently, nothing else very exciting had ever happened in my part of Wyoming, the Big Horn Basin.

The long series of battles with the Sioux and their allies that ended with the Battle of Little Big Horn, all took place on the other side of the Big Horn Mountains. The Lewis and Clark expedition had come no closer than the Yellowstone River, and the countless wagons that rolled over the Oregon Trail had followed the North Platte with no concern for the Basin, a few miles to the north. Chief Joseph and his people in their pathetic flight might have had a glimpse of the Big Horn Basin as they outwitted several regiments of cavalry and escaped to the northeast. And yet the Big Horn Basin was the first part of Wyoming that was known definitely to have been explored by a white man and the last section to be settled. Years later, after I had been working in New York for some time and had found it necessary to develop an outside interest that could offset the worries of an export credit man, I began a concentrated study of just what did happen in the Big Horn Basin. Mr. Edward Eberstadt, well known as a dealer in Western Americana and as a Western historian, encouraged my interest in Wyoming history, and nearly nine years ago suggested that as a native of the Colter country I should try to identify the trail John Colter had followed when he made his epic journey and discovered Yellowstone Park.

The proposal came about due to my chance remark, after reading Stallo Vinton's book on Colter (published in 1926), that it was too bad Vinton had not known there were hot water springs near Cody, Wyoming, and that there had at one time been a great deal of thermal activity there. Mr. Vinton himself then proposed that I should prepare a study of Colter's activities on the basis of the source material cited in his book and my geographical knowledge of the region. The original idea was to try and refute some of the impractical theories that have been put forth about Colter's route by comparing a modern map with William Clark's valiant attempt to portray an involved area he had never seen. We planned to prepare a dry-as-dust treatise on Colter's activities that would be of interest possibly and solely to other specialized students of the period.

When one commutes to New York, has a wife and two active boys, not to mention a home to maintain, there is not too much spare time available for historical research. Thus, it was not surprising that about five years later I had only completed the first draft of three chapters. Mr. Vinton then died suddenly, thereby ending what little collaboration had occurred.

I had been haunted by the concept of the book that I, as a youngster in Wyoming, would have wanted to read at the time I became interested in John Colter—the first white man to explore the region. Colter could not be studied in isolation. Consequently, after Mr. Vinton's death, I embarked on a much more comprehensive program —trying to dig out and bring together every possible sliver of information about the fur trading expeditions of which Colter was a member, and to employ the latest evidence in establishing the truth about Colter's journeys and the routes he followed.

The revised plan made it necessary to trace down many leads to determine whether or not the source material actually contained any new information. This took time, as much of the data was located in St. Louis, Missouri, and Springfield, Illinois. On one visit I located by good fortune in the Missouri Historical Society the map drawn by Clark in 1808 based on information supplied by George Drouillard.

The new program magnified what had been my major difficulty

from the beginning; namely, the setting down on paper of my information. Here again I was unusually lucky in having two writing cousins, Elizabeth Page and Dr. Stuart Tompkins, who gave generously of their time and experience to point out my mistakes and provide genuinely constructive criticism. Mr. Edward Eberstadt, as I have already said, inveigled me into attempting this book and gave me every possible encouragement, but the theories and conclusions described in these pages are my own.

One of the pleasant surprises in this undertaking was the friendly cooperation I received in every reference library to which I appealed for assistance. Before this experience, I, like so many others, had taken for granted the gracious aid that is yours for the asking in almost every library in the United States. However, I had not anticipated the extent to which complete strangers would spend hours searching their records for collateral material for which a direct request had not been made. The staffs of the Missouri Historical Society, Jefferson Memorial Building, St. Louis; Illinois State Historical Society, Springfield; Library of Congress, Washington, D. C., the Yale University Library and the American Philosophical Society, Philadelphia, Pennsylvania, were noteworthy in this respect. I am also much indebted to the Yale Library for permission to reproduce a part of Clark's manuscript map from which the 1814 map was engraved, pertaining to the Colter Route; and in similar fashion to the Missouri Historical Society for permission to use the map drawn by Clark from data supplied by Drouillard. Much of my research was done in Room 300 of the New York Public Library, and thus I was privileged to share with many others the friendly competence of Messrs. Sylvester Vigilante and Ivor Avellino.

Many Wyoming personal friends have helped by reading parts of the manuscript, seeking out inconsistencies and mistakes in geography that might have crept in. Others have tried to run down legends, locate extinct geysers, tar springs, salt mines, and Colter doodlings, or have supplied odd bits of geographical and historical knowledge. So many have responded to my requests for help that I list these friends in the fear I may have inadvertently omitted one or more names: Mr. and Mrs. George T. Beck and Miss Mary Hogg of

Cody, and the following present or former residents of Basin—Miss Elizabeth Page, Judge and Mrs. Percy Metz, Mr. and Mrs. Con Meloney, Mrs. Tacetta Walker, Dr. and Mrs. M. B. Walker, Miss Lola Homsher, Miss Mildred Brown, Mrs. Alice B. Nash, Mr. Robert Brome, Mr. Harold Gartman, and the late Mrs. Vesta Sabin and Mr. Pete Enders. My parents, Dr. and Mrs. H. T. Harris of Basin have aided not only as indicated above but in sundry other ways.

Four people whom I have never met have been most helpful: Dr. Merrill Burlingame of Montana State College, Bozeman; Mr. Mappes, National Park Historian, Omaha; Mr. Breck Moran of Cody; and the late Mr. J. K. Rollinson, formerly of Cody and the Sunlight Basin.

Mr. Emil Henault and his secretary assisted in the translation of the Pierre Menard letter, and Mr. Malcolm Peter Decker has been a good friend and a wise counselor.

From the above resume, it must be quite apparent that this project would have died aborning years ago without the understanding co-operation of my family. My wife, Lorle, has not only put up with my retiring to my study for hours on weekends but has also patiently typed the manuscript over and over again after each revise.

Hackensack, New Jersey
July, 1952

Addenda

The research and writing of *John Colter* took more than ten years. During that period considerable concern had built up regarding the controversies that had been published, particularly concerning Colter's journey in the winter of 1807-08. I used the original William Clark manuscript map, together with Clark's informal cartographic study of the area south of the Yellowstone River, based definitely on information furnished by George Drouillard, and quite possibly John Colter, as well as my knowledge of the Colter country where I lived as a child. My hope was that I had laid to rest most of the theories, based on maps alone, of how a man in the dead of winter could have made such a five-hundred mile trip.

Several years ago I realized the pitfalls of using maps instead of actually visiting the country. Since I had seen the Pryor Mountains from the dining room windows of my childhood home in Basin, Wyoming, I had assumed that Pryor Gap, through which the railroad first entered the Big Horn Basin, was located high on the mountain. Several summers ago I drove up Sage Creek and through the gap. While driving down Pryor Creek, I realized that no panoramic view of the basin was possible because the gap was in a deep valley.

The drive down the Pryor was through the Crow Indian Reservation. In contrast to Colter's day, the only danger was from the little Crow warriors on their minibikes darting from the borrow pits onto the road.

On my first visit to Cody after *John Colter* was published, I asked friends and relatives what leads had developed regarding the "salt cave" on a tributary of the South Fork of the Stinking Water, now named the Shoshone. They said that considerable interest had been aroused and that some people had done some exploring, but with no real results. With very little conniving my friends arranged an interview with the *Cody Enterprise* that focused on the "salt cave" and William Clark's cryptic notation on his informal Drouillard map.

Some time later I received letters from two professional guides who said they were familiar with the area and would be happy to take me into the high country, accessible only in August due to the deep snow during the balance of the year.

Lack of time and poor health ruled out my personal visit to that remote region that had always fascinated me just from studying maps and listening to big game hunters who had been in there. However, my younger son, Frank, was glad to substitute and he made two trips with Anson Eddy as guide.

Since Eddy had mentioned that the game used what he thought was a salt slick, they collected a lard bucket of soil which was later analyzed by Dr. Harold Walton of the University of Colorado's chemistry department. He advised that the tests showed only three per cent of sodium chloride. What the game sought so eagerly that they had dug holes deeper than a man standing up, was calcium phosphate, required for growing horns each year.

In a personal interview, Ed McNeely, the other guide, described a tributary of the South Fork, just downstream from the East Fork of the Shoshone, where sweet water goes into a rock slide from the north and comes out saline.

Frank Harris, on his second trip, could not locate this rock slide, but had the good fortune to meet Fred Fischer, who was doing geological field work for a doctorate, near Needle and Saddle creeks. He was glad to aid in the search for "fossil salt" for a few days. Unfortunately, Fischer, with his expertise, did not find the salt cave either.

I did have the opportunity, however, to discuss with Anson Eddy, who had spent many winters trapping in the area, the possibility of a man crossing the mountains in the winter. Eddy said that Crescent Creek Pass is passable most of the winter because there are not trees on top and the wind blows the snow away. The other passes onto the Wind River are either rimrocked or have deep snow in the timber. In this connection Anson Eddy showed me a Spanish coin, dated 1781, that he had found several years previously on Crescent Creek Pass. The discovery of artifacts as well as large numbers of stone chips and flakes, obviously remnants from the making of stone arrowheads, indicated that the pass had been used by the Indians.

Although the Crescent Creek Pass was known as a well-traveled trail across the divide, that fact does not prove John Colter used it, but merely shows it was possible. Likewise, the finding of an early Spanish coin is not irrefutable evidence that a Spaniard lost it there. Another possibility is that an Indian, with no understanding of money, chose that location to throw it away.

Fred Fischer was more successful in verifying another challenging and characteristically Clark interest note; namely, the "Blue Bead Quarry." Clark's informal map of the country around Cody clearly places the quarry in the Sunlight Basin where Fischer grew up on a ranch. Fred readily located the source of the blue beads as on Pat O'Hara Creek, named for an old trapper who had lived there for nearly twenty years, but had to leave because there were too damned many women around after a man and his wife settled on a ranch more than a dozen miles away. O'Hara is known to have moved to the Big Horn Canyon, but was not seen again. One possible clue to his fate was the discovery, many years later, of a deserted cabin with a skeleton and an old rifle lying in front of it.

In the museum of the University of Wyoming Fischer showed me samples of chalcedony or calcite taken from deposits near Pat O'Hara Creek. Fischer explained that chalcedomy is formed by deposits laid down in the cavities created as vascular basalt cooled off or, as recent, in a geological sense, lava flow. Later the basalt eroded away leaving the deposits exposed or loose. Most of the deposits, judging from the specimens examined, could be readily used as beads after drilling. Dr. Joe Ben Wheat of the University of Colorado advised the writer that the Indians commonly used minute fragments of obsidian on the end of a stick to drill holes in beads. This procedure was similar to the ancient method of starting fires.

The early literature of the fur trade refers to the Absoroka or Crows, among other names, as the "Blue Bead Indians." Anthropologists have also noted that the Crows have a strong affinity for blue in their decorations. Thus it is possible that the Absaroka squaws obtained their blue beads from the deposits long before the beads began coming in from Europe across the Missouri River.

Every biographer plods through his research with the hope that somehow an unknown branch of family may come up with records and recollections of family lore that have not been published. After publication of

John Colter, descendants of the Colter family in Salt Lake City invited me to visit them. I accepted their invitation and learned that they were familiar with only the generally known facts about Colter, but they did show me a well-executed painting of a judge named Colter who lived in Virginia about the time Colter was there. The fact that the painting was not the work of a rank amateur would lend credence to the belief that Colter came from a family with the means to indulge in the luxury of an oil portrait. Thus one tiny thread of evidence is added that Colter was probably not illiterate.

Several years after *John Colter* was published I received a letter from a retired university professor, a descendant of Joseph Dixon. Frank Dickson's letter, dated January 21, 1956, stated that he was the great-great-grandson of Joseph Dixon or Dickson. Professor Dickson said he had been unable to locate any Dickson family papers that related to Joseph's years on the Upper Missouri, but recalled a family tradition concerning the trapping activities of Dickson with two partners during the years 1804–1807. According to family lore in the winter 1806–1807 Hancock and Colter left Dickson, alone and snow-blind, in a cave while they joined a nearby Indian camp where they spent the coldest months cavorting with the Indian maidens.

Dickson family history also relates that Joseph, after his return from the mountain in 1807, spent some years on the Gasconade and then moved to Illinois in 1818 where he settled on Horse Creek in what is now Sangamon County. In connection with this phase of Joseph's life Professor Dickson referred me to the autobiography of Peter Cartwright, the well-known Methodist preacher and circuit rider.

Cartwright was appointed to the Sangamon Circuit in 1823 and in that year journeyed from Kentucky with two companions to locate his future home. One of his companions was another Methodist minister, "old Father Charles Holliday," by strange coincidence, my great-great-grandfather. Cartwright brought his family to Illinois the following year and took up his duties as a circuit preacher. He found that "old Brother Joseph" was an excellent steward, willing to make the rounds of the new settlements and most helpful in collecting his first salary of forty dollars a year.

The two men spent much time together. Cartwright was very impressed by Dickson's account of his conversion to religion as a result of having found a cure for snow-blindness while in the mountains in a cave. The story must have made a profound impression on Cartwright as more than thirty years later he recounted it, in part, as follows:

"Brother D. had been a real back-woodsman, a frontier settler, a great hunter and trapper to take furs. Among other early and enterprising trappers, he prepared himself for a hunting and trapping expedition up the Missouri River and its tributaries, which at that early day was an un-broken Indian country, and many of them hostile to the whites. He made himself a canoe or dug-out, to ascend the rivers, laid his traps, ammunition, and all the necessary fixtures for such a trip, and he and two other partners slowly ascended the Missouri. After ascending this stream for hundreds of miles, and escaping many dangerous ambuscades of the Indians, winter came on with great severity. They dug in the ground and buried their furs and skins at different points to keep them from being stolen by the Indians. They then dug a deep hole on the sunny side of a hill, gathered their winter meat and fuel, their leaves and grass, and carried them into the hole, and took up their winter quarters. The snows were very deep, the weather intensely cold; but they wintered in comparative safety till returning spring, which they hailed with transports of joy. They were robbed several times by the Indians, had several battles with them, and killed two or three of them. The next fall his partners fell out with him, bought a canoe of the Indians, left him alone, descended the river, dug up their furs, and returned home. Dixon fortunately secured most of the ammunition they had on hand. He again found a dreaded winter approaching. He resorted to the former winter's experiment, and dug his cave in the side of a steep hill, laid up his winter provisions, and took up his winter quarters all alone. In this perilous condition, his eyes became inflamed, and were very much affected from constant gazing on the almost perpetual snows around him, until, such was their diseased state, he could not see anything. Here he was utterly helpless and hopeless. He began to reflect on his dreadful condition, which he felt was nothing but certain death, and realized himself to be a great sinner and unprepared to die. For the first time in his life, he kneeled down and asked God for mercy and deliverance from this awful condition . . ."

Cartwright continues the narrative with a detailed description of the experience. "A strong impression" told him to take the inner bark of a tree standing at the door of the cave, prepare a lotion and wash his eyes with it. He awakened the next morning with the inflammation subsiding and his sight entirely restored soon afterward. In gratitude Dickson pledged to serve God faithfully for the rest of his life.

The balance of the story, in Cartwright's words, follows:

"When the weather opened for trapping he said he had astonishing good luck; took a great amount of the very best furs; and collecting them, began to descend the river. He had an Indian village to pass on the bank of the river, and as they were a deceitful, sly, bad tribe of Indians, he determined to keep his canoe as far from their shore as possible. They made many friendly signs for him to stop, so he concluded to land and traded a little with them. He had his rifle well loaded, and was a very strong man. When his canoe struck the bank a large, stout Indian jumped into it, and others were following. He, accordingly, shoved off, when one on the bank raised his rifle and aimed to shoot him. As quick as thought Dixon jerked the Indian that was in the canoe between him and the other that raised his rifle; the gun fired, and lodged its contents in the heart of the large Indian in the canoe, who fell overboard dead. Dixon paddled with all speed down the river, and escaped being robbed or killed. When he returned to St. Louis he sold his furs for several thousand dollars, and returned to his family, after having been absent nearly three years."

Thus, by good fortune, we have three different accounts of the partnership of Dickson, Hancock, and Colter and their experiences during the winter of 1806–1807. Frank Dickson said he was unable to find any family papers that mentioned Joseph's exploits in the mountains. Since it was quite possible that Joseph Dixon was known to Charles Holliday, I searched the Holliday papers in my possession, but to no avail. Consequently, it is necessary to bear in mind that only one account was secondhand and that Cartwright had undoubtedly used the story in his sermons during the thirty years that elapsed before it was committed to paper.

The Dickson version is based solely on family tradition which perforce entails several generations passing on the stories to their descendants. When one tries to verify certain aspects of family lore, as I have done within my own family tradition, it immediately becomes apparent that at least one raconteur in the sequence of relatings has either embellished or modified some facets. Thus, when one studies the three accounts with the above factors in mind, the initial reaction is surprise that there is so much agreement on essential facts.

The major discrepancy is whether Colter or Dickson went off on his own, but the stories do not preclude the possibility that both men went their separate ways. Cartwright did not say that Dickson had been deserted by his companions when he endured the miserable experience of snow-blindness. It is difficult to believe that the preacher would not have emphasized such perfidy if he had been told about it on those lonely horseback rides in Illinois.

Cartwright also refers to a second winter in the mountains, after the partnership of three was formed, which did not occur. In this same connection it is important to remember that Dickson and Hancock were observed trapping as a team by a reliable witness after John Colter had joined the Lisa expedition. Furthermore, there is nothing in the known facts of Colter's life to suggest he would deliberately leave a helpless, snow-blind companion alone in a cave.

The first winter camp of the Lewis and Clark Expedition, across the Mississippi and eighteen miles upstream from St. Louis, has always struck students of the hitherto known papers as an unusually dull and dreary way to prepare for a journey to the Pacific coast. The discovery of William Clark's original journals for Camp Dubois in a forgotten desk in an attic in St. Paul has given scholars considerable new details of the period, even though the journal entries were more like reminder notes than final diary entries.

Captain Clark spent much of his time making astronomical observations while his men erected cabins and bartered for food with neighbors. The nearest were only three miles away. Clark corresponded with Captain Lewis who was enjoying the limited social life of St. Louis. He sent his letters either through the post office at relatively nearby Cahokia, or in the care of carefully selected men travelling by piroque. After delivering the letters they returned upstream with the supplies Lewis had purchased.

John Colter made several trips to town in this fashion. He also did his share of deer hunting on the Wood River. The hunters also bagged many turkeys, squirrels, and rabbits; the latter apparently comprised a substantial part of the party's diet.

Men from the neighboring farms frequently challenged the hunters in shooting contests that ended with the challengers going home penniless, as Clark proudly noted. Colter was among the good marksmen listed. He was also cited among the six men who celebrated the New Year by getting drunk. However, the men were not punished for following an old established tradition. Colter was not one of the two men whose drinking ended in a fight and resulted the next day in having to build a log cabin for the newly acquired washwoman.

On January 17, 1804, Clark made an entry, among many of that busy day, that seemed to indicate that he had loaned three shillings each to Colter and Drouillard, the interpreter. This seems to indicate the esteem William Clark had for John Colter. The debt must have been discharged properly since Colter borrowed later from Clark, after the expedition had been disbanded.

Camp Dubois was apparently located opposite the mouth of the Missouri River, enabling Clark to entertain many of the passengers of boats plying both rivers. Many of the neighbors brought their wives to the encampment. While the wives traded for butter, eggs, and similar food items, the men provided Clark with geographic information of the Upper Missouri. These social calls were not as interesting as the shooting contests. The men were pressed for amusement during that winter which was so cold that some of Clark's wine bottles froze. The daily ration of whiskey was inadequate to offset the penetrating chill. Consequently, more than one "whiskey shop" in the vicinity was well patronized.

Therefore it is not surprising that the Captain's journal entry of March 29th read, as follows:

"Rained last night a violent wind from the north this morning with rain, some hail we have a trial of John Shields, John Colter & Frasure which take up the greater part of the day, in the evening we walk to Higgens a blustering day all day, the blacksmiths return with part of the work finished, river continues to rise, cloudy Day."

William Clark normally conveyed his meanings quite clearly. However, his notations on the following day were exceptions:

"Friday 30th March 1804. a fair day I write engagements & Capt. Lewis I loaded (?) a small pr of Pistols to prevent (?) the consignments do injury Prior is very sick I sent out R Fields to kill a squirwl to make him soup I red the orders on parade this evening J. Sh(Shields) &

J. Co(Colter) asked the forgiveness & promised to doe better in future."

Clark didn't explain why he had to load his pistols, but the two entries reveal a good deal about Clark as a leader.

On May sixth John Colter delivered a letter to Clark, written by an angry Meriwether Lewis. The red-headed Clark must have been strained to the utmost in controlling his temper over an enclosure Lewis forwarded from Washington. Lewis wrote:

"My dear friend,

I send you herewith inclosed your commission accompanyed by the Secretary of War's letter; it is not such as I wished or had reason to expect; but so it is—a further explanation when I join you. I think it will be best to let none of our party or any other persons know anything about the grade. You will observe that the rank has no effect upon your compensation, which by G-d, shall be equal to my own."

The balance of the letter deals with sundry last minute details of preparing for the journey and reflects more explicitly Lewis's irritation. The letter also states that it was carried by Colter and Reed, presumably in the piroque.

The letter from the Secretary of War in addition to asserting that the co-leaders' compensation would be equal, also gave a not very convincing explanation why Clark's commission was that of a Second Lieutenant of Artillery instead of Captain. It did infer that political chicanery motivated a cantankerous Congress to enact such a petty deed. Clark's pride had further cause to suffer since he had previously held a captain's commission and Lewis had served under his command as an ensign.

Clark's reaction could only be surmised until the correspondence between Clark and Biddle regarding the publication of the narrative account of the Lewis and Clark Expedition that was published in 1962. Responding to Biddle's specific inquiry, Clark summed up his sentiments:

"My feelings on this occasion was as might be expected. I wished the expidetion suckcess, and from the assurance of Capt. Lewis, that in every respect my situation Command, etc. etc. should be equal to his viewing the commission as mearly calculated to autherise punishment to the soldiers if necessary, I Proceeded. No difficuelty took place on our rout relative to this point."

The party began their ascent of the Missouri on the fourteenth of May. In reviewing the account of the journey up the Missouri for additional information that might be revealed in Clark's *Field Notes,* the author realized that he had inadvertently stated that the two serious obstacles to travel up the river were synonymous; namely "sawyers and embraras." The sawyers were trees that had fallen into the stream, but continued to be held to the bank by their roots. Embaras was the very apt name the French engagees gave the piles of logs that gather on the upstream side of islands and confine the current into a narrow, rushing channel, most difficult to navigate either ascending or descending the river. Embaras can be translated as embarassing, which seems quite appropriate on this occasion.

In connection with the discussion of the sulphur processing plant along the road west of Cody, Wyoming and the Colter route, it should be explained that the plant was torn down several years ago.

One of the pleasant surprises for me after the publication of *John Colter* was the discovery that many people who had read the book treated me at first meeting like an old friend. Some years ago David Lavender came to Boulder for a Writers' Conference and we found time for a pleasant evening discussing western history.

Some years later Lavender found a letter among the Langlois Papers in the Jefferson Memorial Library in St. Louis and was kind enough to loan me a photostatic copy as he realized its importance to my study of Manuel Lisa's activities while Colter was in the mountains in his employ.

For many years it was believed that Henry's 1810 expedition across the continental divide was the first time that Americans had trapped the streams of the west slope of the Rocky Mountains. A long letter written by Pierre Menard to Adrien Langlois, his business partner and agent at Kaskia, dated October 7, 1809, corrects this error. The letter was written at "Fort Mandanne" and in the beginning discussed personal and business matters. Later, while describing the general experiences of the Lisa Expedition, the letter continued, in translation, as follows:

"The savages do no hunting and are lazy if one is able to put them to beaver hats. There is, however, much to be done here for two years and thereafter more and more often all the reports of the trapping around here nothing at all to compare with that of the lower Missouri. Our men of the first Society, which we found here tell us that one can not imagine the quantity of beaver there is but there is the difficulty of the Blackfeet savages who steal often and who came to our men last spring to make a little fortune. They were obliged to conceal the beginning of the trapping after having been looted not only of their beaver, but also of their horses, traps, ammunition etc. etc.. Except a party of 4 men of whom Case, brother of B. Fortin, was one. He had a cache at the end of October of last year: 20 of beaver and must have at present on hand 50 bales of it. His cache are in the 3 Fourche (Three Forks) but there has been no news of this since last year. However, Mr. Benite tells us he believed them to be in the region of the Taite Plate (Flat Head) and that we will find them this winter.

"Another party of three men have trapped in the upper Missouri and have cached beaver from the Missouri all the way to the 'riviere des Espagnall' (river of the Spanish). This they say incurs no risk whatsoever. The rest of the men after having been looted in the Three Forks, came back to Fort Manuel. After re-equiping they formed a party with Bauvis and Snaguinet and went also to the county of the Spanish River where they say there is much beaver.

"M. Chauplin, a respectable fellow according to all reports, is with the Crows in the third range of mountains and has with him 3 to 4 bales of beaver.

"Mr. Benite is here, having abandoned the fort after having cached his effects and is waiting for us here. He has only 10 robes and 15 skins with him. Mr. Henry left from here with 40 horses and as many men and as for me I leave for above with 50 men to join them. If there is ice this will not prevent us from reaching Fort Manuel which is 200 leagues from here by above. And from there in the spring will go trapping in the Three Forks until 15 June which is the date I leave to go to Illinois—a date which I wish had arrived long before this, not because I cannot resign myself to hardship in order to make money, but the manner of some of our associates displeases me. I would prefer that all the trappers behave honestly, something which is not the case here and often causes some difficulty. This displeases me almost as much as my absence from my family and from all my friends and all of these little difficulties do not gain you anything, on the contrary much is lost and I am annoyed that I am obliged and forced to tell you that we have tricks of the trade (tour de main) 3 times out of four with the engagees and the hunters. Thank God that will end. I am almost sure that I will have no such difficulties with the party I will command. I notice that all of these diffi-culties are disagreeable and that we lose much by them, because it is necessary always to proceed with what is just. I have much confidence in M. Henery. He fits in perfectly as much by reason of his sense of humor as his honesty and his frank manner and his . . . I must tell you also that in spite of the fact that I do not have the highest opinion of our expedition no one knows better than I the advantages and resources of the Missouri. There is no doubt that if a person finds the means to . . . them he will make for himself a great fortune. The whole thing depends upon the way it is done . . . If it is well done one will succeed but if one makes mistakes one can be ruined. I cannot tell you any more about our expedition for the present but will wait to tell you next spring, that is to say in July, the success or disadvantage of our enterprise. Requesting you as always to encourage La Fleur to take good care of the . . . and an-imals and also I entrust to your good judgment my family especially Odill who has the greatest need of it and to let you and my family in no way suffer. Entreating you to assure Mme. Langlois of my respect and your dear children. Kiss for me my daughter Florence and believe in me with the greatest confidence.

Your servant and friend,
Pierre Menard

"P.S. Try to make Dularo and get for him the payment for the . . . which he owes and sell it to our society which will have need of it this spring. Have sent to us also some tobacco.

"Write to me my dear Langlois this spring by all occasions for com-ing up the Missouri. I will find your letters when I go to the . . . and tell me the news."

The balance of the letter refers to family and personal business affairs in Illinois. While he succeeded in giving a picture of the fur trade, Men-ard's handwriting was not of the best, particularly when dashing off a hurried letter. To make matters worse, he wrote phonetically and spelled erratically in French, as was customary with his American contempo-raries writing in English. Since I learned my French by reading and not by ear, I was forced to enlist the assistance of others more familiar with spoken French for both of the Menard letters. Peggy Shipley of Boulder was kind enough to translate the phonics into more or less modern French, but one word did elude our knowledge.

The reference to the "Spanish River" raises several questions. First, how did Menard's informant know it was a stream whose waters eventually would drain either into the Gulf of Mexico or the Pacific Ocean? Years later it was determined that water that originated on Three Ocean Pass actually went into the Atlantic Ocean as well.

Another very pertinent question is, did the name, "Spanish" indicate that there was a Spanish settlement or trading post lower down on the stream? William Clark's note regarding the "salt cave" from which the Spaniards had been taking salt for their settlement twenty-two days journey pack train, or roughly four hundred miles, would logically suggest a trading post on the Green River as a distinct possibility. The Spanish were extremely secretive about their far-flung small trading posts, but there is some reason to believe that at one time there had been such a post on the lower Green River.

Anyone familiar with the region would be inclined to think the headwaters of the Snake River were much more accessible from the upper Missouri and Yellowstone rivers. There are no indications, however, that the Spanish ever got as far north and west to build a post on the Snake.

SOURCES FOR THE NEW INFORMATION IN ADDENDA.

Cartwright, Peter. *Autobiography*. With an introduction, bibliography, and index by Charles L. Wallis. Nashville, Abingdon Press, 1956.

Clark, William. *The Field Notes of Captain William Clark, 1803–1805*. Edited with an introduction and notes by Ernest Staples Osgood. New Haven, Yale University Press, 1964.

Jackson, Donald Dean, Ed. *Letters of the Lewis and Clark Expedition with Related Documents, 1783–1854*. Urbana, University of Illinois Press, 1962.

Lewis, Meriwether.

The Journals of Captain Meriwether Lewis and Sergeant John Ordway; Kept on the Expedition of Western Exploration, 1803–1806. Edited with introduction and notes by Milo M. Quaife. Madison, State Historical Society of Wisconsin, 1965 (c 1916).

Burton Harris
Boulder, Colorado, June 1977

JOHN COLTER

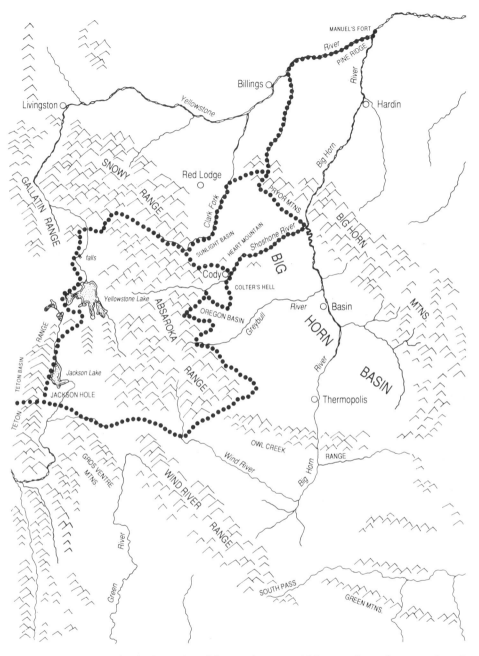

Colter's route is shown by the heavy dotted line on the map, which was redrawn from a section of *Landforms of the United States*, prepared at the Institute of Geographical Exploration, Harvard University, by Erwin Raisz.

Chapter One

Stuffing Dudes

There could be no more appropriate tribute to John Colter than the fact that for a century his legend has descended verbally from one generation to another. Over a period of only seven years, Colter so impressed the men who trapped and battled Indians with him by his awesome solitary journeys and spectacular escapes, that his deeds had become legendary while he was still in the mountains.

Sincere admiration is the only possible reason why Colter's contemporaries, most of whom had had somewhat similar experiences, should have related to all newcomers the essential details of his exploits. The trappers were rarely afflicted with blushing modesty, and preferred as a rule to extol their own accomplishments.

The old trappers who stayed in the mountains after beaver hats went out of style, and served as guides for the soldiers and goldminers and immigrants, would not have bothered to discuss any of Colter's feats with their charges unless they were outstanding. The soldiers and prospectors, in turn, retold the same stories to the settlers and cowpunchers, together with an account of the difficulties they themselves had overcome. Later, the ranchers implanted in their dude-wrangler grandchildren a proper respect for Colter's role as discoverer of Yellowstone Park and Colter's Hell.

The stories about John Colter inevitably attained astounding proportions in the countless retellings; according to some versions of the legend, there must have been times when the wholly fictitious Paul Bunyan and his ox Babe would have been hard pressed to equal what the mortal man Colter did single-handed. This was the result of every narrator adding little personal touches from his own knowledge.

The trappers, with their wide experience, and ample time to concoct imaginative interpretations, brought the art of telling stories to its highest stage of perfection. The effectiveness of yarns of this type depends to a considerable degree upon the circumstances under which they are related. The ideal setting is for both the narrator and his attentive audience to be watching the ever futile struggles of a camp-fire against the overpowering shadows of the night.

In some western states this technique of elaboration to the point where it merges into untruth, is called "stuffing dudes." Every native-born westerner numbers among his inalienable rights the license to use this technique upon occasion, and considers it a gross breach of hospitality if a visitor leaves without having had a few whoppers thrown in with the usual descriptions of the country and its customs. Several subjects are rarely discussed under such circumstances without stretching the truth, and in telling the Colter legend, by tradition it has become almost compulsory to exaggerate. And since no one can study Colter's accomplishments without being affected to some degree by the contagious desire to improve on truth, I have thought it wise to work off my touch of the disease in Chapter One. Stern searchers after fact are hereby directed to begin reading at Chapter Two.

An old time cowman might relate the *legend* of John Colter in some such manner as this:

"And there was the time when John Colter was jumped by two Indians on the Stinking Water. Old Colter was a-squattin' down alongside a beaver pond, doctorin' up one of them lures with that come-hither-beaver stuff the old trappers carried in a bottle strung 'round their necks, when out of the tail of his eye he seen a bush startin' to shake but he knowed the wind wasn't blowin' that hard. So just as calm as a stuffed mule he started linin' up the best way to make a run for his gun—a-leanin' agin a tree a good rope's throw away—and if anybody should'a knowed better, it was Colter.

"But anyway, between him and that rifle he seen a clump a bushes, thrashin' around like ten mangy bears scratchin' themselves with all four paws at once, and a young buck Indian comin' straight at him with a long stick, with the end all decorated with feathers and stuff.

2

Well, sir, an old trapper like Colter, he didn't need no diagram to tell him that when an Indian with hardly no clothes on, waving a *coup* stick, just plows straight through a bunch a buffalo-berry bushes, he definitely ain't goin' to no tea party.

"So, sudden like, Colter figured that at least two Indians was between him and his gun and the rest of his party, so he better git goin' in another direction; and he just slung that heavy old iron trap right at the nearest Indian and lit out across that there beaver pond.

"Well, them poor beaver must a thought a herd a buffalo was stampedin', the way Colter jumped, splashed, swum and dived through that little pond, slingin' mud, water and sticks in all directions. Colter he had already sized up that puddle, and knowed that it just weren't deep enough or big enough for him to swim under water a piece, and then hide somewheres with just his nose outa water as he done one time on the Three Forks of the Missouri. He just had to keep goin', and hope that none a the arrows he stopped when he come up for air would do more than just pretty him up a bit.

"But he clumb out the other side without stoppin' nothin', and started lookin' around and then he seen he was really in for it. Them two Indians wasn't shootin' arrows at him at all, but was crossin' on the riffle below the dam so dainty-like that they hardly wet their moccasins. They was fixin' to run him down and bust him over the head with that fancy *coup* stick, as that counted heavier than just a plain scalpin'.

"Course Colter knowed that with that feathered stick you had to hit a horse fly just right to cripple him, but that once he got rapped with it, then them two would probably catch him, tie him up, and let the squaws kill him slow and painful-like; and if it took a week, the better the women would like it. Naturally, Colter didn't hanker fer none a that stuff, so he cuts right up the little draw to the top of the bench and starts to run.

"I've heared it said that Colter had to go at least two miles before he even got warmed up, and I disrecollect how long it took for him to get his second wind, but anyways he was beginnin' to put distance

3

between him and them two Indians, when he starts havin' trouble with the bottom of his pants. He was wearin' a brand-new buckskin suit he had just gotten off a little Crow gal fer a few beads and female doodads; I don't rightfully know if the deal covered anything else; but that there suit was just fresh offa an old buck deer and hadn't been tanned so good, so with all that water from the beaver pond, it started them pants legs to stretchin' longer and longer. So Colter he just has to slow down and try to hold up his pants, but it wasn't long until he had about two feet of leather floppin' around on the end of each leg, so then he tries to take 'em off, but can't untie the rattle-snake skin suspenders.

"So all he could do was to jump and scramble around. By this time them two Indian bucks was a really gainin' and Colter he just kept goin' the best he could. Finally, about the time he started steppin' on the front of his shirt, he tripped over a runty little sagebrush that shouldn't have bothered nothin' bigger than a baby ant, and took an awful fall in a cactus bed. Maybe you don't know it, but it's a lot easier to git into a cactus bed than git out, and by the time Colter was on his feet there was one Indian buck all set to whack him with that *coup* stick. So what does old Colter do but let him have a big gob a tabaccer juice right between the eyes and then grab the second Indian, take good aim and blind him with the rest of his chaw.

"Well, sir, it just wouldn't be possible to find two more surprised Indians. They was blind as a cave full of bats, and the hollerin' and runnin' around and frantic rubbin' that went on would a been funny, if Colter's pride hadn't been hurt by them two catchin' him because of his floppy pants. But then he decided he just wasn't mad enough to scalp 'em, so he grabbed a holt of both of 'em, cracked their heads together a few times, took all their knives, and bows and arrows, and then headed them for the high badlands. Just so there was no mistake, he give each one a swift kick in the pants, except they didn't have no pants on, and it ain't no fun kickin' tough Indians with only moccasins. Cow boots would a been much better, but then you can't run far with cow boots, no matter who's chasin' you.

"Well, that Colter he was such a powerful feller, he just took them Indian bows and busted them across his knee and then broke

4

the arrows and tomahawks and started back to pick up his traps and find his gun.

"Old Colter was a funny cuss. You know he went back to camp that night and didn't say nothin' about what had happened? The reason was because of what happened when he got back from a trip he took by hisself once in the dead a winter—the time he walked more than five hundred miles and only discovered Yellowstone Park, Wind River Valley, Jackson Hole and a few other places, when all he was supposed to be doin' was to look up a few Indians and tell 'em they was buildin' a fort on the Big Horn.

"Well, sir, there was one of them French *fiancées* or engaged men or whatever you call 'em, who was always a joshin' Colter about Colter's Hell. That was 'cause when Colter got back he told everyone about them geysers squirtin' hot water all over the landscape, and about the boilin' tar springs, and the flames jumpin' right outa the ground while the earth trembled and growled underneath, and how you could scald your foot just by breakin' through a piece of stuff that looked like stone. Of course, them old trappers used to spend a lot of time thinkin' up good stories, and so they figured that durin' all the months he was by hisself, Colter had got a mite looney, if he weren't just as crazy as a bedbug, anyway.

"But then some a them fellers had knowed Colter when he was with Lewis and Clark, and he just didn't have no reputation as a liar at all. Anyway, Colter he finally got so mad that he took some of his friends over to the Stinking Water and showed 'em a few geysers and such-like around where the river comes out of the canyon between Cedar Mountain and the Rattlesnake, just above where Cody is now. Naturally that shut up all them old trappers. They seen that Colter wasn't lyin', and so they began tellin' all the newcomers about Colter's Hell; and some a those fellers really worked at spinnin' yarns, so much so that Colter himself hardly knowed he'd ever seen what they was talkin' about. But there was always some dumb skull that didn't have the guts to go and see fer hisself, and was always makin' dirty cracks, like the French feller that just stayed around camp, cuttin' wood, cleanin' pots and doin' all the dirty jobs.

"Well, this particular cuss was so unusual worthless, that some

5

folks used to say that if his mother had knowed when he was born just what a no-good skunk he was goin' to grow up to, that she would have knocked him in the head and sold her milk. Now it comes hard to git more no account than that. John Colter was a feller that could hang onto his temper real good, but when he got riled up he was worse than a wildcat after a turpentine bath, so he just kept still and didn't say nothin' to nobody. You want to know how come I know all about it? It was thisaway.

"I heard 'bout old Colter gittin' away from them two Indians from my Grandpa, who first started prospectin' in the Big Horns right after the Civil War. He told me one time that he was a followin' a trace of gold up a little creek and he bumped into an old trapper that had holed-up in a little shack up there, 'cause he didn't want no white woman around. Now this trapper (I fergit his name) told Grandpa that old Colter had learned him how to trap beaver before he dried out behind the ears. He stuffed him full a stuff about Colter.

"And that's how I come to know about Colter's escapin' from the Indians with a good chaw, and also how them old trappers used to gallivant around in the snow when it was only thirty below. Grandpa told me about one trapper fallin' in the creek one mornin'—he wasn't quite sure that it was Colter—but anyway, he scrambled out of there fast and then found that his buckskin pants was froze so solid that he made a terrible racket and cut hisself every step, and then he slipped on some ice and busted them frozen leather pants into a thousand little pieces. Well, even a trapper that ain't seen soap in ten years has got some feelin's and this one he just lit out for his camp a couple a miles away and would a had no trouble at all, even if he had cut hisself bad when he fell, 'cause the blood froze in all them wounds; but he darned near bled to death when he thawed out.

"Grandpa used to say that John Colter was just about the toughest man in the mountains and that when he made that trip to Colter's . Hell alone, all he had to sleep in was a four point Hudson Bay blanket. He'd get down in the holler under a big pine tree and bur- row into the snow and then just drop off to sleep like a baby. As a matter of fact, Grandpa told me that Colter gave up usin' a four point after that trip, 'cause he used to sweat somethin' awful unless it was twenty below and the wind was blowin'.

"Grandpa wasn't the only one to tell me that Colter was a good hand with a rifle. I don't know if Colter ever had one of them Hawkins's or not—the barrel that after five years took puny-sized cannon balls, and kicked like all the mules in Missouri put together if the barrel didn't blow up in your face. Most trappers would never bother to shoot a beaver because you had to hit 'em where they couldn't flop into the water and sink to the bottom, and naturally a few bullet holes in the good middle of the skin just ruined the worth of that pelt. Colter, he took care of that by just hittin' 'em in the eye so the ball came out through the other eye. For a time they say Colter tried hittin' one eye so that the bullet came out the mouth, but he gave that up after a time when he found he was gettin' so many ricochets off the beavers' teeth.

"All them old timers never stopped talkin' about how good a hunter old Colter was, and they always laid the discovery of how to kill side-hill gophers to Colter. It happened he seen a bunch a Indian bucks comin' through the snow with nothin' on but a pair of moccasins and that there cloth they wore around the middle stuck full of knives, and them leather-bound rocks tied to a stick that some people call tomahawks, but they were skull-crackers if you ever seen one. Well, Colter he took to the timber and kept a-goin' as fast as he could, but he reckoned that any bunch of Indians runnin' around in that weather in their bare skin was mad about somethin'.

"Now Colter hadn't et for a couple of days and he just couldn't get far enough away from that outfit to shoot any game without their hearin' the rifle shot. After a time he was gainin', when about three miles away he seen a side-hill gopher. This critter was a-comin' along the side of the hill and it was plain as daylight just where he was goin', so Colter hid behind a boulder along his trail. He had seen 'em before but never took the time to study their habits much, so as he waited with a hunk a greasewood in his hand, he watched the gopher comin' along the side of that hill.

"Well, sir, he at first thought his eyes was playin' him tricks, but soon there just was no doubt about it at all. That gopher was trottin'

7

along that steep hill standin' straight up 'cause his inside legs was shorter than the outside. Colter, he figured them gophers had lived so long on steep hills their legs had adjusted theirselves to the slope, but he was studyin' the matter so hard he almost let the gopher pass, and could only hit him a glancin' blow. But the gopher was took by surprise so bad that he tried to turn around and ended up rollin' down to the bottom of the hill.

"Old Colter he kept right after the gopher until they come to a level bit a ground and then the gopher just kept a-runnin' around in a circle. Now Colter really hated to do it, but he needed meat awful bad so he just hit that poor little side-hill gopher on the head every time he come around until he fixed up his supper without firin' his gun.

"There don't seem to be nobody but me that's heared about what Colter seen in the Sunlight Basin. When Grandpa told me this story, he said I better see this place for myself before I started talkin' about it. I ain't never had the time to git over into that part a the Basin, but I figure as that old trapper that told Grandpa about it said he seen it many times, then it's all right I should let you in on it. Colter was trappin' one time way up in the Sunlight Basin when he come onto a little creek with a beaver pond. He had plenty a time, so he sat down on top of the cliff and started studyin' them beaver.

"All them trappers was always tryin' to figure out if they was an engineer beaver that bossed all the others around, marked each tree to be gnawed down and calculated just where she would drop. Well, sir, he soon seen that them beaver just didn't act like other beaver. Most a the time you see a beaver he is just a-workin' or a-gnawin' away or a-swimmin' or a-beatin' his tail, but here there was five beaver all lined up just a-sittin' there and a-starin' at an old tree. The others was a-workin' away as usual, but all of a sudden there was a big commotion and all them beaver started bangin' their tails and yippin' and yappin' as loud as beaver can yip and yap, and soon he seen they was all crowdin' around one beaver. This beaver had the sleekest fur and Colter was fixin' to git him some way, even if he had to shoot him and dive for him afterwards. But then he seen that all them beaver was watchin' this glossy feller run up to a tree and just make the chips fly, and then tackle another bigger tree and kept that up so it looked like it had snowed.

"Colter he started wonderin' just how long the beaver was goin' to keep chawin' wood, when all of a sudden the noise stopped and all them beaver was lined up behind that one who had been doin' all the gnawin'. That slick beaver just sat and looked at that tree between two rocks that didn't have no branches. There wasn't a sound from anywhere, except the water tricklin' through the dam. All at once that young beaver he run up to that tree and started to gnaw, but it made the queerest noise and the sparks started flyin' out, and then he dropped on the ground and didn't move a muscle. Then the darndest racket started, that sounded most like fifty Indian squaws a-hollerin' and a-bellerin' after all their men folk got scalped. Well, finally, two beaver come up and pushed and pulled that beaver into line with the other five that had just sat and stared at that old tree all the time.

"Well, Colter, he seen the other beaver goin' off about their business very sad and down in the mouth and he just couldn't restrain his curiosity no more, so he clumb down to see closer. As soon as they heard Colter, all them workin' beaver jumped in the pond and disappeared except them six lined up starin' at that tree. When he got closer he seen the ground was covered with white stuff near that tree, but it wasn't wood chips; it was busted beaver teeth and that tree was petrified, and was held up by two rocks.

"Well, Colter, he picked up that glossy feller by the scruff a his neck and put him out a his misery. Them other beaver he seen when he got close up was all grey and their fur was moth-eaten and they was awful poor and skinny. Well, sir, he found them beaver was just completely frustrated, and couldn't do nothin' but set there and stare. They couldn't even eat as their teeth had growed back so fast and long they made bars across their mouths, and they was just starving to death. Well, sir, Colter, he found out that about once a month them beaver made a ceremony of some young buck takin' a crack at that petrified tree, but they all ended the same way; busted their teeth, and then sat there and starved to death. That was how Colter discovered Crazy Beaver Creek."

In my mythical version of the Colter legend there has been a slight use of the "stuffing dudes" technique. However, let it be understood that this is the only instance in this book where the luxury of improving the story has been indulged. There will be legitimate inference, but no more witting invention. In the event anyone seriously desires to study the habits of the lop-sided gopher, it should be said that it would be a waste of time to look for them. Likewise it is not recommended that anyone should wear out many maps or boots in a search for the lugubrious beaver colony on Crazy Beaver Creek. It is, however, a fact that beaver must use their teeth constantly for gnawing wood, otherwise the rapidly-growing teeth form bars across the mouth. Finally, the late E. C. Burroughs, formerly of Basin, Wyoming, and one of the last of the leather craftsmen who made a work of art out of a saddle, reported years ago that on a hunting trip in the Sunlight Basin, he found a petrified tree standing straight up because it was supported between two rocks.

Chapter Two

With Lewis and Clark

Until a lie detector is devised that will analyse the printed page, the extent to which the legend of John Colter has permeated western literature cannot be assayed. Many books, written with more concern for entertainment than the accurate reporting of historical events, include at least one fanciful version of a Colter exploit. Their authors, once in full creative flight, rarely retard it by earthbound references to dusty source material. In many instances, it is a waste of time to seek the unmentioned authorities for the lurid anecdotes, and upon occasion the question arises whether the author may not have stimulated his invention by something more potent than black coffee.

Grave historians are popularly supposed to have winnowed every fact they have written down with the same majestic impartiality that a giant combine separates a field of ripened grain into sacks of wheat, straw and windblown chaff. The truth is, however, that just as the threshing machine occasionally sorts into the grain sack a few weeds and pebbles, the serious writer also incorporates into his text fragments of a legend or popular conception of an event, without a trace of authority. During extended research into, and assembly of, indisputable Colter sources, it appeared that historians as highly regarded as Coutant and Hubert Bancroft were not above making positive statements without the slightest qualification, although study of their cited authorities revealed clearly that what they said could only have been conjecture. New material, subsequently discovered, proves this beyond a doubt.

The strong appeal of Colter's extraordinary exploits and the scarcity of first-hand information are the obvious reasons for this situation. When one considers that the first written record about

John Colter that has come to light so far, is his enlistment in the Lewis and Clark expedition on October 15, 1803,[1] it is not strange that many writers resorted to some fabrication. At the time of his enlistment Colter was probably close to thirty years old. The exact date of his birth is not known, but Thomas James who knew him in 1809 estimated he was then about thirty-five.[2]

This assumption, that he was born around 1770, is consistent with the family belief that his birth took place in Virginia between 1770 and 1775. More than twenty years ago, Stallo Vinton, during the preparation of his book on John Colter,[3] made an exhaustive search for members of the Colter family and obtained from them what scant information about the discoverer of the Yellowstone had come down in the family traditions. By their testimony, the founder of the family in America was Micajah Coalter, who was believed to have come to Virginia from Ireland about 1700, although he was actually of Scottish descent. The Coalter family had various holdings of land around Staunton, Virginia, in the district known as "Stuart's Draft." The modification in the spelling of the name to Colter evidently began with Michael, the eldest son of Micajah Coalter, who was also the grandfather of John Colter. There were some members of the family who used the spelling, Coulter.

The changes in spelling brought about by several generations within the family were nothing in comparison to those achieved by Captain William Clark as he grimly made his daily journal entries, in compliance with the rules laid down for the expedition by President Thomas Jefferson. The self-educated captain created much confusion regarding the proper spelling of Colter's name, by using the three commonly known versions as well as inventing several more which were original with him. Writing in an era when considerable latitude in spelling was permissible in educated circles, Clark was exceptional in the variety of ways he could form the same word on the same page. This trait has loosened a flood of "sics" and learned sneers from most of the scholars who have worked on the original Lewis and Clark journals. The pedagogue who prefers to turn his back on the world that surrounds him and employ the less painful method of absorbing knowledge by reading, usually is unable to comprehend what rare courage the proud and sensitive Clark was displaying every time he made his copious journal entries, regardless of grammar and orthography. They also ignore the fact that, despite Clark's erratic spelling, his writing is often more effective than that of the well-educated Meriwether Lewis.

There are available two slim bits of evidence that Colter knew how to read and write. Two signatures in the possession of the Missouri State Historical Society support the contention that he was able to write at least his name.[4] These same small specimens of his writing also ended the controversy about its correct spelling. Since their discovery, his name has been spelled as John Colter. Aside from the circumstance that it is an exceptional person who can write but not read, the proof of his reading ability depends solely upon a deduction. Among the items that made up the pathetically brief list of personal effects which were sold at auction after Colter's death, were three books, titles not indicated.[5] There is nothing in Colter's career to prompt the faintest suspicion that he would ever have acquired books he could not read to impress his neighbors.

The good possibility that Colter was not a stranger to a schoolroom is furthermore consistent with the few isolated bits of family lore that are available. Additional data from the same source reveal that the family was probably in reasonably comfortable circumstances, as they were landowners, and one of Colter's cousins was a doctor, while another had been a judge. Thus there is nothing to substantiate the rather commonly held conception that John Colter was an illiterate backwoodsman, who knew no more practical application for a writing quill than to pick his teeth with it.

Such information as we have points to the probability that Colter was brought up on a farm, and this assumption is in keeping with the tradition of his outstanding feats of woodsmanship that have persisted around Staunton, Virginia. In fact, his competence in the woods is also a part of the family legend, together with the proud knowledge that he was a member of the Lewis and Clark expedition. Colter never returned to his home in Virginia and this undoubtedly explains why the family possesses no first-hand information about his most spectacular achievements.

The final contribution from the family recollections is, that for unknown reasons and at an unspecified time, Colter accompanied his cousins, the two Ray brothers, to Maysville, Kentucky, there to intercept Meriwether Lewis on his way down the Ohio.

There is no question, however, that John Colter enlisted as a private in the expedition on October 15, 1803, at Maysville.[6] Unfortunately, Captain Lewis, who had brought the keel boat down the river, did not make any entries in his diary from September 18th to November 11th.[7] This inexplicable gap in an otherwise detailed journal deprives us of any detailed analysis of Colter's qualifications, as was given for several others. Our disappointment at not having available what should have been an excellent summary of Colter's background and experience should not make us too severe on the young captain. When Lewis resumed his daily notation, he made not the slightest reference to the cause of his lapse, but if ever a man had an ample assortment of alibis for not keeping his journal, it was Meriwether Lewis. Some months before, while Lewis was the President's private secretary, Thomas Jefferson had selected him to organize in secret an expedition to the Pacific, and, if necessary, go up the Missouri River without the knowledge of the Spaniards who still controlled the Louisiana Territory. The President, with his insatiable interest in innumerable subjects, had superimposed upon the primary objective, a vast number of specific instructions for detailed studies along botanical, zoological, geological, geographical, ethnological and anthropological lines, to mention only the major fields of interest. In addition, Jefferson arranged for Lewis to take cram courses in mathematics, celestial observation, and kindred subjects from the outstanding scholars of the day.

After a few weeks of struggling to assimilate an enormous mass of special knowledge, Lewis hastened to Pittsburgh to arrange for the construction of a keel boat. There he found no rest for his agitated mind, as he grappled with the involved problem of keeping the best builder sober long enough to finish the keel boat. His hopes for a restful voyage down the Ohio were soon a sour memory, as he and his makeshift crew struggled with the countless sandbars that filled the Ohio while at the lowest water level in years. Furthermore, he was not then aware that Clark, his old neighbor and one-time commander, had decided to share with him the joint command of the expedition.

Such variegated worries and problems should entitle anyone to a prolonged sick headache, and in Lewis's case might have justified his indulging in a final spell of melancholia, before he became subject to the inflexible military discipline that dictated the conduct of the expedition as soon as it was formally organized. There is also the chance that he did not so indulge himself, but rather had an attack of malaria.

In view of the hiatus in Lewis's journal, we must turn to Thomas James for a description of John Colter, the man. James knew Colter as a member of the Missouri Fur Company in 1809, or after he had had the maturing experience of six years in the mountains. However, his estimate is quite important, as it was formed in the enforced intimacy of a small trapping party invading the territory of the hostile Blackfeet. James described him as: "about thirty-five years of age, five feet ten inches in height and wore an open, ingenious, and pleasing countenance of the Daniel Boone stamp. Nature had formed him, like Boone, for hardy indurance of fatigue, privation and perils." The two most outstanding achievements of Colter were performed alone; therefore, the following comments of James are most pertinent: "His veracity was never questioned among us and his character was that of a true American backwoodsman." [8] James added that Colter had to a supreme degree that instantaneous coordination which was always possessed by those pioneers who lived to die with their boots off and in their own beds.

We may infer some of the qualifications that Colter must have demonstrated before he was permitted to sign his name to the expedition's roster. Lewis, in a letter to William Clark dated June 19, 1803, set down the standards both captains used in selecting recruits as, "good hunters, stout, healthy, unmarried men, accustomed to the woods and capable of bearing bodily fatigue in a pretty considerable degree." [9] Rich men's sons seeking adventure were specifically excluded by the realistic leaders as they chose the civilians and soldiers who made up the roster from the frontier settlements and army posts along the Ohio River.

William Clark joined the party at Louisville, Kentucky. In agreeing to accept the dual command of the expedition with Captain Lewis, Clark had magnanimously swallowed an enormous quantity of injured pride. Lewis had offered him the dual and equal command on the strength of Jefferson's promise that both men would receive captain's commissions, but a cantankerous Congress chose to make Lewis a full captain and Clark a second lieutenant. This capricious act was bitter gall to Clark who had resigned a captain's commission some years before, and had had Lewis serving under him as an ensign. Lewis gave Clark his word that regardless of the commissions, the two men would in all respects share the command, and there is no indication that the bargain was not scrupulously fulfilled.[10]

Thus the two boyhood friends, with rare mutual trust, surmounted a contemptible bit of political chicanery and led the expedition past an involved diplomatic tangle at St. Louis to an encampment on the Illinois side of the Mississippi, at the mouth of the Wood River. Arriving in December, the party hastened to construct shelters for the long damp winter months, while the practiced soldiers began teaching the newly enlisted civilians the meaning of strict military discipline. John Colter was one of the first civilians to enlist in the expedition. The two Field brothers, Reuben and Joseph, actually head the roster. The camp had been placed strategically beyond the jurisdiction of the Spanish governor in St. Louis, and was well situated for training the men and preparing for the long journey ahead. The men may have failed to appreciate this factor, as they lived and drilled in a virtual wilderness, just a few miles from the lively town of St. Louis and other less enterprising villages along the river. Toward the end of February, boredom and the natural desire for a last fling, brought about a relaxation in discipline that ended in Captain Lewis making several entries in his orderly book, dated March 3, 1804. Two men who subsequently took leading roles in many aspects of the expedition's activities—Reuben Fields and John Shields— were strongly censured for disciplinary reasons. Four others were confined to camp for ten days because their hunting activities had for some time centered around "a neighboring wiskey shop." John Colter was one of the culprits, and the other three were, Bolye, Wiser and Robinson.[11]

While the men absorbed their rigorous training program and experienced the peculiarities of Illinois mud in the early spring, some complicated European diplomatic developments were finally communicated officially to the Spanish governor at St. Louis. In March, 1804, he received properly signed and sealed confirmation of what everyone had known for weeks, that Spain had relinquished her rights in the Louisiana Territory to France. Napoleon's representatives had been more promptly advised of the succeeding change; thus the day after they received jurisdiction of the territory, they transferred title to the American representatives and thereby recognized one of Jefferson's most outstanding and audacious accomplishments. Consequently, three flags flew over the territory in a twenty-four hour period.

Captain Lewis, by means of frequent trips to St. Louis, had kept abreast of the diplomatic developments and in the process enjoyed an active social life. The transfer of the territory to the United States eliminated many problems for the leaders and enabled them to concentrate on the accumulation of requisite supplies. It was discovered that thermometers and barometers were needed, and none could be procured. The versatile Dr. Saugrain supplied the lack by making the instruments from materials he had on hand. The two captains were far more delighted than the resourceful doctor's wife, for he obtained the needed mercury by scraping the back off her best mirror, imported from France. The erudite doctor also aided the expedition by producing a supply of the newly invented sulphur matches.[12]

The expedition got under way on May 14, 1804. John Colter had been assigned to the command of Sergeant Ordway, whose squad became the crew of the large bateau. This vessel, better known as a keel boat, was fifty-five feet long and drew three feet of water. There was a large square sail to be used when there was a following wind, otherwise the boat was propelled by twenty-two oars or hauled by the cordelle line, drawn by men walking on the bank. Colter's assignment to such unromantic labor may not have been alone the result of his misdirected hunting, as John Shields was one of the two official hunters during the first few weeks.

The flotilla ended its "shakedown cruise" by stopping at St. Charles on the Missouri for a few days to rearrange the cargoes, add supplies that had been overlooked, and await Captain Lewis' arrival, since he had been delayed several days in St. Louis. This small town, with its population of over four hundred, was the last glimpse of urban living the party was to see for many months. There were some clearings and trading posts along the river after leaving St. Charles, but the expedition soon settled down to laborious effort as they tried to average better than ten miles a day against the Missouri's current.

John Colter evidently accepted with grace the drudgery incumbent upon a member of the crew, and his name was mentioned in the journals for the first time, after the departure, on June 29. He was listed as a member of the court-martial that sentenced Collins and Hall respectively to 100 and 50 lashes. The extent to which Colter had redeemed himself is emphasized by the fact that the two men were tried because Collins had kept such conscientious watch over the whisky barrel that both he and Hall had become thoroughly saturated with its contents.[13]

Joseph Whitehouse, in his brief but vivid journal, described an event on July 7, 1804, that probably had much to do with Colter being mentioned frequently thereafter as one of the party's hunters. Whitehouse's ungrammatical, but pithy comment was: "towards evening a man espy'd a wolf lying a sleep with the noise of oars racing he awoke stood to [k]no[w] [w]hat was a coming captn Lewis shot at him wounded the animal, Colter like ways killed him it was thought he was mad when the first bawl struck him he snap'd at his hind part Roed 15 miles." [14] There were other incidents attesting to Colter's marksmanship, but none more graphic.

One member of the expedition was an obvious exception to the exacting conditions that governed the two captains in the selection of their command. George Shannon was from a good family in Pennsylvania, but lacked the primary prerequisite of a woodsman—a good sense of direction. On August 28, Shannon and George Drouillard, or Dweyer as both captains usually spelled the name, were searching for the party's two horses. Drouillard became separated from Shannon and, despite his unusual tracking ability, was unable to pick up the trail of Shannon or the two horses. Later, it developed that Shannon had found the horses, but was then lost himself and started upstream under the mistaken belief the boats were ahead of him.[15]

The following day, John Colter was ordered to take some provisions and overtake Shannon. Five days later, or September 3, the captains noted that tracks had been found indicating that Shannon and the horses were still heading upstream with Colter doggedly following. On September 6, Whitehouse, in one of the last entries before he gave up his unequal battle with grammar and spelling, mentioned that Colter had rejoined the party without having found Shannon. On the same day, Sergeant Gass stated, as usual without mentioning any names, that they had found Colter's camp with a scaffold of neatly dried meat.[16] Sergeant Ordway, in his thorough way, carefully item- ized Colter's bag of game as: "one buffelow, one elk, 3 deer one wolf 5 turkies and one goose one beaver also." [17]

While Colter had killed far more game than he could possibly eat, Shannon, when found on September 11, was almost starved, not hav- ing had any food but wild grapes and one rabbit. The small creature that would not have represented one good meal for an outdoor man, had been hit with a piece of hardwood that Shannon had found could be fired from his gun. He had futilely shot away all his lead bullets. Later, Shannon learned how to shoot straight, and also how to read sign, as well as smell out the country enough to locate the evening camp site.

These incidents must have satisfied the co-captains that Colter was more valuable as a hunter, ranging along the course of the river in search of game for food and the supplementary geographical informa- tion that broadened the scope of their maps, than pulling a heavy oar. Dating from the time that Shannon was lost, John Colter was regularly mentioned as a hunter.

In fact on September 24, Colter killed four elk and innocently began a series of occurrences that ended in one of the most ticklish situations met with on the entire trip.[18] The elk had been killed on a small island and while the meat was being loaded into the boats, Colter discovered that his horse, tethered on the river bank, had been stolen. Subsequently it was learned that five Teton Sioux, from a band that had been threatening trouble for several days, had taken the horse. The captains attempted to cajole and placate with a few presents the Sioux bent on loot, but the sullen, irascible disposition of the Indians yielded nothing to diplomatic finesse. Then all members of the party demonstrated their willingness to fight if necessary. The piratical Tetons, having been faced and glared down, there began the appropriate and prolonged exchanges of social amenities which included hours of dancing, smoking, speech-making and feasting. During the several bouts of gorging, puppies, a Sioux delicacy, were served, but the whites did not relish the tribute, and at the conclusion of the festivities departed upriver without the stolen horse.

The tribes above the Tetons were in a much better humor, so the expedition arrived on October 26 at the Mandan villages without any further unpleasant experiences. The relatively gentle Mandans, living in their large earthen lodges, had long before established themselves as friendly hosts; thus it was inevitable that the captains should have planned to go into winter quarters with these light-skinned and brown-haired people. The winter camp was constructed in the form of an enclosed triangular fort, a short distance from the main village, and was named Fort Mandan.[19]

The hunters had to be out for game almost constantly and there were several stolen-horse alarms to stir up those who remained in the fort. These also had to entertain or watch a continuous stream of visitors from the Mandans, as well as the Gros Ventre of the Missouri and the Minnetarees, now designated as the Hidatsa. The preparations for the explorations ahead were interrupted by polite calls from traders of the Northwest Company, who were wintering in the circular log houses of the Mandans and Gros Ventre. The two captains greeted them more or less cordially; then courteously, but firmly, informed them of the government's policy, and pointed out that they were on American soil.[20]

The jack-of-all-trades of the expedition, John Shields, improvised his own tools, repaired equipment and fabricated trade goods for the

Indians. His gifted hands and mechanical mind eventually were of more benefit to the expedition than several extra boatloads of trade goods. Sacajawea,* the wife of the newly acquired interpreter, Toussaint Charbonneau, gave birth to her first son and so added gynecology and pediatrics to the cares of the captains. York, the negro slave of Captain Clark, enthralled all the Indians, especially the squaws, with his kinky hair, phenomenal strength and color that would not rub off.

The journal entries of all the diarists were on the sketchy side during the winter months at Fort Mandan. There is not a single mention of Colter's name during the stay at the triangular fort. Thus he must have been satisfied with his normal holiday ration from the

---

* Pronounced in Shoshone as Sa-ca-jaw-ea, according to Dr. John Roberts, Missionary Clergyman of the Episcopal Church on the Wind River Reservation for the Arapahoe and Shoshone from 1883 until his death three years ago. Dr. Roberts spoke both Shoshone and Arapahoe fluently, as well as his native Welch, both North and South. In an interview on July 12, 1946, at his home which had formerly been the school for Shoshone girls, Dr. Roberts was at first quite reluctant to talk about his early experiences, but finally, after a familiarity with Wyoming history had been proven, he spoke freely of Chief Washakie of the Shoshones and Black Coal, an Arapahoe leader, whom he regarded as the peer of the Shoshone in several respects, and his equal in others, including statesmanship. My notes quote Dr. Roberts directly, as follows: "I knew Sacajawea well; there is no doubt in my mind that she is the Shoshone woman who went with Lewis and Clark. Some commercial man at the Mandans wrote that the Snake wife of Charbonneau died. He was a Frenchman who lived with the Indians and may have had several wives." Dr. Roberts elaborated on the above by saying that he had known Sacajawea well during the last year of her life, and that he, as well as other whites on the reservation, had been reluctant to believe her story until she told of many aspects of that trip that would not have been known to anyone unless they had actually participated, since there was no mention of them in the published journals. He said that the Rev. James Patten had known her much longer than he and that he also was certain she was the guide on the expedition. I also knew Mr. Patten as he lived in the next block from my home in Basin, Wyoming. He left Basin when I was a boy, and I, unfortunately, have no recollection of having discussed Indians with him. During the same period. Mrs. Alice B. Nash gave me a warbonnet that had belonged to Andy Basil, the son of the five-year-old nephew Sacajawea had adopted. Mrs. Nash had spent several years on the reservation and has a very high regard for Dr. Roberts and his work. For a more detailed discussion, see Dr. Grace Raymond Hebard's "Sacajawea: Guide of the Lewis and Clark Expedition," Arthur H. Clark Co., 1933.

An important factor to be considered in this question is the credibility of Dr. Roberts. His standing among the people in Wyoming who were acquainted with him and his selfless devotion to helping the Indians adjust themselves to an unwanted mode of living, is of the highest, and numbered among his admirers are some who ordinarily have little regard for churchmen. His indomitable spirit was apparent when I first saw him, standing in the chicken yard in clerical garb, cutting down tall weeds with a sickle so that the snakes would not get at his chickens. At that time he was in his nineties, and his sight had failed to the point where he had difficulty distinguishing objects smaller than doors and windows. His life, consecrated to helping his fellow man, both Indian and white, deserves a thorough study.

whisky barrel, and behaved himself in other respects. If he was not always discreet, he was at least lucky, since he is not numbered among the men who received treatment for various ailments.

The severe winter finally passed and the boats were with difficulty released from the thick ice along the shore. Packs were again filled for the canoes and pirogues with which the party was to proceed up the river. On April 7, the keel boat cast off, laden with letters, reports, maps, and chests crammed with the hides and bones of strange animals such as the antelope for Thomas Jefferson.

The rapacious current had no sooner borne the keel boat out of sight in the direction of home, before the flotilla of canoes and pirogues began anew the task of mounting the Missouri. Paddles, long sweeping oars, poles and cordelling lines taut over the men's inadequately covered shoulders, impelled and hauled the wooden craft past the drab hills split by the green-fringed river. John Colter was among the men who had good reason to debate the eternal problem of whether the paddle was part of him or he a part of the paddle. Until the boats reached the Great Falls of the Missouri, Colter's name was never included among the hunters and did not reappear until the men were conveying the packs and canoes over the portage. The wheels for a vehicle had been made by sawing circular pieces out of a log, and this contraption, which bore some resemblance to a cart, was used to transport the heavier equipment to the river above the falls.

Colter was then relieved of this duty and joined the hunters in their campaign to provide dried elk meat for the mountain crossing that lay ahead. Captain Lewis also needed many elk skins for his pet project, the iron boat frame. Sufficient hides were obtained to cover the frame, but his iron boat was doomed to sail no further than to the bottom of the river, since pitch to caulk the seams could not be found. Lewis accepted with philosophy the drowning of his long cherished scheme and promptly set about locating a large tree which the expert axemen could shape into a canoe.

The further the party had progressed up the Missouri, the more "white bears" they encountered, and with each meeting their respect increased for the dangerous, powerful beast now known as the grizzly.

Several members of the expedition learned very soon that unless they killed the grizzly in his tracks with the one shot possible from a flintlock rifle, they had to get out of reach up a tree to avoid being torn apart. Captain Clark was leading a group of hunters on an island above the falls when a "white bear" attacked Willard, who promptly fled to the camp. Clark, aware that Colter was alone on the lower end of the island, immediately collected his men and went to Colter's assistance. Colter had been unable to find a large tree and had therefore made an ignominious but effective retreat into deep water. He was able to get back on the island only after the bear retreated to the brush as Clark and his men approached. Other members had to resort to jumping into the water to escape from grizzlies, a fact for which Colter must have been grateful, as otherwise he would have been the sole butt of many expertly conducted joshing sessions around the campfire.[22]

The little fleet of canoes ascended the Missouri to the Three Forks and then continued up the Jefferson as far as it was possible to paddle or drag the canoes. From that point, Captain Lewis and two companions went on foot until they finally succeeded in establishing communication with the Lemhi Shoshone. The large herds of horses owned by this branch of the Snake Indians represented the expedition's sole chance of transporting their goods and baggage onto the navigable streams of the Pacific slope. This meeting on the mountain top was given unexpected drama by the reunion of the Shoshone woman Sacajawea, not only with her people, but also with their chief, Cameahwait, her brother, from whom she had been separated by capture years before.

Shortage of food forced the captains to curtail the ceremonies on the continental divide, and Clark set out with a small party to test the feasibility of descending the nearby Salmon River by canoe. Several days of following the rushing waters of the Salmon through rough country, and the paucity of dried salmon—the only food obtainable from the few Indians encountered—soon convinced Captain Clark that this route was quite impracticable. He, therefore, wrote a letter to Captain Lewis, stating his findings as well as his recommendations for their future course, which were based on information from the Indian guides. Colter was selected to take the message back to the

Shoshone camp. This was actually a promotion for Colter, as it signified that he had advanced to that select group whose members the two captains considered competent to undertake difficult assignments on their own.[23]

Lewis had succeeded in obtaining by barter all of the horses and Indian saddles that were needed, by the time the two groups were reunited. The route proposed by Captain Clark was adopted, and an old Shoshone was persuaded to act as guide. The expedition, now mounted on horseback, followed the meandering Indian and game trails that wound through the Bitter Root Mountains to a navigable branch of the Columbia River. Game was scarce and the already familiar sensations of empty stomachs were aggravated by the altitude.

The hunters ranged far ahead and parallel to the main body as they gradually descended the Bitter Root Mountains into the Flat Head country. Colter, while seeking game, met three Tushepaw Flat Heads pursuing two Shoshone Indians who had stolen twenty-three head of horses. The Indians became alarmed upon seeing Colter and strung their bows for instant action. Colter soon relieved their fears by following the Indian custom of laying his gun on the ground and advancing with empty hands outstretched. By means of the sign language he was not only able to explain where his party was going, but also to bring the Indians into camp. There, one of the braves was prevailed upon to abandon the serious business of chasing horse-thieves and possible scalps to become their guide. The Shoshone guide was no longer in familiar or friendly territory and was anxious to return to his tribe. Thus Colter's impromptu diplomacy secured for the party a competent guide at a time when the scarcity of game and rapidly approaching winter made it imperative that they descend from the mountains.[24]

Two weeks later, on September 24,[25] Colter was ordered to go back along the trail to hunt for some lost horses and retrieve a canister of powder that had been left behind at an old camp. Three days later, Colter rejoined the main party where they had camped with a Nez Percé village. He had found one horse and the lead container which kept the powder dry, and later could be melted down for bullets. This clever ammunition case was typical of the careful planning and preparation which made the expedition successful. Colter had also brought in a deer, half of which he gave to the Nez Percé, while the balance went into nourishing solid food for the many members of the expedition sick with dysentery.[26]

The Chopunnish Nez Percé had gladly shared their limited food supplies with the half-starved strangers who had descended upon them from the mountains, but their strange diet of camas roots and salmon was too much for digestive systems accustomed to meat and very little of that. On many different occasions, John Colter had demonstrated that he possessed extraordinary stamina, and during this period of recuperation he and Drouillard were the only ones able to leave the camp and hunt day after day. The conscientious captains administered to the needs of their men with scrupulous devotion. The fact that they usually prescribed bloodlettings, purges, Doctor Rush's pills and even some Indian sweat baths, and followed out their drastic treatments with vigor, undoubtedly resulted in no one's reporting sick unless he could no longer walk. Colter's name never appeared on the sick list during the entire journey and this healthy constitution had much to do with his subsequent accomplishments.

The men gradually became adjusted to the diet of roots and dried salmon, and no sooner were they able to leave their sleeping robes than they began hacking away at one of the five large trees that had been felled to make canoes. The task was completed before all of the men were back on their feet, but arrangements were soon concluded for leaving the horses with their Indian hosts and caching the saddles and other surplus equipment. The boats were launched on the Kooskooskee or Clearwater on October 7, and the expedition set out on the last stage of the journey. The following day a large tributary now known as Potlatch Creek was named Colter's Creek.[27] Most members of the party had their services honored in similar fashion by the co-captains.

The rapids of the Kooskooskee immediately put all the expert boatmen to most rigorous tests which were passed with a minimum of accidents, but which had to be repeated during the rapid descent of the Snake and later the Columbia. No sooner were the broad tidal waters of the Columbia reached, than strong winds and driving rain forced the heavily loaded canoes ashore. The storm continued for several days with such violence that the party could not move to more adequate shelter and secure anchorage for their boats. The men spent a week, crowded on narrow rocky beaches or on drift logs, not entirely out of reach of the thrusting waves. Worn, rotten sleeping robes and over-turned canoes afforded little protection from the driving rain and effectively retained the water, so that the men were soaking wet and thoroughly miserable.

The wretchedness of their situation was climaxed by the daily sight of the Indians skillfully paddling their canoes up and down the river, alternately riding the crest of the waves and disappearing from view. Several men volunteered to make the desperate attempt to round the headland with a light Indian canoe. Willard, Shannon and Colter after several trials succeeded in passing the headland, and continued on to search for a good harbor as well as some white men from the expected trading ships.

Colter, returning alone to report on their discoveries, arrived just as a small party of Indians was visiting with the men of the expedition. Their behavior had from the very beginning aroused suspicions, for two squaws refused to come ashore preferring to stay in the canoes and bob up and down with the waves. Both captains concluded that the natives had taken something from the party down the river, and Colter confirmed their deductions by relating that his gig and basket had been stolen. One of the men on shore kept his gun trained on the Indians while Colter searched their canoes and recovered the stolen property.[28]

After the move to a more comfortable location was completed, Captain Clark announced that all those who desired to see the actual waters of the Pacific Ocean should join his party. Ten men, including Colter, Shannon and York, signified their wish to see the actual goal of the long journey. Sacajawea, displaying far more interest than her husband, begged to be taken along, and her coaxing was rewarded by permission to join the party. Clark commented that all of the others were content to view that part of the ocean that could be seen from their campsite, and, as he inferred, from a reclining position.[29]

Upon the return of the party from the short but arduous trip to the shore, Captain Lewis set out with several hunters, including Colter, to find a suitable location for the winter fort. Later it was decided to erect Fort Clatsop on the opposite bank of the river. During the construction of the fort, Colter escaped the drudgery of swinging an axe, as he was one of the several hunters who were ordered to tramp the surrounding hills in search of elk and deer. Since it rained almost constantly, he probably conducted an unending debate with himself as to whether he really was among the lucky ones. During the wet winter months, the journals of the two captains made frequent mention of the hunters spending days in succession away from the fort. Extraordinary efforts were being made, not only to supply the men with adequate meals, but also to prepare a large supply of jerked meat to take up the river on the return. Ample quantities of game were often obtained, but the meat usually spoiled before they had enough sunny weather to dry it properly.

In order to preserve the meat, a salt-still had been set up on the coast. The salt makers, by dint of constant effort and attention to their small, improvised still, eventually produced several bushels of salt. The oozing, wet winter days were spent in constant watch for a trading ship, irrespective of other activities. Captain Lewis had in his possession what was probably the broadest letter of credit ever issued. It had been written by Jefferson as President, and committed the United States government for any amount that Lewis chose to draw. However, any worrying that the Treasury department officials may have done about the possibilities inherent in such an unrestricted document was wasted, as no trading vessels arrived in the Columbia while the expedition was there. The party had counted heavily on buying trade goods on the coast, and was therefore seriously embarrassed by the uninterrupted stream of Indians trying to sell everything they owned or controlled to the white men. The already depleted stock of barter goods had to be doled out carefully, to make the indispensable presents to the ranking chiefs and to purchase from the squaws those articles of clothing that the men were unable to make properly for themselves. The captains employed their leisure time in compiling with painstaking care their voluminous notes on all conceivable subjects, or copying what the other had written so as to have an extra record of all pertinent data.

Finally, on March 23, 1806, the canoes were again loaded. The men, surfeited with the rain and clinging dampness, were now anxious to start back home. During the last weeks of the stay at Fort Clatsop those men who were not actively engaged in hunting or tending the salt-still had acquired a number of ailments, most of which originated from inactivity. In contrast to the majority, Colter had to reconcile himself to an abrupt change from the liberty of a hunter privileged to stay out and roam for days, to the narrow confines of paddling a canoe. The next mention of Colter was on April 8, when a stiff wind forced the boats to the protection of the shore. Colter was among the four hunters selected to try and replenish the meat supply, but all he got was the welcome chance to stretch his legs.[30] The next day the expedition was having breakfast in the village of the Wahclellah, when Colter noticed a tomahawk that had been stolen the previous November. He immediately seized the tomahawk and held on to it until other members of the party intervened, despite the spirited objections and struggles of the Indians.[31]

As the canoes ascended the river, food became scarcer. The prepared supplies had been eaten and they found it impossible to buy sufficient roots and salmon from the Indians. The Indians did not have enough for themselves, and with the acute shortage of trade goods, the leaders were unable to bargain effectively. Consequently, their ideas about the principal table delicacy of the Sioux underwent a profound change, and dogmeat came to be regarded as a delectable dish. In fact, Lewis became so provoked at one Indian for jeering his men while eating it (because his tribe preferred to starve rather than consume canines) that he struck the tormentor and almost precipitated a serious fight. The food situation improved after they succeeded in trading for a few horses to be eaten on the last stage of the return to the Chopunnish village overland.

Early in May, as the expedition was nearing the place where the saddles and supplies had been cached, the captains bought a young colt which was destined to provide the evening meal. The wild young animal was entrusted to the care of Drouillard and Colter. The prospect of a good evening meal would normally make for a genial mood, but for reasons undisclosed by the captains in their diaries, the two men quarreled. The leaders omitted any further reference to the instigator or the victor. This was the only instance where Colter became involved in a personal altercation that merited comment in the journals, whereas Drouillard's name was mentioned in several similar fracases. George Drouillard, the official hunter and interpreter, was half Pawnee—the balance was presumed to have been French. He was not subject to the strict discipline of the military personnel, and it would have been in character for him to have rubbed in his special privileges while he and Colter, with nerves already sharp from hunger, tried to cope with the antics of their animated supper.[32]

The horses of the expedition were punctually restored to them by the Nez Percé chief, Twisted Hair, but not so fat and rested as anticipated. The young Indian bucks had been racing them. Some of the caches were found to have been opened and robbed. However, it is to the eternal credit of the Nez Percé that most all of the missing articles were eventually returned.

The salmon had not arrived in the Kooskooskee when the party arrived, and the Indians were extremely low on food. Therefore, the hunters combed the hills and valleys for miles around for deer and bear, while more substantial shelters than were customary for the usual overnight bivouac were being prepared in the camp. The snow was deep in the Bitter Root Mountains and generous supplies of jerked meat had to be available for the return crossing.

Permission was granted daily to a select few members of the expedition to visit the Nez Percé village some distance away and trade for their own account. Months before, each man had been given small, easily-carried trade goods that served as spending money. The dearth of trade goods had magnified the value of the trinkets that remained; all the men scraped the bottom of their pockets for anything with bartering possibilities. The captains wisely encouraged the men to exploit their own individual relationships with the Indians in the hopes of obtaining the largest possible return from meager assets. On June 5, Lewis noted in his journal that Colter and Bratten had been fortunate in their trading for roots and bread, and had made a good return.[33]

The scarcity of game, coupled with the lack of articles for trade, created a serious problem, which the leaders met with an uninhibited versatility. The expedition had for some time resembled a traveling medicine show more than a military unit, as the appeal of Peter Cruzatte's fiddle had been frequently exploited; and now the men were encouraged to put on their boisterous dances around the campfires every night for enrapt Indian audiences which should have been well qualified as judges of such demonstrations. Another source of revenue was the thriving business Captain Clark conducted in bottles of eyewash. Many tribes had an unpleasant custom of killing unsuccessful medicine men; consequently Clark's active medical practice for all conceivable ailments required as much courage as technical knowledge. In the case of the eyewash he was on safe ground, for the Indians were badly in need of any possible relief from the irritation to their eyes of smoke-filled lodges and a most improper diet.

After one abortive start, the expedition succeeded in reaching the high country where they found that enough snow had melted to permit the passage of the horses. Reluctant to spend another winter in the wilderness, the party pushed on through the still deep snow, despite an almost total lack of game.

During one difficult passage over the Bitter Roots, Colter's horse fell with him while crossing a creek. Both horse and rider were rolled down stream among the rocks for a considerable distance by the rushing, icy water. Fortunately, Colter suffered no serious injury although his blanket was carried away by the current. Demonstrating the practical, instantaneous judgment that characterized him, Colter held on to his rifle rather than the blanket. At this stage, a gun was of far more value than a blanket, even though it was early spring in the mountains.[34]

By afternoon of the same day, Colter had so far recovered from his unexpected bath that he joined Gibson on a fishing excursion. The venture was productive of a single salmon—one which had expended all its substance keeping alive in the mountain stream throughout the winter, rather than one completing its migration from the warm ocean waters with bones well protected against the frigid waters. The men had been so persistent in their attempts to provide fish for their dinner, they had not only broken several gigs, but had experimented a long time before they were convinced that it is almost impossible to shoot fish, except in a barrel.[35]

Upon reaching the Clark's River, now called the Bitter Root, or St. Mary's River, the expedition divided in accordance with a prearranged plan. Captain Lewis took nine men and crossed over to the Falls of the Missouri where the pirogues had been cached. Captain Clark continued up the Bitter Root with the balance of the party, among them Colter. This party proceeded to the head of the Jefferson River, where the canoes and supplies concealed on the westward trip were entrusted to Sergeant Ordway and his men. The descent of the Jefferson by canoe and horseback was most pleasant, notably to those who, after many months of privation, were again supplied with chewing tobacco lifted from the caches.

The party again divided at the Three Forks of the Missouri. Captain Clark's group ascended the Gallatin River under the competent guidance of Sacajawea, and then crossed over to the Yellowstone River by what is now known as Bozeman's Pass. Inelegant but sturdy boats were built at the Yellowstone, and the bulk of the party embarked on the swift waters of that river; on the other hand, Sergeant Pryor and two men undertook to bring their horses overland to the Mandan villages. The Crows, in later years noted for their friendship for the whites, signalized the occasion by an adroit theft of their horses. Sergeant Pryor's party had to resort to bull boats made of branches and skins as a result of this demonstration of the Crow's most outstanding talent.

Colter was one of the nine men under the command of Sergeant Ordway ordered to take the six canoes to the Great Falls of the Missouri. The Sergeant's lively journal reveals this trip, away from the driving captains and without pressing time limitations, as one of the most pleasant phases of the entire journey. The canoes floated quietly along with the men only rarely using the paddles, but on the alert for all manner of game. The Sergeant's daily entries consisted largely of such items as: "Colter killed a panther and a deer and a rattlesnake." [36]

The idyll terminated all too soon and the small party undertook to convey the baggage and canoes to the less turbulent waters below the falls. Ropes were employed to let down some of the canoes through the rapids, but on July 26, 1806, Sergeant Ordway observed: "Colter and Potts went at running the canoes down the rapids to the white peroque near the carsh." [37] Whenever the small canoes were used by the expedition, Colter's name was conspicuous by its absence from the list of hunters, implying that though an excellent shot, it was preferable he handled a paddle. The casual decision to run the canoes over the falls and the fact that Colter's name was never mentioned in connection with a canoe that ran afoul of the rocks, is rather conclusive evidence that he was competent in a light boat.

Captain Lewis had been urged in his orders to explore the sources of the Marias River, and for this reason he set off on the northerly course of that stream with Drouillard and the Field brothers. Sergeant Gass was left in charge at the lower deposit to await the arrival of Sergeant Ordway's party. Lewis, after having accomplished his purpose as well as time, the weather, and a shortage of game would permit, turned south toward the Missouri. While descending the South Fork of the Marias River, they encountered a party of eight Blackfeet Indians with whom they made all possible peace overtures. Against their desires, they encamped with the Indians for the night and with constant vigilance all went well until early dawn. Joseph Fields, on guard while the others slept, carelessly left his rifle beside his sleeping brother and turned his back. The Blackfeet immediately seized the party's four rifles, and the three men awakened at Field's shout to find themselves armed only with knives and pistols. During the ensuing struggle Reuben Fields fatally stabbed one Indian in the heart and Captain Lewis, having wrenched his rifle from one Blackfeet, finally killed another who refused to release his horse despite repeated warnings. The small command was hastily assembled as the Indians fled. It was found no one had been seriously hurt and one horse had been stolen. However, they had acquired two guns and most of the Blackfeet horses. The fresh horses enabled them to make a precipitate retreat from the scene of battle to the relative safety of the Missouri, and the combined parties of Sergeants Ordway and Gass.

Captain Lewis was understandably anxious to leave the Blackfeet country and hurried the preparations for departure. The two smallest canoes were sent down the river on July 29, the two Field brothers in one, and Colter and Collins in the other. Their orders were to hunt meat and prepare elk hides to cover canoes and protect the men from the weather. On August 3, the main party passed the canoe of Colter and Collins without their knowledge, as the men were hunting away from the bank. Since the two had not caught up by August 5, Captain Lewis ordered the main group to lay over and wait for them. However, the party set out again at noon. There was a possibility that the two men had passed in the night, as had almost happened in the case of Sergeant Ordway.[38]

Arriving at the mouth of the Yellowstone, August 7, Captain Lewis found that an onslaught of mosquitoes had driven Captain Clark and his party on down the Missouri from the appointed meeting place. Lewis's party continued on in pursuit of Captain Clark, after leaving a note wrapped in leather for Collins and Colter, secured to a pole stuck in the sand at the junction of the two rivers. His own near escape naturally made Captain Lewis apprehensive about the safety of the two men and he confided to his journal that "Colter and Collins have not yet overtaken us I fear some misfortune has happened them for their previous fidelity and orderly deportment induces me to believe that they would not thus intentionally delay." [39]

On August 12, 1806, Lewis described the events of a day of great importance to John Colter. "Being anxious to overtake Capt. Clark, who from the appearance of his camps could be no great distance before me, we set out early and proceeded with all possible expedition. At eight A.M. the bowman informed me that there was a canoe and a camp he believed of white men on the north east shore. I directed the peroque and canoes to come too at this place and found it to be the camp of two hunters from the Illinois by name Joseph Dickson [sic] and Forrest Hancock. These men informed me that Capt. Clark had passed them about noon the day before. They also informed me that they had left the Illnois in the summer of 1804, since which time they had been ascending the Missouri, hunting and trapping beaver; and that they had been rob[b]ed by the Indians and the former wounded last winter by the Tetons of the Birnt woods; that they had hitherto been unsuccessful in their voyage having as yet caught but little beaver, but were still determined to proceed. I gave them a brief description

33

of the Missouri, a list of distances of the most conspicuous streams and remarkable places on the river above and pointed out to them the places where the beaver most abounded. I also gave them a file and a couple of pounds of powder with some lead. These articles which they assured me they were in great want of. I remained with these men an hour and half, when I took leave of them and proceeded. While I halted with these men, Colter and Collins who separated from us on the 3rd inst. rejoined us. They were well, no accident having happened. They informed me that after proceeding the first day and not overtaking us, they had concluded that we were behind and had delayed several days in waiting for us, and had thus been unable to join us until the present mome[n]t." [40]

Thus did Captain Lewis calmly report the first meeting with white men since the expedition had left Fort Mandan, and the appearance of two men for whose safety he had been much concerned. Restrained comment was typical of both captains and only rarely did events cause them to lose their dispassionate objectivity.

Shortly after the meeting with Dixon and Hancock, the myopic Peter Cruzatte blasted away at what he evidently thought was an elk, but which unfortunately proved to be the leather suit of Captain Lewis. The rifle shot entered the fleshy part of his thigh, but did not prevent Lewis from organizing a defense against the Indian attack of which he believed himself to have been the first victim.

The joy aroused in Captain Clark's party at the sight of Lewis's boats, quickly changed to concern when the leader's figure was missed, since he was lying on the bottom of the boat. Subsequently the drastic treatment by Captain Clark, despite frequent faintings on the part of the patient, brought about such rapid recovery that Lewis was able to be about by the time they reached the earthen lodges of the Mandans. Surrounded with their log palisades and cultivated fields, the permanent dwellings of the Indian traders of the Missouri reminded the travelers that they were rapidly returning to civilization.

Chapter Three

Winter on the Yellowstone

The two trappers from Illinois, Dixon and Hancock, talked continually to all the enlisted men during the descent to the Mandan villages, but their most attentive listener was John Colter. The two trappers were low on ammunition after two years of hunting and trapping on the Missouri River. Measured in beaver skins their luck had been bad, but in the sense of still being alive after escaping from the Teton Sioux with no more serious hurt than a slight wound in Dixon's leg, they had enjoyed a bonanza of fortune.

The partners from Illinois had analyzed their situation after meeting Captain Clark, and concluded that not only did they need more ammunition and sundry other supplies, but that they should try to recruit another man into the partnership. Sergeant Ordway's journal entry [1] reveals that in their sales talk to the enlisted men, the two trappers emphasized the furs they had already "carshed" in the ground, and subtly played down their narrow escapes and the serious losses of property they had sustained. Lewis and Clark were perhaps more persistent in asking pertinent questions, as their accounts of the success of the trappers were far more somber than that of Ordway.

Earlier entries in Sergeant Ordway's journal disclose Colter's reason for listening so attentively to the proposal of Dixon and Hancock. Ordway's diary was published exactly as he wrote it; thus it was not edited into a model of propriety as was that of Sergeant Gass.[2] His daily entries from the time the party recovered their boats on the return trip relate in detail the extent of trapping for their own gain undertaken by many members of the expedition. The journals of Lewis and Clark refer only to trapping done by Drouillard, the official hunter, but give no explanation as to why he concentrated so intensively on obtaining zoological specimens of beaver and ignored other animals.

35

Traps cannot be set out and the catch cleaned and skinned surreptitiously. The iron traps of that period were heavy and cumbersome. Such noisy, weighty objects could not have formed a part of the minutely regulated baggage of the expedition without the full consent of the two captains. There is only one logical answer, and that to the distinct credit of Lewis and Clark. They had wisely decided that the enlisted men, earning only five dollars a month, could not be expected to cruise on streams swarming with beaver, the most stable unit of frontier currency, and not be tempted to procure some skins for themselves. This considerate decision was contrary to army regulations, but it may be presumed the men's trapping activities did not interfere with the progress of the expedition.

Ordway's journal contains many entries itemizing Colter's bag of game and beaver. Therefore, it could not have been a surprise when, on August 5, 1806, John Colter applied to Captain Clark to join Dixon and Hancock. In view of the unwarranted interpretation that Biddle placed on Colter's action when writing the narrative of the expedition, Clark's frank comments are most important: "Colter one of our men expressed a desire to join some trappers (the two Illinois men we met, and who now came down to us) who offered to become shearers with [him] and furnish traps etc. the offer [was] a very advantagious one, to him, his services could be dispensed with from this down and as we were disposed to be of service to anyone of our party who had performed their duty as well as Colter had done, we agreed to allow him the privilage provided no one of the party would ask or expect a similar permission to which they all agreed that they wished Colter every suckcess and that as we did not wish any of them to separate untill we should arrive at St. Louis they would not apply or expect it etc." [3]

Years later, Nicholas Biddle, in the seclusion of his study in Philadelphia, and perhaps fatigued from the hardships of the expedition he had vicariously undergone as well as worn from months of effort condensing the voluminous journals into a readable narrative, described Colter's leaving the expedition as follows: "The example of this man shows how easily men may be weaned from the habits of civilized life to the ruder but scarcely less fascinating manners of the woods. This hunter has been now absent for many years from the frontiers, and might naturally be presumed to have some anxiety, or some curiosity at least, to return to his friends and his country; yet, just at the moment when he is approaching the frontiers, he is tempted by a hunting scheme to give up those delightful prospects, and go back without the least reluctance to the solitude of the woods." [4] Thus Biddle endowed Colter with a reputation for being callous and devoid of normal human feelings, an appraisal that gained wide acceptance. This estimate may also have been inspired by George Shannon, who assisted Biddle in preparing the Lewis and Clark narrative and conceivably did not share the sentiments of other members of the expedition. The other journal writers made comments similar to Clark's, and none gave the slightest intimation that they regarded Colter's joining the two trappers as anything more than the action of a man taking advantage of an excellent business opportunity.

Ordway commented that Colter and his two companions were determined to stay up the river at least two years "until they make a fortune." Ordway also remarked that the officers and men had given Colter enough supplies for two years as well as a great number of other articles.[5] Knives, powder horns, hatchets and other small, personal utensils used by a man living in the open, become precious and take on an importance to the proprietor far beyond their intrinsic worth. They are not often donated to a person embarking on an addlepated enterprise with little chance of success.

The partnership of Dixon, Hancock and Colter started out with about twenty traps, adequate tools for building canoes, a two years' supply of ammunition and other necessary equipment. The principal asset of the partnership consisted of their position, just before the fall trapping season, only a few weeks' journey from the richest beaver streams in the Rockies.

The supplies in the large part must have been paid for by the beaver skins Colter and the others had obtained, and any excess settled privately with Lewis and Clark against Colter's discharge pay. The expedition records show that Colter earned $5.00 per month and that he was entitled to $179.33⅓, or the equivalent of 35 months and 26 days of service.[6] His name was carried on the roster from October 15,

1803, to October 10, 1806, the latter date being the time when the entire expedition was discharged in St. Louis. Thus Colter was officially mustered out about two months after he left the party at the Mandan villages. There is no evidence that the discrepancy was questioned, but if it was, the two captains undoubtedly justified the technical overpayment by pointing out that Colter was one of the select few singled out by Thomas Jefferson for special praise.

In 1807, Congress passed a law providing for double pay to all members of the expedition and land grants of 320 acres each to all of the enlisted men.[7] This action of Congress caused Lewis and Clark to cancel the original settlement made with Colter, and Meriwether Lewis personally assumed the obligation to John Colter. After Lewis's death and Colter's return to St. Louis, the court determined that there was a balance due Colter from Lewis's estate of $377.60.[8]

On August 17, 1806, the now reduced command of Lewis and Clark loaded and tied together their canoes, collected their Indian guests, and bade farewell to Sacajawea and her son, to Charbonneau, her husband and master, and to John Colter. The three trappers did not stand on the river bank waving forlornly to the expedition until the canoes and their crews merged into identity with the yellow waters and the dirty brown banks. It may be presumed that they embarked immediately in their own small boats and lunged into the rhythmic drudgery of overcoming the relentless current of the Missouri.

As the unknown number of canoes propelled by the three partners slowly disappeared from the sight of the watching Mandans, it could not have occurred to John Colter that his name was thereafter to appear on the pages of historical records only on infrequent and patternless occasions. Only by falling into a sinkhole could Colter have created a greater contrast than that between the minutely chronicled experiences of the Lewis and Clark expedition and the virtually unknown course of the three trappers on the upper Missouri and Yellowstone Rivers. Whether or not the extra equipment donated to the triumvirate included any of the ungainly materials then required for keeping a diary in ink, is not known. All members of the Lewis and

Clark party had been encouraged to keep journals, but if Colter ever made any comments in a chunky leather-bound notebook of his own, this information has escaped notice. We move into a period of inference and possibility.

Unfortunately, no private papers of John Colter have ever been found; in fact, it is pure conjecture to say that they ever existed. His companions were equally reticent about recording their activities on the Yellowstone, at least none of their private papers have been cited or published. Colter himself met several literate individuals who published accounts of their experiences in the mountains and on the Missouri, and all of them made some reference to at least one of his more widely known exploits. Nevertheless, none of the writers gave a detailed chronological account of his activities after leaving the Mandan villages for the valley of the Yellowstone.

The distinct impression is gained from reading the comments of those who personally knew John Colter that he was a shy, quiet and reserved man who had little to say about anything, except perhaps under the stimulus of a roisterous trappers' celebration and the expansive properties of what the Indians so aptly called "fire water." Thus Colter's inherent reticence may have discouraged more than one writer who was anxious to learn the full story of his mountain years.

Since Colter could not have been much over forty when he died, he was far from that state of desuetude where, having lost his former strength and vigor, he could only maintain his place among his intimates by recounting the journeys and excitements of his trapping years. The serious historian normally distrusts the reminiscences of an old man in his dotage, but in the case of John Colter, even a distorted and unreliable yarn would be most welcome. Although it might be filled with many inaccuracies it would at least give us a more connected outline of his mountain years than we now possess. Actually, the years following the winter Colter spent with Dixon and Hancock on the Yellowstone are better known, but there are many consecutive months that cannot be accounted for, even by presupposing that they were spent trapping or enduring the pervading cold and the discomforts of a winter camp. This factor prompts the otherwise incongruous wish that Colter had been given to more of those displays of temper or drunkenness required to gain mention or condemnation in the commentaries on fur-trapping expeditions.

As the trapping partnership of three worked its way up to the mouth of the Yellowstone River, Dixon and Hancock, too well aware of the disasters that grizzlies, Indians, blizzards, floods, disease, or broken bones and guns could inflict upon a small party, may be presumed to have labored without brooding over such subjects.

As for Colter, were he given to introspection, he could look back on his time with Lewis and Clark as the best of experience; in retrospect, he could only congratulate himself on having had such excellent training for his trapping venture under so many highly skilled specialists with years of experience on the untamed side of the frontier.

Idle dreaming does not seem in keeping with what is known of Colter's personality. Rather his pragmatical nature might have forced his thinking on to the question of whether it was advisable for the partnership to continue up the Missouri or follow the Yellowstone River. Dixon and Hancock had already decided to proceed up the Upper Missouri when Colter joined them. In fact, all three men were inclined by preference to keep to the right bank of the Missouri when they reached the mouth of the Yellowstone, and make their gamble for furs and fortune on the Upper Missouri.

The zest with which the Blackfeet were reputed to enter into sanguinary activity and the likelihood that their earlier ill-fated attempt to rob Lewis's party had made them more unfriendly must have been the deciding factors. Although the streams of the Yellowstone Valley had not been reported to be quite so black with sleek beaver as the Missouri, that region, because of the reputation its inhabitants bore for being relatively friendly, was obviously a more advantageous location. The Crows were acknowledged by their neighbors as able to build the most graceful tipis and as being adroit at stealing horses. Since the trappers had no horses, but were relying on canoes, they had little to fear from the exercise of this specialty.

However, the three men may have soon started cursing their lack of horses, as it could not have taken them long to learn something that had escaped Captain Clark—that the current of the Yellowstone was much more rapid than that of the Missouri. The narrower stream-bed and faster water-flow created new problems and fewer slack-water eddies.

Man is not the only mammal with a generous quotient of curiosity, although his inquisitiveness has the farthest scope. High among the most absorbing topics of interest for man has always been the question of who had been there before him. There was no question of this being the first party on the Yellowstone, as Captain Clark had just a few weeks before descended the stream. And the three may have heard from the Mandans, Hidatsa or Gros Ventre of the Missouri, of the trading expedition of Antoine Larocque to the Upper Yellowstone country.[9]

In the spring of 1805, François Antoine Larocque, an employee of the Northwest Company attached to Fort de La Bosse on the Assiniboine River, with two companions visited the Mandans and Gros Ventre villages on the Missouri. The Crows, who are linguistic cousins of the Hidatsa or Gros Ventre, had just completed their annual visit for bartering purposes and some social affairs as the three traders arrived from the North. Le Borgne, the Gros Ventre chief with one eye and a reputation that matched his sinister appearance, persuaded the Crows to permit Larocque and one companion, as well as several Hidatsa, to join the band of more than six hundred Absaroka on their return journey to the region they considered home. The Crows rather reluctantly took the trader and his friends along the trail across country by way of the Knife, Little Missouri, Powder and Tongue Rivers. Crossing the Wolf or Chetish Mountains, an offshoot of the Big Horn Range, the party forded the Big Horn River near the lower canyon and then continued northward to the Yellowstone. The final trading session took place on an island in the river, at the conclusion of which Larocque thanked the Crows for their many kindnesses, and quickly returned to the Missouri by much the same route. Subsequently, Larocque made his way back to the fort on the Assiniboine, and not long afterwards gave up the fur business and retired, ultimately to a monastery in eastern Canada.

41

Historians for more than a century have considered Colter, Dixon and Hancock the fourth party of whites on the Yellowstone River. The honor of having been the first white man to see the valley of the Yellowstone has long been conceded to Charles Le Raye on the strength of a book written by Colonel Jervis Cutler and published in 1812.[10] The bulk of the volume is devoted to the Colonel's description of the territories of Ohio, Indiana, and Louisiana, but it also contains a journal that the author states in the foreword was handed to him by a silent and unknown traveling companion. In this journal, which is said to have been impulsively handed to a complete stranger, Le Raye recounts his capture by the Sioux on the Osage River and his later extensive travels.

Le Raye stated that the Bois Brulé band of the Sioux took him as a slave-captive on a visit to the Gros Ventre villages on the Missouri, and that while there he obtained permission from his master to accompany a French trader named Pardo, who lived with the Sioux, on a trip to the Yellowstone country. Le Raye and Pardo, in company with three Sioux, were said to have joined a band of Hidatsa on a visit to the Crows. Considering that Lewis and Clark spent a great deal of time during the winter of 1804 and 1805 trying to reconcile the traditional enemies, the Hidatsa and the Sioux, relations between the two tribes must have deteriorated with astounding rapidity for them to have become implacable traditional enemies within two years. Le Raye's story also reveals that for a slave-captive he enjoyed so much of the confidence of his captor, a chief, that he was loaned a musket and two horses with the understanding that all furs obtained would be shared.

Le Raye's narrative relates that his party, totaling forty-three persons, left the Missouri on July 3, 1802, and rode across country until it reached the Yellowstone River. Here the party joined with a band of the "Paunch Indians," which various scholars have identified as the Crows or Absaroka Indians. Le Raye described the village of these Indians located on the Big Horn River as consisting of: "43 huts. These huts were sunk 3 feet below the surface of the ground but otherwise are built nearly similar to those of the Gros Ventre." [11]

The Absaroka were justly famous for their graceful and comfortable skin tipis and at this period had been a nomadic people for generations. Their traditions state that many years before they had lived with the Hidatsa, and had then inhabited earth-lodges. The separation into separate bands is variously attributed to a quarrel over a woman, or a dead buffalo, or a combination of both time-honored causes for disputes. In later years none of the visitors to the Crows made any mention of their living in sunken huts, and it seems significant that the Crow name for the Gros Ventre of the Missouri literally is translated as "earth-lodges" or "dirt lodges." [12]

Le Raye also told of seeing a group of sixteen captive Flat Head Indians and gave a detailed account of how their deformities were created by strapping boards on their babies' heads. Quite apart from its being unusual for plains Indians to take prisoners in such numbers, the tribes from the Pacific slope that habitually came over the Rockies to hunt had abandoned the practice of head-binding generations before the coming of the white men. Nor did these same Indians wear bones through the septum of their noses, although it was a practice of some of the tribes on the lower Columbia.

Furtive, wretched and misshapen creatures were also described by Le Raye, with the explanation that they were called Snakes because they customarily lived in caves and had to be dragged out to be exterminated like reptiles. Few white men ever saw these lowly, defenseless Indians, better known at Sheep Eaters,[13] who definitely were known to have lived in the Rockies and possibly in the Big Horns. The large tribe of Snake or Shoshone Indians were composed of a number of widespread bands speaking approximately the same language, but whose culture and repute ranged from the Lemhi, rich with many horses, to the abject Sheep Eater and Digger Indians, whose diet often of necessity included grasshoppers and ants.

Similar pitiful, timorous creatures were mentioned by Thomas James and James O. Pattie. Among the various reasons for discrediting Pattie's assertion that he was on the Yellowstone is his vivid description of the abnormalities of the Flat Head and Snake Indians he said he saw on the Yellowstone.[14] Thomas James recounts much of the same fanciful nonsense, and both are essentially the identical account attributed by Colonel Cutler to Le Raye. There is no question of James having been on the Yellowstone; thus we must assign responsibility to their editors who wrote with lively imaginations and little regard for accurate reporting. Comparable lurid stories were told in other books of the same period, perhaps due to a reluctance to admit that Africa contained any more freakish wonders than did North America.

The many statements that are contrary to known conditions and Indian customs create a serious doubt that Le Raye ever saw the Yellowstone valley, although any single one of the discrepancies might be condoned. In fact, there are sound reasons for believing that Charles Le Raye never saw the Sioux and, further, that he never existed anywhere except in the mind of Colonel Cutler. George E. Hyde, an authority on the early history of all branches of the Sioux or Dakotas, expressed his conviction that Le Raye was never a captive of that tribe. He further states that he has never located any other references to the several traders Le Raye alleged were living with the Sioux at that time, including Pardo.[15]

The purported Le Raye journal was published in 1812, or seven years after Larocque's visit to the Yellowstone, and many white men are known to have visited the Mandan and Gros Ventre villages before the publication date. Thus, the nearest approach to a factual basis for Le Raye's account of his captivity with the Sioux was probably the picturesque misinformation that was bandied about the St. Louis taverns patronized by trappers, whenever gullible listeners were present, willing to buy drinks for the narrators as long as their yarns were entertaining.

The stories the three trappers, Colter, Dixon, and Hancock, swapped around their campfires most likely were more apt to be of a practical nature. Men who were risking so much could be expected to make a concentrated study of the habits and traits of their quarry, the beaver. Since Colter and his partners devoted so many months almost exclusively to gathering furs, and so little otherwise is known of their activities, we shall here summarize their way of life as trappers and what they must have learned about the beaver.

The aquatic rodent who had the misfortune to bear a fur from which were made top-heavy, ungainly hats, then the epitome of elegance in London and on the continent, possessed qualities that absorb the attention of many people aside from those interested in acquiring their pelts for gain. The accomplishments of this wily animal, best known for building dams across streams that maintain a minimum water level all year around, have caused the loss of incalculable hours of sleep to interested observers, for beavers normally do their building in the wee small hours of the night. Those who have spent many hours patiently watching and cross-examining other students of the beavers' capabilities, credit them with a remarkable adaptability in solving complicated engineering and construction problems.

Colter was at this stage more familiar with the beaver ponds formed by erecting a structure of poles anchored to the bottom with mud, and of branches then woven so tightly that the seepage of water could be regulated with twigs held into place by daubs of grass and mud. John Colter could hardly be expected to have understood the engineering principle that inspired the beaver to build their dams straight across a sluggish brook, but curved upstream when the current was rapid. Dams hundreds of feet in length, impounding water that covered several acres and protecting divers brush-heap lodges, each perched on a minute islet of dry land, should have ceased being a novelty long before Colter had seen the Pacific slope of the Rockies. He may not have had the rare good fortune to see one of the solid bank dams, maintained by so many generations of beaver that the bottom parts had become petrified, but he could not possibly have failed to note the canals that led away from the old established ponds through the adjacent land covered with conical stumps of trees that had long since satisfied the beavers' bark hunger.

The canals are dug as straight as the land contours permit, and so deep that they are well filled with water at the pond's minimum water level. The channels extend into the fringes of the wooded section and are used as waterways to transport the winter supplies of bark, which are buried at the bottom of the pond and consumed when the ice confines the beaver to their lodges and burrows. There is ample evidence that such canals are constructed by young beaver couples

45

who have elected to construct their own pond and lodge with the assistance of their elder relatives, but whose ancestral habitat had possessed adequate numbers of willows and cottonwoods within rolling and dragging distance of the water, without requiring the digging of additional waterways. The ingenuity of young beaver in figuring out the solution to involved problems with which their forefathers had not been confronted in many generations is considered one of the best proofs that the *genus castor americanus* has the ability to reason. Such achievements have resulted in the beaver being credited with far more intelligence than it possesses; but the argument as to whether the beaver's accomplishments are due to an ability to think, or to a highly developed instinct, seems more entertaining than conclusive.

Dams and lodges are constructed and kept in repair; burrows, canals and slides are excavated; trees and shrubs are gnawed down and into maneuverable segments; reserve food supplies are accumulated and stocks of barkless sticks stored for emergency repairs: all with a minimum of confusion. Casual observers have assumed that such smooth performances were the result of able supervision on the part of one or more individual beaver. However, those who have studied carefully the seemingly tireless activities of the beaver concur in the belief that there is no director or engineer acting in a supervisory capacity. In fact, the nearest semblance to an organized unit is the family group which is usually estimated at seven or eight members, comprising the two parents and the young who have not found mates or been forced to shift for themselves.

Students of the beaver point out that positive identification of individuals is complicated by the fact that it is often necessary to dissect beaver to determine if they are male or female. The loud whacking of the tail on the water as a warning of danger is apparently the principal means of communication. The beaver's tail, a broad, horny appendage, is used as a paddle, a rudder, and to slap mud and branches into place, but it is not so versatile that it can be used as a trowel or tray. Mud and sticks are carried in the tiny front paws clutched to the chest or tucked under the beaver's chin. The webbed hind legs are much larger than the front, and with powerful strokes propel the beaver and his burdens through the water at a rapid rate of speed.

46

The beaver is so thoroughly streamlined that it looks like a grotesque exaggeration of what the advertising men refer to as the "stenographers' spread." This squashed appearance is most pronounced when the beaver perches on his tail and gnaws his way around a tree with all the dignity of an English lord whose cane seat has collapsed at the races.

The consequences of catching the front feet of a beaver in the trap were serious, as the beaver would often drag the trap into deep water or into dense brush and then gnaw or pull loose the frail limb, thereby causing the trapper to lose not only his quarry but his trap as well. Traps were not only expensive in Colter's time but almost irreplaceable. Therefore, the trappers devised many different methods of forcing the beaver to spring the traps with their rear feet. The most common technique was to place the trap in the water just below a slide, and attach the ring on the other end of the chain to a pole with a fork or similar obstruction on the top end. The object was to allow the beaver to drag the trap into deep water where the animal drowned quickly, but could be retrieved readily by use of the pole. Many trappers placed over the trip-pan a stick smudged with castor essence extracted from a previous victim. This attracted other beaver so strongly that they would rear up on their hind legs to reach it, thereby stepping into the trap with legs so sturdy they rarely could be broken or bitten off. The early trappers wore a small bottle around their necks on a leather thong in which to carry their supply of castor.

Dixon and Hancock, who had trapped for two years on the Missouri, probably could explain to Colter many different systems of setting traps, based on their experiences with the river-bank beaver with which they were then more familiar. Whenever the beaver found a stream that provided deep water and a cut bank throughout the year, they did not build dams but dug burrows into the bank—the entrance about two feet below the September water level, or the lowest in the year. In conjunction with the store of branches for the winter feeding when the ice closed them in, the beaver also erected a false lodge to mislead his enemies. Normally, the real lodge or home was in a burrow some distance back from the water and with an air vent close to the surface. The burrows were commonly dug under the roots of a tree which gave protection and the necessary reinforcement that permitted the burrow to be well concealed although but a few inches underground. Some observers maintain that the beaver pile twigs and branches over the air vent to prevent the deep snow from shutting off the air.

The two men from Illinois may have taught Colter the curious technique usually employed for locating the burrows of the bank beaver by tapping on the ice with a chisel and axe until a hidden burrow altered the tone of the metallic blows. This same method could also be used on some ponds, as the beaver also dug burrows along the edges of the ponds and out of the canals as well. Burrows afforded better protection than a lodge, and also were frequently lived in by those spinsters and bachelors who had not succeeded in finding mates but had been forced by their parents to forage for themselves and make room for the younger additions to the family. These burrows, like the lodges, usually had at least two exits. One was straight to permit easy dragging-in of branches as food, and also afforded a rapid means of flight in the event a marten made his appearance.

The trappers understood that the amazing constructions of the beaver were solely for the purpose of concealment from their natural enemies. Neither they, nor those who have subsequently studied the varied abilities of the beaver, can reconcile such indisputable skill in self-concealment with the virtually complete lack of will to defend themselves when actually attacked. The teeth of the beaver only have enamel on the outside; thus with the continual gnawing of wood, the edges attain a razor sharpness and the jaw muscles the power to force these dental chisels through large pieces of wood. With such powerful weapons, it is astonishing that the animal when cornered by an enemy is said to cower in paralysed fright, incapable of making but the weakest fight for its life.

The beaver are woefully deficient in fighting spirit, but they display unusual good sense in other directions. Although their reputation for industry is firmly established, during the hot summer months the beaver go off on lazy, carefree pleasure trips through the surrounding countryside. Around the beginning of September they return to

48

their lodges and resume their mending routines. This vacation period represents such a decided contrast to the unremitting drudgery of the balance of the year, that it suggests the possibility of being an instinctive antidote for the months of laboring in the murky ice-sealed waters, or huddling in the cold, clammy darkness of the burrows and brush heap lodges.[16]

The beaver should have completed all major repairs and the submerging of sweet bark branches by the time Colter and his companions arrived at the mouth of the Big Horn. The trappers' progress up the Yellowstone would have been governed by the frequency of beaver signs, and these would have been encouraging in their fatiguing struggle with the flight of the river from the mountains. The individual trapping techniques of the three men should have become well-defined after weeks of experimentation. John Colter could have put aside his unusual specialty of shooting beaver. The beaver ponds on the Atlantic slope were much deeper than those on the Pacific side of the Rockies; hence the most expert marksman had to dive all too frequently to retrieve his prey, and the pelt might have acquired damaging bullet holes. Ammunition was entirely too precious to be expended on such sport and there could have been no pleasure in plunging into ice-fringed water. In fact, the trappers had quite enough wading to do in setting their traps in the approved manner.

By the end of November, winter has taken uncontested possession of the Yellowstone valley. The winds sweep down from the north with increasing regularity and give shrill warning of the blizzards that might follow. The power of the wind is shown by the nearly horizontal departure of the last, rattly, dry leaves to be wrenched from the cottonwoods, and the way such snow as has fallen on the level ground is forced into the clumps of sagebrush, or swept into the sculptured drifts that fill the gulches and draws.

The drive of the masses of cold air is such that it penetrates the warmest garments and forces the hardiest to cover their faces to avoid freezing. The trappers wore a colorful combination of buckskin suits, woolen blanket capotes, fur caps and fur-lined moccasins and leggings, of designs evolved from their individual fancy and the style of Indian tribes with which they had been associated. Their life of nearly constant traveling and the weight limitations imposed by pack horses and saddle bags, however, forced them to make up any clothing deficiencies with the toughening and numbing effects of constant exposure upon the skin. Those who had the misfortune to freeze some part of their bodies very likely devised some extraordinary covering to protect the sensitive portion from the pain that thereafter accompanied each subsequent experience of freezing temperatures.

The more ambitious trappers under these circumstances looked forward expectantly to the time when thick ice on the ponds eliminated the need of wading, and prompted the use of other means of killing beaver. There were few topics on which the thick-hided trappers exhibited any reluctance to discourse down to the last gory detail, but the process by which they crossed on the ice to beaver lodges, closed it exits with poles and then, after tearing off the roof, clubbed to death the entrapped inhabitants, was rarely a voluntary subject of conversation. Apparently, even calloused professionals were loath to admit unsporting conduct of this kind. Before such wholesale operations became commonplace, Colter and his partners should have decided in principle which of the two possible methods of spending the severe winter months should be employed. The trappers always asserted that beaver skins taken during the coldest winter months were less valuable than those acquired in the fall or early spring. The fur was said to be too thick, but it would be astonishing if this conclusion was not a sophistry derived from the danger and discomfort of trapping in sub-zero weather. Wading into icy waters several times a day to unload or reset beaver traps, and then spending the remaining hours of daylight hunting for game with leather moccasins and pants legs frozen stiff, would tax the nerves and flesh of any man. The trapper's hide was of necessity barely human, but there was a limit to even his incredible endurance.

The trio had been in the mountains for years and their need for new and more garments must have become distressingly apparent with every gust of chilling wind. Since they were hundreds of miles from the nearest trading post, the only other possible source of clothing would have been one of the Indian camps along the Yellowstone

River. The prospect of seeing another human face after so many months of intimate living would also have represented a welcome interlude for the three trappers.

Trapper parties frequently joined with a band of friendly Indians during the summer and winter months when beaver fur was either too thin or too thick. Convivial gregariousness was just one of the good reasons the trappers had for visiting Indian villages. Most of the plains Indians eventually learned how to trap and skin the pelts in demand with the fur companies, and the bartering sessions were invariably lively, if they did not degenerate into bloody violence. The squaws brought out their tanned robes and other beaded work, from which the trappers replenished their wardrobes with much noisy haggling and the darting swift gestures of the sign talkers.

Although many westerners do realize the courage the trappers exhibited every time they went into the mountains, the way of the trappers with Indian women is almost invariably condemned. The popular concept of this phase of the trapper's life is that they had fewer morals than a mink, and more restricted interests than a buck sheep. This judgment on the basis of city standards shows no consideration for the vast difference in prevailing circumstances.

The early trappers lived for years in the mountains without returning to the settlements or visiting trading posts. In order to survive, they had to adopt many Indian customs, and under such conditions, it is not surprising that many of them acquired a companion, housekeeper and mistress, all in the same person. Normally, there was very little romance about the forming of such relationships, as the trappers paid to the girl's father or brother the stipulated number of horses, or perhaps a rifle. The price of a comely maid with a knowledge of several languages might be three or four horses. Although horses were expensive for the trappers to buy, and they were not encouraged to steal them, it was a good investment. The squaw took care of a trapper's lodge, made his clothes, cleaned his beaver skins and did all of the cooking. Aside from menial labors, an Indian woman materially aided her mate by acting as interpreter and diplomat with the Indians, as well as supplying a most welcome knowledge of beaver streams. These women earned many times over the bright cloths, gaudy finery and silver-mounted saddles which they inveigled their trappers into buying at the annual rendezvous, perhaps at the expense of the major portion of the year's catch of beaver plews. The trappers apparently derived as much satisfaction as their squaws from the envious looks of the other Indian women. In accordance with Indian *mores*, many of the trappers tried the experiment of having several wives at the same time, but only the most expert could afford the luxury of several squaws and keep them sufficiently well dressed so that they considered themselves more fortunate than their friends who only had Indian husbands.

There is ample evidence that the squaws felt themselves to be better treated by the white trappers than they would have been in the lodge of one of their own tribesmen. Separation and re-marriage in most of the plains tribes was a relatively simple affair and did not always entail the return of the horses that constituted the original payment. On such matters there were widely divergent opinions among the plains tribes. Thus, it was beneath the dignity of a Crow chief to notice the unfaithfulness of one of his wives; whereas, in another tribe, the same offense might result in the wife losing her life, or at least having her nose cut off. Temporary liaisons were condoned in many bands, and it is possible that John Colter may have indulged in relationships of this type, though he is not known to have set up housekeeping with an Indian woman.

The attitude in the settlements was that, regardless of whether or not such affairs were arranged in strict conformity with Indian morality, since the trappers knew better, they should have set a better example. The features of the trappers' conduct that were most censured were the facility with which squaws were changed and the maintenance of two or more women at the same time. Another object of criticism, and quite justifiably so, was the practice of some trappers of just riding away from the squaw and his children, leaving them no means of support. However, the trappers held that these strictures would have been more acceptable had a more tolerant understanding been demonstrated toward those mountain men who took their Indian wives to the settlements, legalized the relationship with an official ceremony, and strove to educate their children. Rare courage and unlimited patience were needed by those trappers who eventually succeeded in getting their families accepted by their all-white neighbors.

Thus did the outstanding accomplishments of the trappers become obscured, if not obliterated, by a rigid application of the norms of an entirely different social structure. The man of today, harassed with alimony payments, legal fees, and conflicting state divorce laws, might conclude that, all things considered, the lot of the trapper was not too unpleasant. Therefore, before he yearns too enthusiastically for the good old days, he should weigh a philosophical dissertation on the subject by a trapper with a great deal of experience, as follows: "For twenty years I packed a squaw along. Not one, but a many. First I had a Blackfoot—the darndest slut as ever cried for fofarraw. I lodge-poled her on Colter's Creek, and made her quit. My buffler hoss, and as good as four packs of beaver, I gave for old Bull-tail's daughter. He was head chief of the Ricaree, and came nicely round me. Thar wasn't enough scarlet cloth, nor beads, nor vermilion in Sublette's packs for her. Traps wouldn't buy her all the fofarraw she wanted; and in two years I'd sold her to Cross-Eagle for one of Jake Hawken's guns—this very one I hold in my hands. Then I tried the Sioux, the Shian, and a Digger from the other side, who made the best moccasin as ever I wore. She was the best of all, and was rubbed out by the Yutas in the Bayou Salade. Bad was the best; and after she was gone under I tried no more." [17]

Colter, Dixon and Hancock actually did not stay long with the Indians that winter, but adopted the much less exciting procedure of locating in a secluded valley. Tall grass and sweet cottonwoods nearby were important, as they attracted game during the deep snow months.

There are relatively few wintering places on the upper Yellowstone above the Big Horn River and this has tempted those students of Colter's life, also familiar with the country, to guess where he spent the winter. One notable surmise of this character is contained in the History of Wyoming, by Hubert Howe Bancroft.[18] This historian stated, or at least endorsed, the assertion of one of his assistants that Colter, Dixon and Hancock wintered on the headwaters of

Pryor's Fork. Since the mountain Crows were well known to have preferred to pass the winter months on the upper tributaries of Pryor's Fork, or Creek as some would have it, Bancroft's statement, which is not substantiated by any of his quoted sources, represents a logical and shrewd guess.

Fortunately we have more than conjecture to justify the belief that Colter and his partners spent the worst of the winter of 1806–1807 on the Clark's Fork of the Yellowstone. The late J. K. Rollinson, who wrote two books on Wyoming history, is our authority. In a personal letter, Mr. Rollinson related that in 1902 he became acquainted with Dave Fleming, one of the first locaters at Miner's Camp, now Cooke City, Montana.[19] Fleming was then in his late seventies and he informed Rollinson that he was the stepson of either Hancock or Dixon. Unfortunately, Mr. Rollinson could not recall after so many years which of Colter's two partners was Fleming's stepfather. Nevertheless, it seems more likely that it was Hancock, as Joseph Dixon is known to have given up the fur trade at an early date and to have moved from Illinois to Wisconsin in 1827.[20]

Dave Fleming told Rollinson that when he was about ten years old, his stepfather took him on an expedition into the mountains, since after the death of his mother there was no one to take care of him in the settlements. The small party of trappers attended a rendezvous on the upper waters of Green River, and from there proceeded to the Yellowstone at Coulson Landing near the city of Billings. One winter, young Fleming accompanied the men to the mouth of the Clark's Fork Canyon, where it breaks out of the Absaroka Mountains. The party made camp, and Fleming's stepfather told him that on that very spot Colter and his two associates had spent the winter. They had constructed a combination lean-to and cabin by erecting two walls against the side of a cliff so as to take advantage of a recess in the rock. Perhaps they enclosed a portion of one of the several limestone caves to be seen in the canyon walls, and it is possible that further evidence of Colter's known habit of doodling on rocks may eventually be found that will mark more precisely the location of the first semi-permanent dwelling on the Clark's Fork.

Rollinson, who was for several years forest ranger in the Sunlight

Basin, stated that the reason he remembered Fleming's story so clearly after so many years was the fact that John Colter was evidently the first white man to enter the Sunlight Basin. Fleming quoted his stepfather as having said that, during the winter of 1806–1807, Colter became bored with the confined temporary shelter and went up the canyon by himself into the Sunlight Basin. Colter made good use of this experience the following year.

This characteristic solitary trip, undertaken apparently for no better reason than to have something to do, suggests that Colter may have found himself always the outsider in relation to the two men who had lived together at least two years in close association. An inability to get along in the enforced intimacy of a party of three would be accentuated by the vast expanses of empty country around them. This would be also a logical cause for the dissolution of the partnership, which is known to have occurred. The only other shred of information available is the fact that the venture was not profitable. It is difficult to believe that they did not have the opportunity to take many beaver skins; however, the serious problem would have been that of transporting them down the river. Beaver pelts were usually compressed into heavy bundles that were awkward to handle and transport in a canoe, or bull boat made of branches and hides. Consequently, one mishap like the overturning of a canoe may have destroyed the bales of beaver, or again the Indians could have taken their pelts from them by force.

The gamble for a fortune in furs was unsuccessful for Colter, Dixon and Hancock. The returns from their trapping efforts in no way compensated for the risks involved, and their newly acquired geographic understanding had uncertain resale value. Although a large part of the Rocky Mountain region was first explored by such tiny bands of men, following the streams to their sources and then down the next adjacent ones as far as beaver sign was in evidence, these men rarely kept journals or drew maps of the country they had passed through. In fact, good beaver streams were a closely guarded trade secret and their location was usually only imprinted on the trapper's photographic memory. The relatively few trappers' journals that have survived reveal how thoroughly the early trapping parties had followed the western streams, and further illustrate how little unknown territory there would have been for later government expeditions to explore if the trappers had committed to paper their vast knowledge of the water courses on both slopes of the Rockies.

Far from being held in high esteem by the later inhabitants of the regions they discovered, the trappers enjoy a most unsavory reputation. In the minds of the present-day westerners, the proper associates of a fur trapper live in the depths of a prairie dog hole, and there have been few monuments erected for them, although many towns and localities still bear their names. One reason for this disdain might be termed an occupational liability, as the skinning and cleaning of game permeates the clothing and body with secretions that give off a distinctly unpleasant odor. The one so afflicted is unaware of his malodorous state, until he congregates with others in an over-heated room on a rare visit to a settlement and notices the distressed expressions of the townspeople.

The association of unavoidable, disagreeable smells and the judgment of the general public, are in many cases quite unwarranted. The situation is also an excellent example of the truism that a few bad eggs will spoil the entire lot. Not too many trappers chose to live in the mountains because the sheriff would have been their principal welcomer in their home communities. Some of these men had fled from the consequences of a single mistake, but thereafter conducted themselves with sufficient discretion that their decent-citizen consciences were not bothersome. On the other hand, many entered into the life of the mountain men with full appreciation of the opportunities afforded by the lack of law and order. We now recognize that many of the vicious characters who did so much to give all the trappers a bad name were psychotic personalities, free to exercise their abnormal impulses on a scale that had only been envisioned in their wildest hallucinations. They were the ones who set forth, in order to excuse their thrill-inspired killings, the rationalization that the only good Indian was a dead Indian.

Renegade white men were not the only ones who ambushed unsuspecting passersby for reasons that did not stem from either a desire for revenge or self-protection. Many trappers, working alone or in small parties, were seized by roving bands of Indian braves, stripped of all their possessions, and left lifeless and scalpless for the vultures and wolves. Occasionally, a trapper's gun, horse and clothing would be taken, but in a spirit of sportsmanship the Marquis of Queensberry would never have recognized, the victim was given the opportunity of trying to walk, naked and defenceless, to a friendly camp. The motivation for such attacks was often the desire of several young warriors to improve their standing with their tribe. In order for the young men to advance they had to prove their fighting ability and courage in actual combat, and if the tribe as a whole was not involved in a war with one of their neighbors, they periodically would set out, singly or in small bands, in search of some one to attack or rob. Each tribe had its own distinctive method for computing the valor of the warriors, and ratings were even assigned to the different ways of stealing horses. For example, it counted little to take one from the common herd, whereas it was considered most difficult to make off with one tied to the owner's tipi. The plains Indians usually gave far more recognition to the man who would strike his enemy with a relatively harmless *coup* stick than to the one who actually killed him. Many bands regarded the taking of scalps as one of the lowest accomplishments of a warrior. In fact it was permissible for the first to reach a fallen enemy to grasp a handful of the victim's hair, cut a circular incision and wrench the hair and skin loose. More than one trapper lost his scalp, but not his life, and thereafter concealed his loss with a tight fitting cap, showing no other ill effects than sagging facial muscles.

The principal wealth of the plains Indians at the time the white men first came into contact with them was their herds of horses. Each man was required to steal or take by force the horses with which he would satisfy the demand of his selected mate's father or brother. Thus the urge to increase their wealth, and to add new feats of valor to their war chants to be sung and enacted with a complete lack of modesty before the assembled tribe on festive occasions, inspired many war parties when the tribe was nominally at peace. There were few chiefs who could control the young men and eliminate these aggressive excursions, which continually resulted in violations of the peace treaties of later years. The attacks of young warriors seeking glory and wealth could not be predicted, and represented the most serious danger to which Colter, Dixon and Hancock were exposed.

These factors and a quarrel with his partners, prompted Colter to pile his furs and traps into his canoe and follow the broken ice down the Yellowstone to the angry flood waters of the Missouri.

Chapter Four

Fort Raymond

The slender canoe swept downstream in the grip of the current still bloated and arrogant with spring run-off water. John Colter, the only occupant, dipped his paddle from time to time, as often for something to do as to steer the craft across the converging waters of the River Platte. His solitary routine ended when he saw the bare masts of keel boats tied to the bank and the smoke of cooking fires.

Colter instinctively began digging his paddle deep into the swirling tan waters, and impelled his canoe with rapid strokes toward the keel boats. He was as anxious to learn about this expedition, as the members were to know his identity. Long before his canoe had been hauled a safe distance out of the river, he had discovered that he had several friends in the personnel of the expedition, and had started to catch up with the latest news from the States.

Three men who had been with Lewis and Clark—George Drouillard, John Potts and Peter Wiser—were members of the party ascending the river, which is often referred to as the Lisa and Drouillard expedition. Drouillard held a semi-official position, by reason of acting as proxy for two of the regular partners of the Missouri Fur Trading Company of St. Louis. The organizer of the company and leader of the fur trading venture was Manuel Lisa.

The party had stopped at the mouth of the Platte to overhaul their boats in accordance with the custom of the early day boatmen. Heavy timber did not grow in continuous stretches along the river bottom above the Platte, and ash trees were rarely found beyond that point. Thus, experienced river men always cut at least one extra mast of ash for each keel boat. The mouth of the Platte was also regarded as the boundary line between the Upper and Lower Missouri. The neophytes among the crew were often initiated into the mysteries of the upper river in boisterous fashion by the old timers. Heads shaven clean and involuntary baths in the river were the usual initiation stunts, similar to the traditional ceremonies on board a ship crossing the Equator.

And so, by mere coincidence John Colter met the expedition at the very boundary line of the Upper Missouri, and his decision to sign on as a member brought his years of continuous stay in that region to a total of six. His action at this juncture, on the threshold of the settlements, nearly justifies Biddle's comments on his character, as he could not have hoped for large financial returns from his association with Lisa's company. There is no record of the inducements that Lisa offered Colter, but they must have been substantially more than the $500 contract that was given to Le Compt.[1] Since Colter had trapped on the headwaters of the Missouri and the Yellowstone, his knowledge of that region would be invaluable.

When the weathered men of the Lewis and Clark expedition returned to St. Louis in the fall of 1806, no one had listened more attentively than Manuel Lisa to their reports of abundant beaver on the headwaters of the Missouri and Yellowstone Rivers. On the strength of this information, Lisa formed a partnership with William Morrison and Pierre Menard, with a reputed capital of $16,000. The expedition was composed of forty-two men. Benito Vasquez was actually second in command and the balance of the men, thirty-seven, were French Canadians.

Lisa had an excellent reason for listening so intently to Lewis and Clark. He had come to St. Louis before the close of the century, after some years of trading on the Mississippi. With the assurance of the brash young Spaniard that he was, he had obtained from Delassus, the Spanish Governor, the valuable right to be the sole trader for the Osage Indians on the waters of the Missouri.[2]

Pierre Chouteau, an old established trader with the Osage, thereby lost a business he had enjoyed for years. However, the wily Chouteau was not one to accept adverse fortune calmly, so he built a rival trading establishment on the Arkansas River and persuaded over half of the tribe to move into that region. Since Lisa's grant only covered the waters of the Missouri, he could take no legal action against the maneuver. Some time later, he made the impolitic mistake of writing an impertinent letter to the Governor, which resulted in Lisa languishing several days in jail and did not enhance the Governor's esteem for him.

The transfer of the territory to the United States on March 10, 1804, put an end to Lisa's monopoly, which had never been very profitable. General James Wilkinson became the American governor in 1805, and it was not long before he was referring to Lisa as the "Black Spaniard." [3] For the second time, in characteristic fashion, Lisa had incurred the intense dislike of a man who could do his interests much harm.

Since Manuel Lisa was born in New Orleans of Spanish parents, it is not strange that he should have looked toward the almost legendary city of Santa Fe in his endeavors to develop a new field of business operations. In this scheme, which he never relinquished, he was many years ahead of his time. His plan for development of trade with Santa Fe very likely ran counter to some personal ambitions of Governor Wilkinson, and that accomplished schemer did not hesitate to use his official position to hinder Lisa in every possible way. [4]

H. M. Brackenridge, writing several years later and quoting Lisa, stated that the flotilla made a "tolerable force" [5] when it departed from St. Louis on April 19, 1807, since two boats had joined for company with Lisa's two. However, in a deposition for a law suit some years later, Lisa asserted that his expedition had only one keel boat. [6]

The cargo of food, Indian trading goods, guns and powder was carried in a shallow draft keel boat which had a small cabin for the leader or *bourgeois*, in addition to the limited space for freight. The crew, who propelled the boat with oars, or pushed it with long poles, slept ashore in hastily erected shelters. This type of boat sought the slack water along the bank and the eddies created by the current in the middle of the stream. In rapid water the boat was hauled by men struggling through the brush and trees along the shore, pulling on hand-lines known as cordelles. The heavy, unwieldy boats could usually make no progress against the main current and, in fact, had difficulty crossing from one bank to the other.

The keel boat also carried a square sail which could be used when the wind was sufficiently strong and from the proper direction. The twisting channel of the Missouri would usually put an end to such luxurious cruises, even if the wind did not shift or die down. The specific type of breeze required for the river ahead must have ranked high in the prayers of the French Canadians who specialized in the backbreaking work of handling the keel boat on the river. The high percentage of French names on the roster of Lisa's party was typical of other early-day fur expeditions.

Canoes hewn from logs formed a part of Lisa's force, as the tiny craft were needed to transport the hunters and bring in the game upon which the party almost entirely subsisted. The ever shifting Missouri River also frequently required investigation, to determine the navigable channels around the numerous islands.

The expedition departed from St. Louis on April 19, 1807, but Manuel Lisa is known to have stayed on for an additional two weeks before actually beginning the first of his known twelve trips up the Missouri. Before his death in 1822, he spent seven winters with the Indians in their villages, or in primitive, hastily constructed trading posts. During this entire period Lisa's business methods were the object of criticism and suspicion on the part of his competitors, and the same feelings were shared in more than one instance by his own colleagues. Nonetheless, his extensive experience and proven abilities won him positions with most of the expeditions up the Missouri during his lifetime.

The actual departure of the party was delayed due to the necessity of sending the constable to the *Vide Poche* [empty pocket] district of St. Louis and serving a warrant on one of the *engagés*, Jean Baptiste Bouché, who had not come on board the boat. The practice was to advance the *engagés* some money at the time they signed on for the expedition, to assist their families during their absence. However, the *engagé* frequently changed his mind or had not completed his celebration by sailing time; so the trader had to take legal action and arrange for the constable to bring the recalcitrant, if not incapacitated, recruit on board. In the case of Bouché, Lisa would have saved the constable's fee many times over by going off without him, as from all accounts, he was a complete liability to the expedition. The only good he is known to have accomplished was to have won a judgment against Lisa for three hundred and twenty dollars and fifty cents, which sum represented the approximate wage that a competent *engagé* would have earned for three years' work. This caused Manuel Lisa to make a deposition regarding the expedition for the purpose of appealing the decision. Slivers of information gleaned from the verbose legal jargon of this curious document in both English and French add to our meagre knowledge of the expedition. Even so, the rascality of Bouché had to mellow for a century before the able historian, Judge Walter B. Douglas, put it to good use in his excellent work on Manuel Lisa.[7]

On May 14, 1807, while the expedition was near the mouth of the Osage River, Antoine Bissonet deserted after having hidden blankets and equipment on the shore. In the heat of his anger, Manuel Lisa ordered George Drouillard to follow Bissonet and gave the following instructions before witnesses: "go and bring him back dead or alive."[8] Drouillard succeeded in overtaking Bissonet and did bring him back, but more dead than alive from a gun-shot wound. Repenting of his impulsive orders, Lisa immediately dispatched the gravely wounded Bissonet by canoe to the nearest settlement, but to no avail, as the deserter died on the river not far from St. Charles. Months later, Drouillard was tried for murder but acquitted, possibly owing to the emphasis laid by the defense attorney upon his brilliant record while with Lewis and Clark.

This incident illustrates in somewhat exaggerated fashion the great difference between the lax methods employed by the fur companies and the strict military discipline of the Lewis and Clark expedition. The deserter Bissonet was replaced immediately by a new recruit whose name in after years was to bear one of the blackest reputations in the fur trade. The replacement was Edward Rose, of mixed blood and dubious background, who had lived for several years with the Osage Indians on the river of the same name, and must have been previously known to Lisa.

By the beginning of June the party reached the Kansas River, and there Lisa engaged Francois Le Compt from Madelain. His contract [9] stated that after the completion of three years of service he was to receive $500. The two witnesses to the contract were Francois Hortiz and Robert McClellan.

The constant battle against the powerful current of the Missouri was continued. Falling banks, mercurial sandbars and the deadly "sawyers" added their exasperating dangers to the more obvious perils of the expedition. The "sawyers" were also called "embarras" by the French Canadians and were trees that had fallen into the water with the roots still clinging to the bank. Everyone on the river feared those trees undigested by the rapacious floods, their dead branches groping with the flow of the muddy water for unwary boats and their cargoes.

The great loop of the Missouri approximately doubles the airline distance the crow is reputed to fly from its headwaters to St. Louis. For nearly a generation the fur brigades consumed many months inching their way upstream to the rapid waters of the Upper Missouri, before the Rocky Mountain fur traders found they could save time and distance by traveling overland with pack trains. The broad valley of the Platte represented such a natural highway to the mountains that few trips were necessary for the traders to discover the best routes, and also prove that wagons could readily be taken into the heart of the fur country on the Green. The provision wagons of the fur traders raised the first small plumes of dust beside the sprawling waters of the Platte, which later grew into the choking clouds that on a still day marked the Oregon Trail to the Pacific Coast.

The lines must have been cast off with high spirits when the party headed up river again with Colter on board, as he was a competent guide for both the headwaters of the Missouri and the middle Yellowstone region. Some time later, Lisa made absolutely certain of having available all possible geographical information for the area in which he intended to operate by hiring Forrest Hancock [10] and, possibly, Joseph Dixon, when they were encountered on the upper river.

On July 12, presumably after the party had passed the Platte, the keel boat became damaged in some unknown manner. Jean Baptiste Bouché was ordered to cut twelve pieces of timber for repairing the boat, but refused. He not only disobeyed orders but threatened to incite the Indians whom they should meet against Lisa.

Shortly afterwards, the insufferable Bouché took advantage of the shortage of game to demonstrate his true character. While the party was subsisting on a daily ration of a quarter of a pound of salt pork per man, Bouché surreptitiously removed this scanty supply of meat from the kettles, roasted it to his own taste, and consumed the entire portion. In the face of the officers' disapproval, he then saw to it that a buck, weighing four hundred pounds, was completely eaten in one day by the forty-odd men. Two days later, he refused to spread out some meat to dry in the sun, thus completing his wholly negative contribution to the party's food supply.

Notwithstanding these annoyances, the party arrived in the territory of the ever dangerous Teton Sioux, and Lisa wisely prohibited all solitary hunting trips. The irrepressible Bouché reacted immediately to this situation by absenting himself on a hunting journey of his own for a period of four days, during which time the rest of the party remained tied up alongside the bank and watched the favorable, following wind blow uselessly up the stream. Upon his return, on July 31, Bouché was doubtless informed in great detail of just how many stupid animals he closely resembled. Lisa considered it a logical sequence of this event that in the middle of the night some unidentified person cut the rope tying the keel boat to the bank. Lisa chanced to awaken in sufficient time to save the boat from running aground or capsizing. George Drouillard thwarted a second cowardly attempt a few nights later. Suspicion pointed to Bouché, but there was no conclusive proof. The sum total of Bouché's crimes would seem to equal, if not exceed, the single act of desertion which cost Bissonet his life.

On a good day, a keel boat under sail with a strong tail wind, could make thirty miles. The crew of Lisa's boat unquestionably responded willingly enough to the call for additional speed, since its object was to leave the piratical Teton Sioux behind them.

The Arikara village, situated about 1440 miles from St. Louis, with its palisade of cedar logs and nearby cultivated fields, had represented to earlier expeditions a friendly haven from the truculent Sioux. These relatively industrious people who lived in permanent abodes and cultivated the soil to some extent, in succeeding years gained a reputation for unpredictable behavior. This tribe took the lives of many white travellers during their ferocious and often unprovoked excursions into belligerency.

Lisa and his party were fortunate in that the Arikara, upon their approach, demonstrated their angry mood by lining two or three hundred warriors along the bank of the river. As the boat drew nearer, those braves who had firearms shot across the bow, thereby indicating where the landing should be made.

Based on the first-hand account received from Lisa, Brackenridge has given the following vivid description of their reception: "He accordingly put to shore, but instantly made it known, that no one of them was to enter his boat: the chiefs at the same time appointed warriors to stand guard and keep off the crowd. The women, who always trade amongst these nations came to beach with bags of corn, which they offered: an Indian rushed forward, cut open the bags with his knife, while the women took to flight. Lisa, who was perfectly acquainted with Indian character, knowing that the least appearance of alarm would be dangerous, instantly called his men to arms, pointed a couple of swivels which were fixed on his boats, and made every preparation for defence. The Indians perceiving this, dispersed in confusion; and after some time the chiefs approached with pipes of peace extended before them in their hands. Lisa making signs of reconciliation, they came to him, and according to their custom, stroked him on the shoulders, begging him not to be displeased, declaring that the Indian who had offended him was considered a bad man. This had a good effect, and enabled him to proceed on his voyage without further molestation." [11]

In actual fact, Lisa was far from finished with the episode when the Indians permitted the party to proceed up the river. It happened that there were two parties following: the first under the command of the recently promoted Ensign Nathaniel Pryor, and the second led by Lisa's old rival, Pierre Chouteau. The Arikara attacked both parties and drove them back, thereby preventing Pryor from completing his

INTERIOR OF THE HUT OF A MANDAN CHIEF   Karl Bodmer

ASSINIBOIN AND YANKTON INDIANS   Karl Bodmer

(Lithos.—New York Historical Society)

mission of returning the Mandan chief, Shehaka, to his people. In the encounter several men were wounded and two of Chouteau's brigade were killed. On the basis of a captive Indian squaw's story, Ensign Pryor later asserted that Lisa, in order to protect his own party, had given the Arikara guns and powder. Chouteau alleged that his boat had been stopped by the Arikara because Lisa had informed them his trade goods were on Chouteau's vessel. The business ethics of the fur traders were strictly cutthroat and Lisa managed to hold his own against such competition. However, the facts of this episode, as well as a number of others in which Lisa was accused of sharp practice cannot now be determined.

The Mandan Villages, a relatively short distance up the river, closely resembled those of the Arikara, but the similarity did not extend to the inhabitants. The light complexions and brown hair of the Mandans, so markedly different from their neighbors, convinced some early travellers that the tribe was descended from a lost band of Welsh who had left their native land centuries before. These Mandans were also conspicuous for their mild manners and hospitable habits, by which the Lewis and Clark expedition had profited so much in the winter of 1804 and 1805.

Before the white men visited the Mandan Villages, they had become trading centers for the surrounding tribes. English traders[12] for several years had been making trading trips from the Assiniboine River, supplying them with goods that had improved their ability to trade with their neighbors. Therefore, it would not have required any unusually clever propaganda campaign for the Mandans to have become convinced that Lisa was a business rival whose activities would harm their commercial interests.

Lisa had gone ashore upon reaching the first village, intending to walk by the earthen huts and visit the fields of maize, squash and tobacco surrounding them, while his boat ascended the river. In the first and second villages he held council with the respective chiefs and gave them the customary presents of tobacco rolls and other articles. Brackenridge describes the unexpected reception in the third village, as follows: "At the third village, his presents were rejected, and the chief demanded some powder, which was refused: Lisa knew that his life was in no danger while his death could not procure them his goods, and resisted their repeated solicitations in a bold and firm manner; he told them that they might kill him, but that his property would be safe. They were finally compelled to accept such presents as he offered." [13]

The party evidently had the good fortune to pass by the Gros Ventre or Hidatsa Villages without incident, as Lisa did not relate any stories about them that Brackenridge felt warranted mention in his account of the trip. However, the expedition did encounter the Assiniboine tribe encamped along the banks of the Missouri. These nomadic people, part of the Sioux tribes, did not build permanent villages but ranged the country to the northwest of the Mandans. The attitude of the tribe was always unpredictable, but Lisa was fortunate since the Indians immediately disclosed their hostility. Their scouts had brought in the news of the approaching boat and the whole prairie, to use Lisa's expression, was "red with them."[14] The entire nation, estimated by Lisa as four or five thousand, came down to the river bank on foot and horseback, all painted for war.

The situation became so tense that Lisa decided to make the first aggressive move. The swivel guns on the boat were charged and all hands were ordered to load their firearms. The boat was suddenly swung directly toward the Assiniboine. When they were only a hundred yards away, a match was put to the swivel and at the same time the small arms were fired. The shots were deliberately aimed high to terrify the Indian audience. The tactics were most successful as "the effect was ludicrous, they fell back, tumbled over each other, and fled to the hills with precipitation." [15] Only a few of the chiefs and warriors remained, but these were sufficient to bring about a council, during which the pipe was ceremoniously smoked with rigid adherence to age-old custom.

Leaving the Assiniboine behind, the expedition resumed its journey up the Missouri. As the brigade neared the mouth of the Yellowstone, John Colter must have been summoned frequently to take part in the deliberations of Lisa, Drouillard and Vasquez; to decide whether they should continue up the Missouri as originally planned, or ascend the Yellowstone. The hostility of the Blackfeet and Colter's experience on the Yellowstone would seem to have dictated the decision to go into the heart of the Crow territory.

The current of the Yellowstone River is more rapid than that of the Missouri. This unpleasant fact undoubtedly provoked continual arguments among the boatmen as to how many prime beaver skins would fully compensate for the difficulties of handling the unwieldy boat against the surging current. The *engagés* could rarely keep their trousers dry as they slipped and stumbled along the muddy, rock-strewn beaches, or waded through the quiet pools of backwater. When the main current raced to undermine in secret the cut banks, the taut cordelle line became a jerking searing cord almost possessed of human cunning. The men had to maintain their hold on the line and at the same time scramble up the crumbling earth to reach the bank over-hanging the water. In later years, the fur traders bought horses from the nearby Crows and thereby spared the ill-clad backs of their men from the galling effects of the cordelle lines. We have no record of Lisa's having used horses for pulling the boats, but it is known that the following summer the company owned a few horses.

For nearly six weeks, perhaps because there was sufficient food, Jean Baptiste Bouché had conducted himself in an acceptable manner. However, on October 10, he demonstrated that his vicious mind had not been idle. On that day Lusignon, an undersized man, provoked a quarrel with Lisa at the instigation of Bouché. It was expected that Lisa would strike Lusignon and in so doing provide Bouché and his friends with an excuse to join the fight and kill Lisa during the *melée*, without exposing themselves to the charge of deliberate murder. Lisa kept his temper for once and frustrated the entire scheme. Bouché subsequently offered two hundred dollars to anyone who would kill Lisa, but there were no claimants for the reward, possibly because everyone knew that Bouché did not have that much money. The epi-sode was terminated when someone took an unsuccessful shot at Lisa from ambush. Lisa had strong suspicions but no conclusive proof of the identity of this early exponent of a practise that in later years became known as "dry gulching."

The brigade arrived at the mouth of the Big Horn River, or La Corne as Lisa called it, in October, 1807. Our authority for this date is the first map drawn by William Clark, August 5, 1808, on the basis of information supplied by George Drouillard,[16] just returned from Fort Raymond. On November 21, 1807, the incorrigible Bouché refused to cut some wooden pins for the roof of a house, and Judge Douglas misinterpreted the statement in Lisa's appeal of the judgment against him obtained by Bouché, as having been the arrival date.[17] Log trading posts were rapidly constructed, but rarely so fast that the roof was on by the end of the first day. Lisa did allege in his appeal that the expedition was delayed a month, and placed the entire responsibility on Bouché. The charge seems grossly exaggerated, although the only thing known to Bouché's credit is the fact that his misdeeds have supplied us with most of our information about the early days of Fort Raymond.

The first permanent building in what is now the state of Montana was a log cabin, consisting of two rooms and a loft. Lisa named the trading fort, Raymond, after his son, though it came to be much better known as Manuel's Fort. The name was also spelled "Remon" by Lisa, who could speak three languages, but was unable to write any of them well. The correct location of Manuel's Fort and the proper date, 1807, are shown on Clark's map in the Biddle edition of the Lewis and Clark narrative.

The *engagés* had hardly begun to find out that a smooth axe-handle could raise painful blisters on hands already heavily calloused, before the hunters had completed their preliminary surveys of the surrounding country and picked out the landmarks that forever after would indicate to them the exact location of the fort. John Colter was possibly one of the hunters who left a quantity of meat on a scaffold located on the south side of the Big Horn, about a mile from the fort. Lisa, having discovered that Bouché was unwilling to use an axe, dispatched him to bring the meat back to the fort. Bouché, of course, refused and as a result the grizzly bears and wolves had a feast at Lisa's expense. In his appeal, Lisa had the audacity to place a value of one thousand dollars on the meat that was destroyed.

This trading fort had coal for fuel, a luxury that was not often encountered on the frontier during that period. There are deposits near the mouth of the Big Horn which could have been worked with little difficulty, at least enough to keep the fort well supplied with fuel. We are again indebted to the obstreperous Bouché for this bit of information, as he refused to tend the coal "kiln."

The established practice among the fur companies had been to build a trading post convenient to one or more tribes, and within the security of the palisades await the coming of the Indians to barter their peltry. Lisa varied this procedure by also sending out his own trappers to hunt for beaver skins. From the point of view of proximity to Indians, the fort was well located in the heart of the Crow country, as that tribe was comparatively peaceful. The Sioux, Cheyennes, and Blackfeet, all came into the Yellowstone Valley to hunt buffalo and theoretically they could have also traded at the new fort; in addition, Nez Percé, Shoshone and Bannocks, in the beginning of the nineteenth century, also made annual trips across the Rockies to make their winter hunt along the Yellowstone. In theory the post was well situated, but in actual practice so many of the tribes were bitter enemies that the trade was largely with the Crows.

The fort was established relatively near both the Rocky Mountains and the Big Horns. The Big Horn River between the lower canyon and the Yellowstone was described by Nathaniel Wyeth, nearly thirty years later, as providing the best trapping on a large stream that he had ever seen in the mountains.[18] Thus the hunters of the party were for some time able to work out of the fort proper.

The expedition's arrival at the wintering ground in October meant that less than two months of the fall trapping season remained. The few pelts the hunters could collect from the traps set near the fort, between their quests for meat to be dried for the severe winter months, must have represented such a poor return on nearly one year's operation for the company that Lisa can be pardoned for attempting desperate measures to reduce the large operating deficit.

The only way the firm could commence quickly the business of gathering furs was by trading with the neighboring Indian tribes, who were probably still ignorant of the trading post then under construction. Early November was obviously not the most propitious time to send men out in search of the various bands of Crows in their winter camps located in secluded valleys or canyons. Nonetheless, we know of at

71

least two emissaries who were sent out that winter, namely: John Colter and Edward Rose.

The little known biography of Edward Rose, "Five Scalps," [19] is our only authority that he was a member of this expedition. The author, Captain R. Holmes, an army officer who knew Rose personally, described him as a sinister-looking individual of mixed blood. The captain asserted that during a fight some unknown person had improved upon nature's handiwork by biting out a piece of his nose, and that Rose was further disfigured by an ugly brand on his forehead. On occasion Rose would enhance the effect by assuming fiendish facial expressions. This morbid histrionic ability, coupled with rash courage and phenomenal strength, gave him prestige among the Indians.

Edward Rose had lived several years with the Osage Indians and was probably well known to Manuel Lisa. Therefore, it was logical that Rose should have been selected as one of the several emissaries sent out to the Crows. Rose was put in charge of a small group of men that transported their trade goods with pack horses to one of the Crow villages, which was presumably near Fort Manuel. The River Crows normally wintered along the Yellowstone Valley, and Rose and his men joined one of their camps with instructions to trade during the extreme cold weather.

Rose and his men held the usual council upon their arrival in the village, and judiciously distributed the gifts customary on such an occasion. Years later, Rose informed Captain Holmes that he had particularly noted that the Crows evidenced a high regard for the donor of the presents. He also related how he had entered into the tribal life with gusto, easily picked up some of the language, and proved to the Crows that "he could run a buffalo or a Blackfoot as well as they could." The Crows professed surprise that a white man could compete with them on equal terms in such activities, and thereby began the subtle campaign of playing upon Rose's ego that ultimately resulted in the failure of his mission. Rose's costly fiasco augmented the importance of John Colter's journey the same winter.

Chapter Five

Colter's Route

The broken rhythm of the *engagés'* axes and the frequent rending crash of a falling tree might lead one to suspect that the unnatural din was the reason why a hunter like Colter shunned the post site during the daylight hours. The freezing nights, however, had thickened the beaver fur to the prime condition prized in St. Louis and London, and the nearby ponds had already experienced the ruthless efficiency of the profit-hungry trappers. In addition, an accomplished tongue lashing by Manuel Lisa was known to await any hunter who was so thoroughly lacking in the pride of his calling as to loaf around the fort during the trapping season. In fact, Lisa was considered capable of demoting such a laggard to the indignity and drudgery of swinging an axe with the lowly *engagés*.

Those familiar with the region, such as Colter and Drouillard, must have lost no time telling the trappers the location of the best beaver streams. Consequently the small trapping parties became more and more infrequent visitors to the log-strewn clearing, as they extended their operations up the Yellowstone and the Big Horn Rivers. Nearly thirty years later, Nathaniel Wyeth described the Big Horn as being one of the best beaver streams he had ever seen. Thus the first catch of pelts may have been taken in phenomenal time, thereby giving the badly worried Lisa and his assistants renewed hope and the courage to carry out their more ambitious plans. A trading expedition to a nearby Crow village is known to have been one of the first schemes put into execution. This venture, led by Edward Rose, was in accordance with Lisa's previous method of operating.

The tiny pack outfit, laden with trade goods and well-justified expectations of success, would have barely wound out of sight into the brush along the river bank, before the aggressive Lisa called in his lieutenants to discuss the next move. Since sufficient horses were available to provide Rose with a pack train, it is likely that some trading had already been done with the Crows who usually owned large herds of horses. The same Indians may have given some information about the favored localities for setting up winter camps. The data derived from this primitive survey, coupled with the company's urgent need of customers with skins for barter, brought the traders to the conclusion that the neighboring tribes had to be advised of the new trading post with all possible speed.

One of the most obvious choices for such an assignment was John Colter; and his advertising tour subsequently became extended into one of the most difficult and hazardous journeys ever deliberately undertaken in western history. The trail he made through approximately five hundred miles of mountainous terrain would not be easy for the hiker of today to follow with the assistance of modern maps and roads. The magnitude of Colter's performance can only be appreciated by bearing in mind that most of the journey was made in the severe winter months, and that in some manner he made his way through jumbled mountain ranges that frequently baffle those who have lived in them all their lives.

The financial arrangements made with Lisa at the Platte would hardly have included compensation for such an expedition, particularly as Colter must have missed the best part of both the fall and spring trapping seasons. Unfortunately, those records of Lisa that are now available contain no informative references to Colter's affairs. Nonetheless, there are no grounds for believing that Lisa either coerced or inveigled Colter into attempting the trip against his will or better judgment. The hunter had already demonstrated that he could make long trips alone, and indeed very likely he had created the impression that he welcomed the opportunity of undertaking difficult assignments by himself. During the previous winter he had perfected the art of living in the open with no more protection than a robe or a blanket. The mere fact that he survived is sufficient proof that he possessed this ability, as subzero weather rarely affords a second chance to rectify mistakes.

Colter did not need much time to stow away in his pack the thirty pounds of equipment and supplies he is known to have carried, but considerable thought must have gone into the selection of trade goods that were so essential.[1] Awls, beads, vermilion and needles would not take up much space, but other articles such as knives and tobacco had to be included even though they were heavier and bulky. The goods Colter took with him were not just samples of the wares available at the trading post, but rather represented the currency with which he made the traditional gifts to his Indian hosts and paid for his supplies of food and clothing. Lead for bullets was another important trading commodity, since some of the Indians had already obtained guns from the British traders to the north; yet Colter could not possibly have carried much more of that heavy metal than his own ammunition requirements.

An active imagination was a definite liability to the professional trapper, as even the dull-witted often had difficulty keeping their composure when it was known that war parties were out seeking the additional deeds of valor needed to increase a warrior's standing with the tribe. It is unlikely that Colter's qualms surpassed those vicariously experienced by the *engagés* in the relative security of the hewn log shelters, as they watched him set out through the sagebrush. All the same, Colter could not have been without some misgivings. During the previous winter he had seen enough of that tangled maze of mountains to realize the task he was undertaking. But however puzzled he may have become on the trip as to his proper direction, he would have been more than perplexed if he had had any notion of the storms of controversy his route was to raise among writers many years later.

The seeds of the arguments that followed were sown by persons other than John Colter. He contributed materially by not giving a detailed account of his trip to any of the several competent writers he encountered, or making certain that his family or friends were able to preserve either his own written version or a crude sketch of his route. In fact, it is not known whether Colter drew a map for William Clark, or just told him of his route. Actually, the fact that neither a journal nor a map exists does not prove that none ever existed, but rather that they may not yet have been discovered.

The traditions that the mountain men have handed down about Colter's feat are supported by a few lamentably brief published accounts and three maps. Some of the less harsh things that have been said about the principal source of information, namely, William Clark's map as published in 1814,[2] are that it is badly out of scale, especially in the region of Colter's Route, and that the courses of several rivers are more artistic than accurate. This map which is entitled, "A Map of Lewis and Clark's Track Across the Western Portion of North America From the Mississippi to the Pacific Ocean," for nearly a hundred years represented the principal tangible evidence of Colter's fabled journey.

The difference is startling between the published map of 1814 and the meticulous field charts drawn by Clark which make no reference to Colter's Route.[3] Each individual field sketch reflects the care with which Clark noted the data that he, as a surveyor, army engineer and experienced woodsman, well knew would be invaluable to any one traveling through the same country. The mouths of the tributary streams were carefully noted and identifying names given to the more important creeks. Conspicuous landmarks such as islands, hills, mountains, and prominent rocks were indicated in a manner quite suggestive of the modern technique of preparing topographical maps. Students of the expedition nearly a century later have been able to retrace parts of the trail that could not be identified from the narrative and journals by themselves.

These field maps, now in the W. R. Coe Collection of Yale University Library, were drawn on many sheets of paper numbered so they could be joined together. These sheets, however, did not form a large square, but rather followed the courses of the principal rivers. Jefferson probably saw the field maps for the first time at the then uncompleted White House in Washington, in February 1807, with both captains vainly trying to answer his flood of questions.

In the spring of 1810, William Clark was in Virginia and conferred with Jefferson about the publication of a report on the expedition. Such a conference could only have taken place at Monticello, the home of the then retired president which so dramatically portrays his personality. Clark brought with him a large comprehensive map, which he had prepared on the basis of his field maps and other available data. Jefferson could not have examined this new map without comparing it with the field charts spread out on the floor of his study. Crawling about on hands and knees with their red hair often touching, is the only way the two men could have studied the maps, following the Missouri around the great bend to the Rocky Mountains, and then down the Columbia to the Pacific, extending through the archway and under Jefferson's suspended bed.

The method of inspecting the field maps was related by Jefferson, several years later, when writing to his friend and fellow scholar, Abbé Correa da Serra.[4] In the same letter Jefferson also stated that he considered the map as being only "tolerably accurate," as regards latitude. He further said that the two captains had only attempted to determine their latitude by celestial observation, having computed the longitude references "merely from estimates of the log-line, time and course."

The Lewis and Clark *Journals*, however, reveal that on more than one occasion, the leaders did attempt to determine their longitudinal position by astronomical observations. The minute details of all such observations had been carefully copied in several different volumes of the notes on express instructions from Jefferson, since he had anticipated that their calculations might have to be either adjusted or corrected by an experienced mathematician. The first attempt to ascertain their longitude, made at Fort Mandan,[5] was a failure, and the contributing causes not only justify Jefferson's precautions, but also indicate the criterion which a spirit of fairness requires be applied to all the Lewis and Clark maps.

An eclipse of the moon took place just after midnight on the morning of January 15, 1805, which afforded an excellent opportunity to compute the longitude of Fort Mandan. Apparently, the two leaders did not anticipate the event and only began timing the eclipse after they had been awakened by the sentry, but they timed it as well as the inadequate light and the congealing effects of a January night in North Dakota permitted. This observation was faithfully performed, although the captains were not sure that their chronometer was correct. Someone had forgotten to wind their one and only chronometer while the expedition was on the lower Missouri, and the captains the same night reset that all-important timepiece by a celestial observation.

Several years later, after having spent months in trying to correct their calculations and readjust their computations on the basis of the readings and his own extensive knowledge of astronomy and mathematics, Dr. Ferdinand Rudolph Hassler expressed the belief that the chronometer had been reset with a difference of over an hour from the correct time at the mouth of the Missouri. Dr. Hassler, an outstanding mathematician and geodetic surveyor, had been selected by Thomas Jefferson to go over the readings and calculations, and Lewis and Clark turned over to him, sometime in 1807, their notes and other data for correction.

The results of Dr. Hassler's studies were communicated months later to Meriwether Lewis in one or more letters. The outcome of this labor was just another item in the extensive list of calamities that stemmed from Meriwether Lewis's untimely death. The original plan had been for Lewis to write a narrative of the expedition which would be published for the personal profit of the two leaders and thereby provide them with more adequate compensation for their activities. Owing to the pressure of his public and private affairs, Lewis had accomplished very little, if any, writing of the narrative. William Clark, the executor of Lewis's estate was unable to locate among his private papers any letter or letters from Hassler.

Consequently, on January 26, 1810, Clark, while in Philadelphia, wrote to Dr. Hassler in Schenectady, to send him if possible any copies or data he might still have in his possession regarding the corrected calculations. There must have been a further exchange of correspondence, since, later in the spring of 1810, Clark turned over to Nicholas Biddle at Fincastle, Virginia, together with the journals, supplementary notes and field charts, a map prepared especially for Dr. Hassler's use and study.[6] Writing years later, Biddle described the map as being smaller than the comprehensive one inspected by Jefferson, but showing the course of the rivers and the parallels of latitude and the longitude meridians. The principal purpose of the chart was to indicate to Hassler the relative position of the various celestial observations.

This map has not been found, but as mathematicians are notoriously absent-minded it is hoped that it may be found in some completely illogical place. The American Philosophical Society and the New York Public Library, Ford Collection, two logical repositories, have no record of the map, but the latter does possess a letter dated August 13, 1810, from John Vaughan, who was assisting in the publication of the narrative on behalf of Jefferson, to Hassler. Vaughan quotes part of the letter, written the previous day, by Nicholas Biddle. Hassler had presented several questions to Biddle, who through Vaughan as intermediary was recommending that the questions be addressed to William Clark in St. Louis. In this same communication, Biddle added his own observation that there was a difference of nearly two degrees between the longitude of Fort Mandan as portrayed on the comprehensive map he was using and that which the journals indicate had been computed.

The realization of such a careless mistake, in conjunction with the additional information he was continually gathering from the fur traders, must have prompted Clark to draw a new comprehensive map. Unfortunately, Clark had not received the corrections from Dr. Hassler by the time the map was completed and forwarded to Biddle on December 10, 1810, with the explanation that "it is made on the same scale of the one you have, containing more country." [7]

Thus the revised and more comprehensive map represented the culmination of Clark's years of effort to put on paper the essence of his geographic knowledge of the vast region west of the Mississippi. Since this was the first map drawn by a man who had actually explored the territory and was the basis for the engraved chart that was published in 1814, there is no other single item among the known Lewis and Clark papers of equal importance. In fact, students have for more than a century searched for Clark's manuscript map with the zeal of a treasure hunter seeking pirate gold. The reason for this map being the most sought after of all the missing documents of western history is that it is the key to the discrepancies between the 1814 map and the data known to have been available to Clark.

This unique manuscript map was found recently, still in a cylindrical lead case bearing the scars of many journeys. It was purchased by

Mr. W. R. Coe and donated to the Yale Library. Those who have seen it and are familiar with William Clark's handwriting believe that he is the only man who could have drawn that map.

The portion of the map showing Colter's Route is shown on the opposite page. This segment provides the answers to many questions regarding the route, and to a question of a general nature that has definite bearing on Colter's Route. Four men, namely, William Clark, Samuel Lewis a cartographer, Samuel Harrison an engraver, and John Vaughan, by their combined efforts produced the 1814 map which was printed off the beautiful copper plate now owned by the American Philosophical Society. Many of the mistakes on the map regarding facts that were known correctly to Clark before December, 1810, have been attributed to the other three men. Most likely they did make errors, but only the completion of a badly needed cartographic study will definitely settle the question.

However, a comparison of the printed 1814 map and that in Clark's handwriting for the region of Colter's Route, will show that the engraver drew the misplaced mountains exactly where Clark indicated. The area of the Big Horn Mountains and Basin was depicted about twice too large, but precisely as Clark had instructed. These errors are difficult to reconcile with Clark's care in drawing his field charts, and the fact that before December, 1810, he had obtained a great deal of geographic information from two different men who had seen the greater part of the Big Horn country. Ironically enough, Clark had prepared in August, 1808, an excellent map of the region from information George Drouillard had given him.[8] A reproduction of this engrossing map follows the Clark map, and little comparison with the modern topographical map on the endpapers is needed before the conclusion is reached that the scale is reasonably accurate. A footnote on the Drouillard map explains the symbol " ठ ," as "days travel or thirty miles," thereby establishing the scale. Furthermore, the chart portrays the essential geography so minutely that today, a person unfamiliar with that country could easily follow the trail of George Drouillard, and, with the additional aid of the 1814 map, the route of John Colter.

Clark is known to have misjudged the speed of the Yellowstone

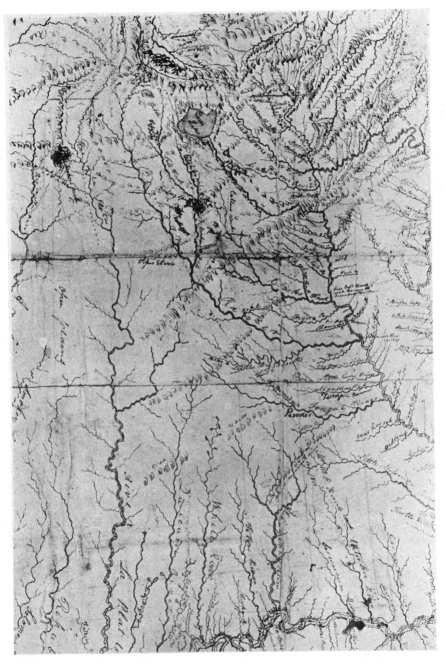

Section from manuscript map by William Clark used as the basis for printed map in the 1814 edition of the *History of the Expedition under the Command of Captains Lewis and Clark. Courtesy*, Yale University Library, W. R. Coe Collection.

Snow in summer covered
the pine and fur

ain country

little big

little Big Horn

confirmation

creek fills with bad
constant stream

ahtelope bend

big   Horn

River   River

fine Plain —

River   River

travil some Creek

Small Creek

20 m

Prior's river

River

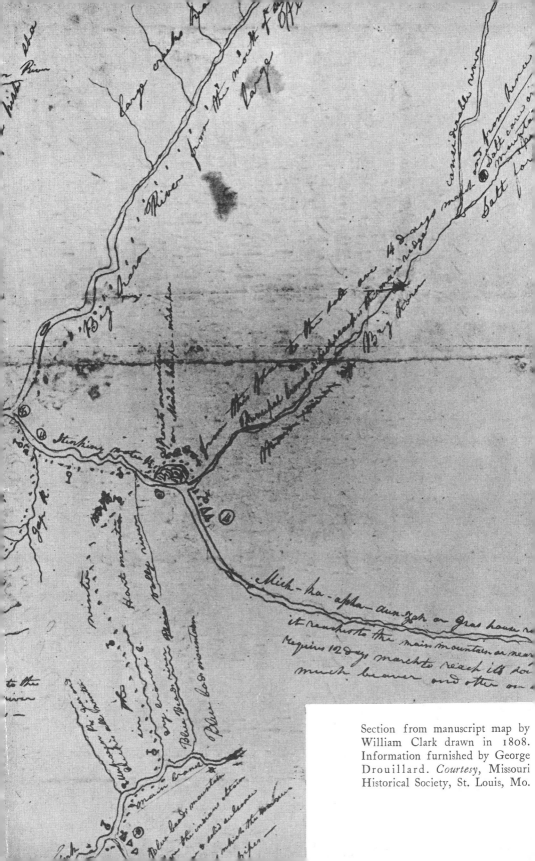

Section from manuscript map by William Clark drawn in 1808. Information furnished by George Drouillard. *Courtesy,* Missouri Historical Society, St. Louis, Mo.

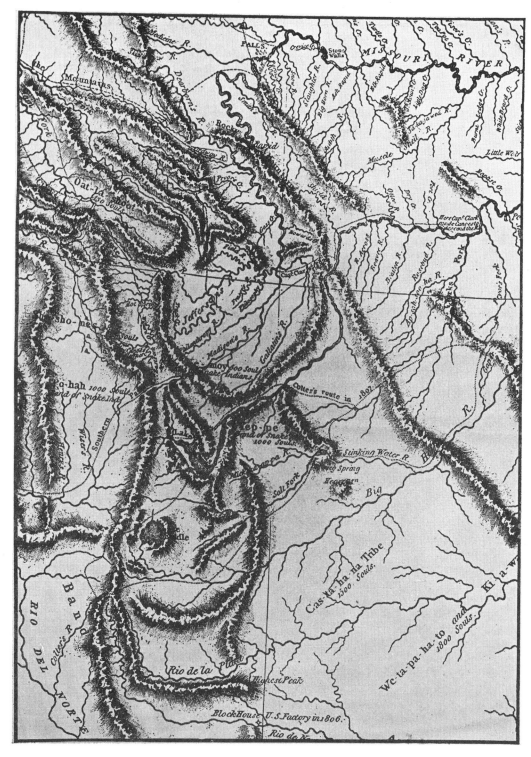

Section from map issued with *History of the Expedition under the Command of Captains Lewis and Clark*. Philadelphia, 1814.

River as he descended it. Thus it is inevitable that his concept of the expanse of country to the south of the river was wrong. However, this factor was subordinate to the conditions under which he prepared his maps. William Clark drew his charts in the spare time that remained after his duties as a major partner in the largest fur company and as a general of the militia had been fulfilled. Furthermore, he was not only a devoted family man, but one of the outstanding hosts in St. Louis also. He was in addition, agent for all the Indians in the Missouri valley, a function he performed so well that the Indian name for St. Louis was "Redhead's Town," and so honestly that the standard he established has never been exceeded and rarely approximated. Condemnation of Clark's map because it cannot be superimposed upon a modern map is carping criticism at its irrational worst.

In his correspondence, Clark repeatedly emphasized that what he had prepared was exactly what the title indicated, namely: "A Map of Lewis and Clark's *Track* Across the western Portion of North America. . . ." The map was used extensively by trappers and explorers for more than fifty years as the best available description of how to proceed from one point to another, and for approximate location of rivers, lakes and mountains; thereby paying it a tribute far more eloquent than words.

A new analysis of the Clark maps is indispensable, not only because of the newly discovered manuscript map, but also to scrape away the sludge of fanciful conjecture that armchair geographers have dumped on "Colter's Route," to the amazement of those who know the country. Some years ago, one commentator, on the basis of comparing with a modern map the pattern of streams drawn by Clark for country he had not seen, and ignoring a misplaced mountain range in that area, came to the conclusion that Colter had gone from the Sunlight Basin to the North Fork of the Shoshone, thence straight across the Wapiti and Hoodoo Ranges to Lake Yellowstone. Big game hunters advise that only a Big Horn sheep could climb those mountains in winter without the aid of a helicopter. Therefore, it is just as preposterous to superimpose a modern map of that region on Clark's map, as it would be to assert that Colter surmounted Wapiti Peak by means of his trusty sky hooks.

However, "Colter's Route" cannot be followed from Clark's map with easy accuracy without taking into consideration the written sources that are deemed reliable. The nearest approach to a written account of Colter's journey is that by Brackenridge, who, although he had met Colter, simply retold the second-hand story he had heard from Manuel Lisa. This tantalizing, brief account reads as follows: "He [Lisa] continued his voyage to the Yellowstone River, where he built a trading fort. He shortly after dispatched Coulter, the hunter before mentioned, to bring some of the Indian nations to trade. This man, with a pack of thirty pounds weight, his gun and some ammunition, went upwards of five hundred miles to the Crow nation; gave them information, and proceeded from them to several other tribes. On his return, a party of Indians in whose company he happened to be was attacked, and he was lamed by a severe wound in the leg; notwithstanding which, he returned to the establishment, entirely alone and without assistance, several hundred miles." [9]

The discoveries made by Colter were of the type that appealed strongly to Brackenridge and it is odd that the author, with his unusual reporting ability, did not extract more information from the hunter after his return from the mountains. John Bradbury, the English botanist, also made no mention of Colter's discoveries, although we can readily forgive Bradbury because he has given us the classic description of Colter's escape from the Blackfeet quoted in Chapter Six.

Brackenridge and Bradbury both talked to John Colter; however, it is likely that part of the information they had about his activities came to them indirectly through Clark. The latter was skilled in the art of extracting geographic knowledge from inarticulate mountain men, and furthermore enjoyed Colter's confidence. There is no indication that Clark made any notes of his conversations with Colter.

Thus the sole surviving record of the data imparted by Colter must have been inserted by Clark on his manuscript map. And yet, various circumstances present cogent reasons for believing that Colter never saw Clark's master map. The most important is the odd error committed by Clark in beginning the dotted line of Colter's Route halfway up Pryor Creek, instead of at the mouth of the Big Horn, the only possible starting point. This indefensible omission results in our not knowing whether Colter set out from Manuel's Fort directly across the hills toward the Pryor Mountains, or followed up the "As-to-pah-oan-zhah" as the Indians called their Elk River, now the Yellowstone. In the latter case, his first stop would have been the mysterious "Pot's establishment" of Drouillard's map, which may have been a small trading and trapping post under the direction of John Potts. Drouillard's map shows that there was an Indian camp above Pompey's Pillar, at the junction of Pryor's Fork with the Yellowstone. Colter would not logically have devoted much time to this band because of their proximity to the trading post.

The trails that ascended Pryor Creek were well traveled, as both the mountain and river branches of the Crows frequently visited the "Mire-pe-awn-zhah," their name for the stream. The headwaters near Pryor Gap were sacred ground to the Absaroka. This region was a favored location for winter camps and its was therefore essential that Colter climb to the summit of Pryor Mountains in his search for Indian customers. This was the first of many difficult and illogical side-trips on Colter's route that have no explanation other than that he was searching for Indians in their winter camps. The exact location of each band was a closely guarded tribal secret. Thus Colter had to visit methodically the principal localities where it was known an abundance of tall grass and sweet cottonwood would attract the game which provided the Indians with their food and clothing.

The easy climb to the top of Pryor Mountains enabled Colter to look down on several other favored camping sites including those at the junction of the Stinking Water and the Big Horn Rivers. From the mountain top, facing south, he saw the empty bed of an ancient inland sea that had been confined on the east by the Big Horn Mountains and on the west by the Rockies. On a clear day he would have been able to distinguish the Owl Creek and Bridger Mountains that form the boundary of the Big Horn Basin, more than a hundred miles to the south. As he absorbed the geography of the immense, eroded area before him, Colter understood why the Indians considered the small mountain on which he stood as part of the "Ammah-hah-pa-ish-sha," or the Red Mountains, since it had been carved off the main chain by the incalculable force that dug the exit from the Basin, the Big Horn Canyon. The derivation of the name Red Mountains was vividly revealed as being the extensive red sandstone formations along the mountains below timber line to the south of the gigantic "W's" of Horse Creek and Shell Creek Canyons.

While on top of the mountain Colter probably took extra precautions that his campfires were made of dry wood and extinguished before sunset. He had no reason for knowing that if he had built four huge bonfires on a prominent point on four successive nights, he might have saved himself many miles of weary walking. This ritualistic display of fires happened to be the signal that had been arranged with Antoine Larocque two years before to announce the return of traders to the Yellowstone valley.[10]

In September, 1805, Larocque, after a profitable trading session on an island in the Yellowstone River above the mouth of the Big Horn, had informed the Absaroka that he intended to trade with them again the following year. Consequently, it was agreed that the arrival of the traders would be announced by lighting four signal fires on four successive nights on the summit of "Amanchabe-clije." This is the way the Indian name for the mountains, which could only be Pryor Mountains from the directions given, registered on Larocque's ear, accustomed to the dissimilar sounds of English and French as well as several northern Indian languages.

Antoine Larocque did not return to the Yellowstone in 1806, owing to a change of policy in the Northwest Company, a modification which was quite possibly one of the immediate results of the Lewis and Clark expedition. There were a number of the Hidatsa aware of the fire-signal agreement with the Crows, but it is unlikely they shared their secret with Lisa since their ugly mood discouraged the trader from lingering in their village. Lisa would have had no scruples in utilizing such a signal had he known of its existence and would have probably set the fires in the belief that even a year later, curiosity would have attracted some bands to the Yellowstone valley.

However, we have no grounds for believing that Colter stayed four nights on the mountain top before he turned toward the west and began to descend the gentle slope of the Pryors where they cease to be mountains and merge into the badlands. This not inconsequential chain of bare, gray hills links with the Absaroka Mountains a few miles away. Water slides off those adobe badlands as if they were mammoth ducks' backs, so unless there had been a recent snowfall, Colter's need of drinking water would have forced him to angle toward the nearby broad fertile valley of the Clark's Fork. The sprawling woods and brush patches along the rushing As-kis-pe-ah-aun-zah, as the Indians called the stream, became more and more familiar as Colter neared the cliff at the mouth of the canyon where he had shared a crude hut the previous winter with Hancock and Dixon. The smoked rocks may have been the only sign he found that white men had dwelt there for months, as the Indians would likely have eradicated all traces of the makeshift cabin.

The memories of the old campsite may have been such that Colter hastened to follow the familiar trail up the side of the mountain. In breaking out of the Sunlight Basin, the Clark's Fork has cut a deep canyon surmounted by a large triangular gap, which from a distance looks as if a gigantic multi-layered sandwich had been wrenched into two uneven segments.

Despite the fact that Colter had seen the gouged enormity of the Sunlight Basin at least once before, he would have been a callous man if he did not pause and absorb again the expanse of canyons, towering swollen hills, and distant mountains that spread out in front of him. As he went down toward the forks of the river, Colter should have alternated his admiration of the view with a more mundane search for the faint wisps of smoke and pony herds that would indicate a camp of Crows at one of their favored spots near the junction of the Ap-sah-roo-ka fork with the main river.

Drouillard visited a large village of Crows at this location the same winter and gave Clark a detailed summary of the attractions of this spot as a wintering place. The notes Clark made on the Drouillard map read: "The camp that the Crow Indians winter—here they find an herb which rises about nine inches high evergreen smells like sage —small and obicular leaf—leaves abundant—fall when horses bite it—this forms the food for the horses and the inducement to the Indians to winter here—abundance of buffaloe, elk, antelope etc."

This graphic note reflects Clark's very personal interest in the stream named for him, and the care with which he incorporated useful details into the map. This chart can be studied for hours without exhausting the geographic, historical and ethnological information it contains.

There is no reason for believing that Colter could have added much to the information Drouillard gave Clark on these Crow villages, as the trapper probably did not prolong his stay in that vicinity. The fear that a heavy snowfall might confine him to the Sunlight Basin until spring unquestionably prompted Colter to visit no longer than the minimum permitted by Indian good manners. The principal trail out of the Basin must have passed close to the blue-bead quarry shown on Drouillard's map from which the Indians obtained the stone they carved into pipe bowls. The Crows grew on Pryor's Fork most of their tobacco which was prepared from Larb leaves, and called "Kinnekinick." The quarry is indicated on the map as near the Blue Bead River, which may be the Pat O'Hara Creek of today. The present name is just as interesting as the first one. Pat O'Hara, an old trapper, lived there for about seventeen years until in the 1870's he disappeared from the Sunlight Basin because a white woman came to live within fifteen miles of his hermit cabin.

Colter very likely used the same trail (shown on the 1808 map) in leaving the Basin, which went up the steep side of Dead Indian Hill—it would be called a mountain anywhere else. The old Indian trail has been almost obliterated by the twisting automobile road and the eroded ruts left by the locked wheels of freight wagons bound for Cooke City during a one-time gold rush to that district, as they slid down the slope impeded only by the drag of a tree trunk chained to the rear axle.

Once Colter had gained the top of the hill he might well have established the precedent followed by most travelers since that time of going to the edge of the nearby cliff and studying once again the topography of the Sunlight Basin. Months later he must have had occasion to review in his excellent photographic memory his last impression of the distant profiles of mountains in the northwest, for the two pointed silhouettes of Pilot Peak and Bald Knobs became all important points of orientation on his return trip.

Turning to the southeast, Colter soon emerged from the scanty timber on the east slope and found that the stunted, twisted jack-pine did not prevent him from looking down once again into the bare, solid, wavelike rows of hills that fill the bottom of the Big Horn Basin. The colors of the scene he had just left were the deep solid greens, grays and blues of pine-covered mountains rising out of a white snow blanket, punctuated by stark, yellowish, sunlit rimrocks; whereas the naked uneven bowl into which he was descending, appeared at first sight to be almost devoid of color. Longer observation, however, revealed that the softly modulated tints of red, gray, and tawny brown, constantly changed as the sun set and the shadows crept out of the valleys in the mountainous edges of the basin.

The gaunt, cold, stone tower that is Heart Mountain blocks off part of the basin, but Colter would not have objected to this; the lonely landmark must have figured prominently in the directions to the Stinking Water he had received from the Absaroka. This isolated peak is located properly on Drouillard's map, who followed the approximate route of the road from Dead Indian Hill to the Stinking Water.

Nevertheless, the 1814 printed map places Heart Mountain to the south of the Stinking Water. Through the manuscript map, the mistake can be traced directly to Clark, as it reveals distinctly that the symbol for Heart Mountain to the south of the river had been scratched out and another redrawn in the proper location and in accord with Drouillard's information. Clark obviously continued to work on his manuscript map after it had been returned by the engraver, and very likely rectified the mistake at the suggestion of one of his trapper friends who had seen the towering landmark.

The use of the name Heart Mountain on maps drawn between 1808 and 1810 conclusively eliminates the contention of some Cody old-timers that it was named either for a trapper or an army officer named Hart. In keeping with his casual spelling, Clark did write it once as Hart, but on the same map he characteristically misspelled several dozen other common words. Most all accounts of early exploration in the Big Horn Basin cite Indian tradition of long standing as the reason for the name Heart Mountain.[11]

Both the Drouillard and the manuscript maps reveal that Clark had been given much information about the region between the present town of Cody and the forks of the Stinking Water. In fact on his master map he tried to insert so much data that the engraver incorrectly interpreted it. One example was the portrayal of a lake at the juncture of the Salt Fork and the North Fork of the Stinking Water. The tourist of today will find nothing incongruous in this, as there has been an irrigation dam in the mouth of the canyon for nearly fifty years, known both as the Shoshone and Buffalo Bill Dam. The maps of the survey before the dam was built do not show any trace of a lake. Clark's manuscript chart, however, plainly proves that the error was due to Clark's having tried to depict far more details of that unusual area than the soft squiggles of his quill pen could delineate.

Although Clark failed in his attempt to put onto paper in words such reports of the region as he had obtained from Colter and Drouillard, the blotch of pen scratches shows that he tried his best to illustrate extraordinary information from his two informants. And well he might have made a special effort, since the region should properly be known today as "Colter's Hell." "Colter's Hell" for nearly fifty years has been regarded as synonymous with Yellowstone Park, but this is a modern invention. Colter actually did discover Yellowstone Park, but that enchanted region for many years has been more in keeping with the trappers' yarns attributed to Colter; hence the transposition of names. George Drouillard, according to the 1808 map, evidently retraced much of Colter's journey into the Sunlight Basin and thence to the Stinking Water. Thus Drouillard is an hitherto unsuspected witness for Colter, as the map Clark drew with his help reflects an extensive knowledge of the country which even then was considered to have been first seen by Colter.

The balance of George Drouillard's itinerary as traced by Clark on the 1808 map represents an important contribution to the little that is known of early exploration of the Big Horn Mountains. Drouillard, after visiting Cedar Mountain, went down the Stinking

Water to Sage Creek, which he captioned Gap River, and it is so shown on the 1814 printed map. Ascending Sage Creek, Drouillard went through Pryor Gap, and from this pass it was an easy trip down Pryor Creek to the Yellowstone River. The map is not clear as to whether Drouillard followed the Yellowstone down to Manuel's Fort, and then returned upstream about halfway before striking eastward up a small stream that empties into the Yellowstone near Pompey's Pillar. In the event he did not go down to Manuel's Fort, he must have encountered a trading party which replenished his supplies of barter goods and ammunition.

The map does show clearly that, in the spring of 1808, Drouillard made a second trip to the east by crossing the Big Horn River at the mouth of the Little Big Horn; and then ascended that stream past the site where the Battle of the Little Big Horn was to occur nearly seventy years later, until an Indian camp was encountered.

The Crows might have been encamped in this region, but the Indians Drouillard visited could have been Sioux, Cheyenne, or Aarapaho. The map indicates that he found several more Indian camps on the Tongue River which he visited, after determining that there were ample beaver in the headwaters of the Little Big Horn. Drouillard's symbols reveal that he spent one night in an Indian village on the north fork of the Tongue River not far from a little lake which charmed him so much that he gave Clark a detailed description. Continuing his exploration, he crossed over to the south fork of the Tongue River where he found other Indian bands, one of which was on the stream the Indians called the Mah-pah-to-awn-zhah and was translated as Otter Creek. This position represents the farthest point of Drouillard's trip, since from there his route led almost due north across country to the headwaters of the Rosebud. Swinging west he struck a stream, E-ze-rah-awn-zha, that may have been Tulloch's Creek, or Fork, which brought him onto the Big Horn River not far from the fort.

Drouillard's trip was patently for the purpose of making a survey of good trapping streams and advising the tribes he met of the trading post. Thus it is not too surprising that when he described to Clark in such detail, Mah-h-pa-mah-pa, the Indian name for Cedar Mountain, as being the Mountain of the Spirits, no notation was made on the map of the hot springs and other wonders that constituted Colter's Hell. The chances are that if Clark disbelieved anyone, it was Drouillard, until his story was corroborated by others, including Colter.

The printed map bears a caption for the area of "Boiling Spring," an understatement that is impossible to surpass. Clark's manuscript map, however, reads, "Boiling Spa." Thus the engraver must have misread the legend or misunderstood Clark's purpose in using an ambiguous word that could be construed in different ways. The most comprehensive definition is, nonetheless, inadequate; as any visitor to the area beginning about halfway between the town of Cody and the mouth of the Shoshone canyon can easily verify.

The only active springs are now in the bottom of the lower canyon, but the tourist does not have to leave his car in order to see that at one time there was extensive thermal activity in all that region. The perfect cone of an extinct geyser stands on the side of a hill just above the road, only a few feet from the sulphur processing plant. Nearby is another unmistakable geyser cone and on the ridge above are extensive travertine formations. In walking the short distance from the road to the perpendicular walls of the lower canyon, the visitor cannot avoid treading on the sulphur-colored soil and being startled by the rumbling echoes of his footsteps that rise from the ground. The lower canyon at this point is dwarfed by the mountain from which the river has made its exit, but the history of the area for thousands of years is revealed with almost indecent plainness in the banks that tower a hundred feet above the water. The layers of yellow in the canyon wall show that thermal springs have been functioning in that locality for centuries. North of the river are several large gaping sink holes that at one time were filled with pools of deep blue water.

In the bottom of the canyon the Demaris Springs not only provide the luxury of a hot-water bathing pool, but also prove that connections still exist with the molten core of the earth, although the ducts have almost closed. The last geyser has been covered by the waters of the river, but in low water can still be seen stubbornly ejecting every few minutes a low column of water above the surface.

The weathered terraces along the foot of the mountains and the testimony of the old-timers that in the past there were many more hot springs than the four that are active today, all prove there has been a gradual decline in thermal activity in that region. More than forty years ago, Cassius Fischer, while making the first geological survey, noted the extensive travertine deposits and extinct springs. He wrote of five or six springs, in contrast to the four functioning today, that were contributing hydrogen sulphide to the river water; these give off a disagreeable odor as a constant reminder why the Indians long ago named the stream the Stinking Water.[12] The Indian name for the river literally meant "the river that ran by the Stinking Water," [13] but was always referred to by the more concise "Stinking Water" from Colter's time until the turn of the century, when the inhabitants of the fast-growing community of Cody petitioned the State legislature to have the name changed to the more euphonious, but no less appropriate, Shoshone River.

The captions "Boiling Spring" or "Boiling Spa" are both incorrect as all evidence leads to the conclusion that Colter saw extensive thermal activity, and "Colter's Hell" was a correct and appropriate title.

As late as 1848, the accomplished Belgian priest, Father De Smet, placed Colter's Hell on the Stinking Water on the strength of information obtained from the few trappers who were left in the mountains at that date. The courageous priest, known as "Black Robe" to the Indians, was on his way to visit the Sioux in 1848 when he wrote the following account: "Near the source of the River Puante [Stinking Water, now called Shoshone] which empties into the Big Horn, and the sulphurous waters of which have probably the same medicinal qualities as the celebrated Blue Lick Springs of Kentucky, is a place called Colter's Hell—from a beaver hunter of that name. This locality is often agitated with subterranean fires. The sulphurous gases which escape in great volumes from the burning soil infect the atmosphere for several miles, and render the earth so barren that even the wild wormwood cannot grow on it. The beaver hunters have assured me that the frequent underground noises and explosions are frightful." [14]

Less precise data was given to Brackenridge by Manuel Lisa, although it is entirely in keeping with the Colter legend, as follows: "Mr. Lisa informed me that he had been told by Indians, and some of his hunters, that about sixty miles from his fort, on the Roche Jaune, at the entrance of a river, there is a mountain which emits flames. This is about two hundred miles from the mouth of the Roche Jaune. In this part of the country, I am well informed that great quantities of sulphur can be procured; it is found not only in caves, but can be scraped off the prairies in the manner of the salt." [15]

In writing his two western classics, Washington Irving relied heavily upon the experiences of many fur traders, although he did not always indicate the source of his information. His description of "Colter's Hell" reads as a statement of fact, rather than the recital of a legend of doubtful veracity, as follows: "The Crow country has other natural curiosities, which are held in superstitious awe by the Indians, and considered great marvels by the trappers. Such is the Burning Mountain, on Powder River, abounding with anthracite coal. Here the earth is hot and cracked; in many places emitting smoke and sulphurous vapors, as if covering concealed fires. A volcanic tract of similar character is found on Stinking River, one of the tributaries of the Big Horn, which takes its unhappy name from the odor derived from sulphurous springs and streams. This last mentioned place was first discovered by Colter, a hunter belonging to Lewis and Clark's exploring party, who came upon it in the course of his lonely wanderings, and gave such an account of its gloomy terrors, its hidden fires, smoking pits, noxious streams, and the all-pervading 'smell of brimstone,' that it received, and has ever since retained among the trappers, the name of 'Colter's Hell!' " [16]

In 1829, Joe Meek crossed the Absaroka Mountains from the Yellowstone River with a party of the Rocky Mountain Fur Company and descended the Stinking Water to the region he identified as Colter's Hell. Just a few days before, Meek had accidentally visited one of the large hot-spring areas in what is now Yellowstone Park, and it is significant that he considered the district near Cody as equally interesting. Meek could tell some whoppers when it came to bears or Indians, but there is no valid reason for adding more than just the usual grain of salt required by all trapper stories to the narrative quoted by Mrs. Victor Fuller: "—and came upon the waters of the Stinking Fork, a branch of this river, [Big Horn] which derives its unfortunate appellation from the fact that it flows through a volcanic tract similar to the one discovered by Meek on the Yellowstone plains. This place afforded as much food for wonder to the whole camp, as the former one had to Joe; and the men unanimously pronounced it the 'back door to that country which divines preach about.' As this volcanic district had previously been seen by one of Lewis and Clark's men, named Colter, while on a solitary hunt, and by him also denominated 'hell,' there must certainly have been something very suggestive in its appearance.

"If the mountains had proven barren, and inhospitably cold, this hot and sulphurous country offered no greater hospitality. In fact, the fumes which pervaded the air rendered it exceedingly noxious to every living thing, and the camp was fain to push on to the main stream of the Bighorn River." [17]

Three reliable authorities, one an eye witness, place Colter's Hell on the Stinking Water. The distances given in Lisa's sensational account, as quoted by Brackenridge, would also locate the region where the sulphur was lying on the ground in the vicinity of Cody. This detail, which apparently taxed Brackenridge's credulity, actually proves that Lisa was discussing Colter's Hell. For years a sulphur factory has operated off and on just out of Cody, only a few feet away from an extinct geyser cone. The plant processes the raw element that is dug from the craters of the old geysers and springs located on the south side of the river.

The vivid manner in which Colter described Colter's Hell to the other trappers attests to the profound impression the sights along the river made on him. Those who have inspected hot springs and geysers closely can readily picture the state of mind in which Colter viewed for the first time the roaring eruption of a column of steaming water high into the air. The playing of a geyser profoundly moves those who see the noisy spectacle for the first time, although they may be familiar with the scientific explanation. This memory is, however, of limited assistance in imagining the reactions of a man with no advance knowledge seeing a geyser in action for the first time. Geysers had been known in Iceland for centuries, but the odds are astronomical against Colter's having previously heard of such a phenomenon.

There is an atmosphere of fantastic unreality about an area teaming with hot springs that is created only in part by the pungent, disagreeable odor of hydrogen sulphide that permeates the air. Solid footsteps belatedly echo back from the ground below, and the ease with which the travertine formations crumble adds to the pervading sense of insecurity. One incautious step may result in a scalded foot. The deep pools of boiling water are surrounded by innumerable little puffers, perpetually coughing and sputtering as a reminder that another, nearby, innocent-appearing mound may suddenly eject tons of scalding water.

Colter's understandable agitation may be the reason for the one statement in the Colter legend that cannot be substantiated. The intensity of Colter's feelings can be pictured as he peered into the deceptive depths of the pools, dodging the steamy emissions of geysers, all the while wondering what possessed him to remain near such awesome curiosities. Perhaps the white flash of a ball of steam rushing to the surface of a pool, persuaded Colter that prudence was the best policy, and he began to retreat hastily from the boiling water that encircled him. Suddenly a plume of steam rose from the ground in front of his moccasins. True, actual flames did not spurt from the earth, but ascribing such a happening to familiar flame would be natural; and it completely set apart the story from the ordinary yarns swapped around the evening campfire.

The jeering comments of incredulous listeners to the other parts of his story may have prompted Colter to throw the flame part in for good measure, and be damned to all of them. The men of the frontier believed that if a yarn told with punctilious respect for the truth fell upon unbelieving ears, it was proper to elaborate on the story and make it a good one.

Many of the trappers associated with Indians so long that they acquired many of their traits. The Indian lack of modesty about their own accomplishments was emulated so thoroughly by some of the trappers that their narratives almost vibrate with the brassy notes of self-adulation. These same men had no hesitancy in giving themselves credit for the praiseworthy deeds of others. Colter's Hell represented a discovery that would have tempted many trappers to preempt the credit, if they had not known full well that all of their contemporaries were aware that the honor belonged to John Colter. Therefore, it is obvious that the traditional ridicule of the stories about Colter's Hell did not originate with his contemporaries, but rather with those who preferred to rely upon the writings of cloistered, learned men and scoffed at the reports of those who told of what they had actually seen.

The legend of Colter's Hell calls for boiling springs, sulphur lying on the ground, flames shooting from the earth, and the great tar spring. Much fun has been poked at the story of the tar springs, since none are known to the present-day residents of the Shoshone valley. Nevertheless, the maps of Drouillard and Clark, by showing the trail winding around Cedar Mountain prove that Colter, if not Drouillard, actually saw at least one of the tar springs. The "boiling tar spring" was not the product of Colter's imagination, but was located on the South Fork of the Stinking Water just above the junction with the North Fork and at the bottom of Cedar Mountain. The entire area has been at the bottom of Shoshone, or Buffalo Bill, Lake for more than forty years. The late J. K. Rollinson, who punched cattle on the upper Stinking Water before the irrigation dam was constructed in 1906, is authority for this statement. Mr. Rollinson described the boiling tar spring, which he saw several times, as being situated with several other hot-water springs that were surrounded by a number of small semi-geyser spouters.[18] Thus the "boiling tar spring" may still be stubbornly contributing a flow of asphalt to the waters of the lake, or again it may have succumbed to adversity and submitted to ignominious burial in the mud at the bottom of the lake.

The dotted line of the trail on Drouillard's map also circles Cedar Mountain, and then stops at an Indian camp between the forks of the Stinking Water. Clark's notes explain that this was one of the favored wintering spots because of an abundance of grass and game. Drouillard gave the Indian name of the North Fork as "Mich-pa-apha-aun-zah, meaning "Grass House river," but with no explanation of the odd name, other than that the river "reaches to the main mountain or nearly it requires 12 days march to reach it sours much beaver and otter on it." [19]

John Colter very possibly visited the same camp of Absaroka before he set off in search of more winter camps up the South Fork of the Stinking Water. Less than a day's journey from the forks he again found the air permeated with the smell of rotten eggs, and in examining this group of springs may have found another malodorous spring that he might have considered a boiling tar spring. This group of springs may now be under the lake or have ceased their flow; they are not known to the present residents of the valley. In 1873, the members of the expedition commanded by Captain William A. Jones examined the springs and their detailed report reads as follows: "Camp 32 July 26 was made on the Stinking Water, near which we found a large spring raised ⅔ feet above the ground, with an abundant flow of a Blackish water of great specific gravity, of strong sulphurous smell (temp. 56°, of air 75°) and depositing black. The water contained soda sulphates and sulphides. The deposit was made up of sulphur and hypo-sulphite of soda. As we approached the river by cretaceous bluffs, an odor of sulpheretted hydrogen became distinctly perceptible in the air, observable several miles away—a number of extinct springs occur here, but the existence of numerous active ones near, besides the last mentioned, was indubitable. The Indians [Shoshone] stated that many large similar ones could be found at the junction of the forks, about 20 miles east of our trail." [20]

This spring with the blackish discharge may have cooled off by the time Captain Jones' surveying party investigated it, while seeking a road into Yellowstone from the Union Pacific Railroad.

The remainder of Colter's Route must be followed from Clark's map of 1810, since George Drouillard turned back towards Manuel's Fort after trading with the Crows camped at the forks of the Stinking Water. Nevertheless, Drouillard's map indicates the extent of Indian information Colter must have possessed as he walked through the luxuriant sagebrush along the river bottom. The farther he went up stream, the more conscious he became of the blue-black mass of the

Ishawooa Mountains crowding in upon him from the right, while the gouged tan hills of the badlands on his left rose to rougher and higher silhouettes in the harsh brightness of the afternoon sun. The way the nearly perpendicular walls of the Ishawooa Mountains lower over the streambed of the South Fork raises a serious doubt in the mind of the stranger that it is possible to follow the stream to its source. Colter must have learned from the Indians that there was a trail that went all the way up the river and then crossed the divide into the Wind River valley. More important, he must have been stimulated by the report that twenty-two days of traveling on that trail would lead him to the Spanish settlements, presumably located on Green River.

The Indians must have told Colter, as they did Drouillard, that about fourteen days of walking from the forks of the Stinking Water would bring him to the "salt cave," situated just above the mouth of "a considerable river" that comes in from the south. Clark's typical note locating this hitherto unknown salt mine on the Drouillard map reads as follows: "Salt cave on the N side of a mountain where the salt is found pure or perfect. The sun never shines is believed to be fossil salt the Spaniards obtain it from this place by passing over the river Collarado—the Indians of the country live on horses altogether."

Spaniards in Wyoming prior to 1808! Once again a tantalizing bit of indefinite information is added to the odd assortment of discoveries of armor, mill races, stone ruins, and the yarn about the Spanish mine on the east slope of the Big Horn Mountains—all so fantastic, it almost seems credible.[21] The salt cave has not been found to date of writing, but it is hoped that some cowpuncher or big-game hunter will eventually locate the salt mine of the Spaniards on the South Fork of the Shoshone.

Drouillard's map distinctly reveals the interest of Clark and doubtless Manuel Lisa in the proximity of the Spaniards. The estimates of travel time quoted from the Indians are most confusing, as a day's travel might mean the distance covered by an entire band moving at a leisurely pace toward better game country, or the forced marches of a war party. The re-occurrence of notes on the map regarding distances and routes to the Spanish settlements, evidence of Clark's concentration on this subject, becomes doubly important when it is

97

recalled that the first overland trade with Santa Fe was transacted by a party sent out by Manuel Lisa in 1812 from his trading post on the Yellowstone at the mouth of the Big Horn.[22]

Clark's note also clears away the previous mystery of the caption on the 1814 map of "Salt Fork" instead of South Fork of the Stinking Water, and the mountain with the word "fossil" almost obscured by the contour marks.

In addition to his search for the salt cave, Colter had to keep continually on the alert for the game on which he depended for food, as well as the thin wisps of smoke that would indicate he was approaching an Indian camp. The Crows regarded the South Fork as one of their favorite winter camp sites as there was an abundance of game, dried grass, and sweet cottonwoods, the bark of which would keep the ponies alive when the snow was deep. The other prerequisite of an ideal wintering spot was an isolated stream, and the South Fork qualifies in this respect without question. In fact, the country is so rugged that those who know it well seriously doubt that Colter, with all his phenomenal strength, could have followed the stream to the divide during the winter months and descended onto the headwaters of the Wind River as the 1814 map indicates. Men like Judge Percy Metz, who have hunted big game for years in that region, say that even if Colter did succeed in surmounting the snow drifts which often exceed a depth of forty feet, he would have been "rim rocked" just below the divide; as the narrow trail that winds up the wall of stone is impassable except in July and August. The printed 1814 map shows that Colter's trail deviated from the South Fork to the southeast. The tangent is more pronounced on the manuscript map.

These facts suggest to those acquainted with the country that Colter only followed the South Fork of the Shoshone for a few days and then, using one of the several Indian and game trails, crossed the badlands into the Greybull River watershed. The headwaters of the Greybull were also popular wintering grounds for the Crows. Colter by using this route would have had infinitely easier traveling and could look for more Indian camps.

The Greybull River, named for a Crow chief, is almost as important a stream as the Stinking Water, but the fact that there is no sign of it on any of the three maps does not disprove the theory. William Clark had already drawn a detailed map of the Big Horn Basin, by the time he talked to John Colter. Thus it is reasonable to assume that Clark did not question Colter too carefully about this region, since he was under the impression that he already possessed complete information, and did not realize that Drouillard, on the basis of his map, would not have seen the Greybull except perhaps from the Pryor Mountains. The omission of the Greybull confirms that Colter did not see either Clark's manuscript map or the one based on Drouillard's data.

In fact, if Colter did take the well-defined trail to the Greybull and then over to the Owl Creek Mountains, he would also have crossed the Gooseberry, Grass Creek and Owl Creek, to name the principal important streams that Clark would have considered worthy of mention on his map. Nevertheless, this route would have saved Colter many miles of struggling with heavy timber and deep snow, as well as afforded a relatively easy crossing of the Owl Creek Mountains over into the Wind River Valley. There are so many practical considerations which could be added to support this theory, that many natives of the region would be hard to convince that even a man with the strength of John Colter could have made his way up the South Fork onto the Wind River during the winter months.

The fact that the route over the low Owl Creek Mountains embraced so many recognized, good, winter-camp sites, accentuates the circumstance that had Colter wanted to go to the Wind River from the Pryors as rapidly as possible, he could have taken one of the several trails up the Big Horn River and made the trip in a matter of a few days rather than weeks. Since this route led almost entirely through open country which rarely has deep snow other than in hard crusted drifts, and except in a blizzard afforded easy traveling, there can be no more positive proof that Colter's involved trail resulted solely from his desire to visit methodically as many Indian camps as possible.

It is obvious that Colter did not see the Wind River Canyon, and further, was unaware of the manner in which the river abruptly changed its direction. None of the three maps makes any mention of the fact that, at the exit of the canyon, the Wind River becomes the Big Horn River. The Indians of the region consistently employed two names for the same stream, and the custom is continued today to the bewilderment of many students of Wyoming geography.

The advantages of the Wind River were explained years later by the Crow Chief, Arapooish, to Robert Campbell, the fur trader, in his eloquent description of the Absaroka country as reported by Washington Irving: "—and when winter comes you can take shelter in the woody bottoms along the rivers; there you will find buffalo meat for yourselves, and cottonwood bark for your horses; or you may winter in the Wind River Valley, where there is salt weed in abundance." [23]

The hardships of the journey to the Wind River may have been only one of the reasons for Colter's lingering days, or possibly weeks, with the hospitable Crows or Shoshone he found encamped among the trees that lined the stream. He had already seen enough hotsprings on the Stinking Water, so that those on the Wind River would not have been too interesting; but the oil seep may have been a different matter. New moccasins, if not a complete outfit, had to be purchased from the squaws, as well as a supply of the light but nourishing pemmican for the mountain passes that lay ahead. Information about the involved geography of the mountains that rise to the west and north of the valley would seem entirely too complicated to be conveyed by the flowing gestures of the sign language, and this knowledge was probably imparted by making miniature contour maps in the dirt around the campfire of Colter's Indian host, or drawing with a burnt stick on a well-tanned deer skin. In addition, Colter probably did all he could to encourage some young brave to visit another band to the west, so that he would have a companion and a competent guide for the difficult terrain at the head of the Wind River.

All available evidence leads to the conclusion that, as far as white men were concerned, Colter made the trip alone, but that for some of the most confusing mountain passages he may have had the companionship of an Indian guide. Inasmuch as the geography of the sections he traversed is so illogical and confused that it frequently baffles those who have been born and brought up in them, it would be more than miraculous if Colter had completed some stages without assistance from the Indians.

While Colter was on the Wind River, the white cap of the dominating peak, which is now named Fremont, was a prominent point of orientation, and he evidently stressed this bit of information when talking to William Clark. Thus it is not strange that such a peak should be conspicuously shown on the 1814 map with the caption, "highest peak." However, the map also indicates that the highest peak was just a few miles north of the block house built by Major Zebulon M. Pike in 1806. The actual site of this block house is now known to have been near Canyon City, Colorado, on the Arkansas River, and the highest peak immediately to the north is still called Pike's Peak. Both the block house site and the peak are situated several hundred miles to the south of the Wind River Valley and Mountains.

The blame for this, the most glaring error in Clark's map, should almost entirely be laid at the door of the ambitious Pike, who took a long change but only succeeded in besmirching his excellent record of exploration on the Mississippi, and later on the Arkansas River. The expedition up the latter river was undertaken under orders from General Wilkinson in 1806–07, and the purpose was to explore the sources of the Arkansas.

On January 5, 1806, Pike and his party were in desperate straits, due to heavy snow and lack of food, near the Royal Gorge of the Arkansas. On that day Pike took his double-barreled gun (his rifle having been broken by a fall on the ice), and climbed to the top of a nearby mountain with the dual purpose of hunting for game and examining the surrounding country. From this vantage point Pike noted the distressing fact that his party's position was only a short distance from an earlier easily identified campsite, despite thirty days of the most laborious travelling. His mind disturbed by this discouraging discovery, his eyes studied the country that lay to the north. In that region he saw the loop of a stream which he called the Yellowstone River on his published map.[24] Many years later, when Pike's original work papers were found in Mexico, it was revealed that this loop of a river, which was probably a tributary of the South Platte, bore no name.[25]

Zebulon Pike extricated himself from his difficult position and turned south. Leaving the Arkansas River, he crossed over to the Rio del Norte (Rio Grande), but pretended that he thought it was the Red River when he encountered a detachment of Spanish soldiers. However, the Spaniards were definitely certain of the geography and escorted Pike to Santa Fe, virtually a prisoner. Pike, subsequently was able to effect his release from the confinement that resulted from his invasion of Spanish soil, and published his report and map in 1810.

In his report Pike made the assertion that the sources of the Platte and Arkansas were in the same chain of mountains that gave birth to the Red River of the Missouri (Yellowstone), the Rio Colorado of California, and the Rio del Norte (Rio Grande). He concluded this discussion with the following unequivocal statement: "I have no hesitation in asserting that I can take a position in the mountains whence I can visit the source of any of these rivers in one day." [26] The logic used by Pike to reach this conclusion, would, if known, make an interesting study.

Some students of Pike's career have surmised that he took the chance of linking his area of exploration with that of Lewis and Clark, because the Missouri and Yellowstone Rivers were then much in the public eye, and some of the Indian information he had collected could be construed to support such an assumption.

Clark, anxious to integrate all of the available information with the data obtained from John Colter, had no reason to suspect that Pike was taking a wild guess and assumed that the "highest peak" was Fremont Peak in the Wind River range. Clark was aware that the segment could not be the Pierre Jaune (Roche Jaune) or Yellowstone, therefore, he quite properly corrected it to Big Horn, a tributary of the Yellowstone, but omitted any reference to the stream's second name, Wind River. In addition, Clark also had equally misleading bits of Indian information, one in especial collected by Lewis that the Yellowstone "has its extreme sources with the North River in the Rocky Mountains, on the confines of New Mexico." [27]

These errors in judgment cannot be attributed to John Colter, and it is equally unfair to hold him responsible for the grievous mistake on the map showing the Wind River, or Big Horn, as heading from

Lake Riddle or Biddle, now called Jackson Lake. Colter ascended to the headwaters of Wind River and then crossed over into Jackson Hole by Togwotee Pass. It is preposterous to assert that Colter, having laboriously followed the stream up the mountain range, could have reported to Clark that the Wind River cut through the mountains and flowed from Jackson Lake.

The manuscript map shows no signs of radical alteration, but does indicate that Clark at some unknown date inserted the trail of the Wilson P. Hunt party, which went overland to found Astoria in 1811. The route of the Astorians is clearly shown from the point in South Dakota where the party left the Missouri, and rode horseback in a southwest direction to avoid the Blackfeet, as Colter and others had counseled. The party crossed over the low southern end of the Big Horn Mountains and started up Wind River just above the Wind River Canyon. Hunt's men were eight days ascending the river and for about four days' travel, the dotted lines for their trail and Colter's route merged.

Near the summit of the Wind River Mountains, Hunt is definitely known to have turned south from the river, and crossed over onto Green River via Union Pass. Shortage of food prompted him to change his original plan of going through Togwotee Pass and down the Gros Ventre, or the way Colter descended into the Jackson Hole. Colter's trail turns north where the Hunt party left the river in accordance with the usual way of using the two passes. Consequently, Clark's manuscript chart settles how Colter crossed the Wind River range, and also excuses him from any responsibility for the fact that Clark indicated that Wind River headed from Jackson Lake, and did not drain into the Snake. In addition to Colter, Clark must have talked to several others who had crossed the Wind River Range, some at least twice; but none of them succeeded in arousing in Clark's mind any suspicion that he might have originally drawn the headwaters of the Wind River wrong, or he would have inserted corrections as he did in other localities.

Thus Clark must have relied too heavily on Indian information for his concept of the region, and overlooked the fact that much of his data was obtained by interpretations and translations of three, and often six, languages, with the help of sign language and rough maps drawn on the ground.

In 1821, Chevalier Lapie prepared a map that was said to have incorporated all of the new geographic knowledge discovered by Wilson P. Hunt, as well as Robert Stuart, who returned east overland from Astoria in 1813 and discovered South Pass. Lapie's map was intended to illustrate the experiences of Hunt and Stuart, extracts of whose journals were translated and printed in volumes ten and twelve of *Nouvelles Annales Des Voyages,* published in Paris in 1821. The routes of both parties are shown so that they can be followed with considerable accuracy, although there are errors on the map—many due to Lapie's own errors.[28] Lapie made the same mistake as Clark in showing the Wind River coming out of Jackson Lake, but in his case it was a more serious error. Lapie had Hunt's journal, which intimates a slow climb up the mountain. Furthermore, there were several men with Hunt quite familiar with the region.

The Lapie map, as well as Clark's, show Stuart's trail eastward going across the Rockies at a point which could only be South Pass. Clark must have inserted this trail, but without a caption, after Stuart's return to St. Louis and after the plate for the map had been engraved. The manuscript map also clarifies several uncertainties about Colter's Route in Jackson Hole. Again, the fact that the dotted line of Hunt's party rejoins Colter's for a space through the Teton Pass (marked Gap on the manuscript chart), establishes incontrovertibly that Colter did cross the Tetons.

There are few gentle slopes in the abrupt rise of the Tetons from the floor of Jackson Hole, and no one would attempt to use the pass in deep snow without compelling reasons. The possibility of encountering Shoshone, Bannocks, or Blackfeet in winter camps on the west side of the Tetons does not seem adequate motivation for Colter's having added the Teton chain to the already long list of mountains he had crossed that same winter. By going into the Jackson Hole he amply fulfilled any reasonable interpretation of Lisa's order to locate the nearby tribes and advise them of the new trading post under construction at the mouth of the Big Horn. Colter's motive for risking such a crossing must have been that unmistakable symbol for permanent

Spanish dwellings, which the Indians described as being located on the "White Men's River," or Spanish River, only twenty-two days' travel from the Forks of the Stinking Water. The maps indicate that Colter made an extensive search for the log or adobe houses he understood were located on a stream that flowed into the Colorado River. It is now apparent that he was searching for Green River, rather than the Snake which flows into the Columbia. According to the chart the first stream he crossed was named Colter's River, and it was shown as a branch of the Rio del Norte (Rio Grande). Clark's second attempt to honor Colter was doomed from the start, as the stream must have been a tributary of Snake River rather than the Rio Grande.

The loop of Colter's route, which begins and ends at Colter's Hell on the Stinking Water, consistently fits in with the normal channels of travel in that section of the Rockies, and with Colter's known objectives, despite the several glaring errors previously cited. The grotesque geography of the printed 1814 map showing the country between Manuel's Fort on the Yellowstone and Colter's Hell, has been the root of all the controversies about his route. The Drouillard map indubitably proves that Colter went to the Stinking Water, and in so doing converts the weakest link in the earlier evidence into the strongest part of the chain. The mass of circumstantial evidence presented by the maps receives an unexpected support at the extremity of the loop in the form of a carved rock.

In 1931, William Beard and his son, residents of Teton Basin, plowed up a stone that had been crudely shaped into the form of a human head. On one side of the stone, rough irregular letters spell out the name John Colter, and the date 1808 has been scratched on the other. Two years later in 1933, Aubrey Lyon, a neighbor of the Beards', obtained the "stone head" in trade for a used pair of riding boots, and later presented it to the museum of the Grand Teton National Park, where it is now one of the principal exhibits.

The stone is a slab of rhyolite lava, 13 inches high, 8 inches wide at the broadest part near the top and 4 inches thick. One edge has been crudely shaped into the form of a man's face in such a way as to suggest that the carver had merely emphasized an already strong facial resemblance by chipping off a few pieces of rock. The authenticity of the Colter stone was established only after an exhaustive investigation by the Park officials.

Those who have examined the stone state that the carvings and inscriptions give every indication of having been exposed to the weather for more than a hundred years. The weathering has affected the carvings, and appears to have penetrated as deep on the worked surfaces as elsewhere. The age of the carvings has been confirmed by the fact that frost has broken off several chips so removing parts of the face and inscription, and these fracture surfaces are also deeply weathered.

Careful investigation by Park authorities has disclosed that at the time the Beards found the stone they had no knowledge of John Colter, and had only kept the "stone head" as a curiosity. The fact that they relinquished their find for a pair of old boots is incompatible with the blatant publicity that would have followed the discovery of a deliberately manufactured relic. Those who discovered the "stone giants" in the past lost no time in announcing their find, and inducing the public to pay their quarters and dimes to view the phenomenon.

The 1808 date further substantiates the belief that Colter worked on the rock, since it has been almost universally assumed that his journey was made in 1807—the date given on Clark's 1814 map. Thus, the average person desiring to fake an historical curiosity would have used the 1807 date. Regardless of whether Colter set out in October or November, it is inconceivable that he could have reached the Teton Basin before 1808, particularly as he was traveling during the worst winter months.

The Colter stone was found about five and a half miles from Tetonia, in the state of Wyoming, just a couple of hundred yards from the Idaho line. The Beards plowed up the relic while clearing aspen and lodgepole pine from their land between the north and south forks of Leigh Creek, in the rolling foothills along the west slope of the Teton Range. There is an outcrop of lava near where the stone was found similar in composition to the Colter stone, which suggests that Colter had sought that secluded spot, some distance from the main trail to Teton Pass, in order to hide out from a storm or a band of Indians on the warpath. He may have chipped away at the rock he

106

found there in order to while away the time before the hostile Indians departed, or the storm passed over.

Brackenridge's lamentably brief article on Colter implies that his first battle with the Blackfeet took place in the Teton Basin. For more than a century it was believed that the battle occurred on the west slope of the Teton Mountains. In 1916, Thomas James's book, *Three Years Among the Indians and Mexicans,*[29] was transformed from a museum piece to an accessible book by the reprint of that date. Only then was it revealed that the battle between the Crows and Blackfeet, in which Colter unwillingly participated, took place near the Three Forks of the Missouri. Standing on the battlefield still littered with human bones, Colter had told James the full story. There is no question that the James version is more conclusive evidence than the deductions made by historians from a secondhand yarn, retold several years after the event by Brackenridge.

When Colter came through Teton Pass on his return, he turned north and set out for Manuel's Fort. The dotted line in Clark's handwriting distinctly shows that he followed along the shoulder of the Tetons above Jackson Lake, until he was able to cross the Snake above the lake. Colter did not need Indian guidance at this point, because there was an excellent Indian trail that followed up the Snake to Shoshone and Heart Lakes, thence over to Yellowstone Lake. The fact that there is no sign of either lake on the Clark maps proves that Colter was being guided by his highly developed sense of orientation, and vague Indian information, but was handicapped by having his best landmark at his back—the pointed, conical peaks the trappers so aptly named the Trois Tetons.

Colter would have had to search a long time to find a more confusing country to fight his way through in the deep snows of ten to fifteen feet that are common, as many summer tourists have learned to their astonishment from the scars, high up on the trees, of the winter sleigh traffic. Snow shoes were a part of his equipment, without the slightest doubt. There were many tribes along the Missouri who made excellent snow shoes, both the long, racing ski-like snow shoes, and the round webs for deep snow.

The most direct way to go from Jackson Lake is via Two Ocean

Pass, but Colter's trail seems too far north for that route. None of the maps are any great help as to his exact route, and if Colter had been able to draw an accurate chart of that labyrinth of streams, hills, ridges and mountains, the map makers would no doubt have reproduced his information in a most confusing fashion. The 1814 printed map depicts mountain ranges by a series of little piles of dirt that resemble nothing more than corrugated angleworms, but give no indication of the respective heights of the different ranges. The same map frequently portrays areas as plains, whereas they are most rugged country in actual fact. The region between Lakes Biddle and Eustis represents an excellent illustration of this misleading but fashionable practice of cartographers of that period.

Indian information was probably the reason for Clark having shown the source of the Salt Fork or South Fork of the Stinking Water as being in the Teton Mountains, although Colter may have contributed to the misunderstanding. Little study of a modern topographical chart for the region is needed to realize that the many streams run in all directions down the slopes of what are more like a series of hills than mountains which constitute the continental divide, and are in many cases overshadowed by neighboring lofty mountains.

Although the maps of Colter's Route are not helpful for this leg of his journey, another manifestation of man's natural urge to leave his mark behind him assists us in following his itinerary. While in the Teton Basin, Colter did some crude sculpturing; on Coulter Creek, he was again seized with the desire to doodle. This time he hacked a large piece of bark off a pine tree, and carved with his knife J C under a large X. This initialed blaze was found by the late Philip Ashton Rollins while on a hunting trip in the 1880's, about fifty feet from the bank of a stream which bears the name "Coulter"; yet, quite consistent with the ironic pattern that dogged Colter all of his life, the stream was not named for him, but for a man prominent in the early development of Yellowstone Park.

Rollins, who later became well known as a writer on various western subjects, examined the blaze carefully with his two guides, Tazewell Woody and John E. Dewing. The two experienced woodsmen, after cleaning away all the accumulation of sap and loose bark, reached the conclusion that the blaze was about eighty years old. The two guides rejected the suggestion that the tree should be cut down in order to determine its age from the growth rings. Subsequently, the huge pine was cut down by employees of the Park, and the blazed section was removed in either 1889 or 1890, to be placed in the Park museum. Unfortunately, the log with Colter's initials was mislaid, and never placed in the museum.[30]

An Indian trail ran north from Coulter Creek to Lewis Lake and finally came out on Yellowstone Lake. The poles of the Indian travois, laden with tipis, baggage, and children, broadened the game trails into distinctive paths that became thereafter known as Indian trails. This was one of the trails the Indians used for passing through the hot-spring area of the Park in much the manner of the modern express highway. Such haste was contrary to their usual meandering trips between campsites, and was due to their great fear of the geysers. For a people who made a fetish of courage, it is an interesting commentary on their mental processes that not only did they refuse to visit the geysers, but actually pretended to be ignorant of their existence. There is evidence that the Indians did visit the wonders of Colter's Hell on the Stinking Water, and would discuss them with the whites, but the concentration of geysers in the Norris Geyser Basins was another matter. The Indians lent no assistance on the several different occasions the geysers were discovered by white men.

The only inhabitants of Yellowstone Park in the vicinity of the lake in Colter's time were the furtive Sheepeaters. The presumption is that this wretched, primitive tribe were outcasts from the various Shoshone bands, and that they lived in the region only because the other tribes shunned the geysers. The Sheepeaters possessed few weapons, and had been cowed so thoroughly by their enemies that their principal method of defending themselves was to cower near geysers they feared no less than their pursuers.

From all accounts it would have been more difficult for Colter to track down a Sheepeater in his hidden, bare shelter and catch him for a guide, than to make his own way through the tangled streams and hills of the area due south of Yellowstone Lake. His lack of a guide seems to explain why Colter missed the main trail to Yellowstone Lake and had to fight his way through some very difficult country until his sense of direction led him to the welcome sight of the large body of water he was seeking. Clark's maps show that as soon as Colter caught sight of the lake from the heights of some mountain such as Chicken Ridge, he veered to the northwest and did not descend to the lake shore.

The curious, elongated shape of Lake Eustis, as depicted on the 1814 printed map (which can only be Yellowstone Lake), is entirely consistent with the impression Colter must have gained by viewing the South Arm and the Thumb from the distant heights. However, the shape of the lake on the printed map for some unaccountable reason does not agree with that of the manuscript map. The region to the south of Yellowstone Lake, despite present-day, well-marked trails and good maps, is still an unpleasant place to visit, due to the innumerable hot springs, swampy terrain and dark stretches of heavy timber. Consequently, it would have taken Colter several weeks of most difficult travel to have determined the intricate outline of Yellowstone Lake.

From the time Colter swung north to circle Yellowstone Lake until he forded the Yellowstone River, he was passing through a region unrivaled in the world for its concentration of outstanding natural phenomena and beautiful scenery. Nevertheless, Clark's map gives little indication that the district was replete with curiosities of a type that always attracted his attenion.

A theory has persisted for years to the effect that Clark did not believe Colter's story about the wonders of the Yellowstone, and refused to invite ridicule for himself and Lewis's memory by placing such fantastic data on the map of the expedition's explorations. Since there is no evidence that Colter visited the geysers on the Firehole River, his report should not have placed any undue strain on Clark's credulity. In addition, Clark's extraordinary open-mindedness about new concepts and his skill in extracting geographic data from hunters are readily apparent to all who have read the complete journals covering the expedition. Therefore, it is preposterous to assume that Clark would have revised his map on the basis of the additional information from Colter whom he knew intimately, if he had had the faintest suspicion that the trapper was not telling the truth. Another assumption that has gained wide acceptance is that Colter refused to tell Clark all he knew of the Yellowstone region because the trappers had ridiculed his stories of Colter's Hell. This theory is obviously of modern invention, since Drouillard's map eliminates all doubt that when the trappers discussed Colter's Hell, they were talking of the area along the Stinking Water, and not Yellowstone Park.

The dotted line of Colter's trail never touches the shores of Yellowstone Lake or Eustis and suggests that he followed the ridges as far as possible, in order to work out the lay of the land and avoid unnecessary walking. The swampy region immediately to the south of the lake creates a depressed feeling among the members of a well-guided party travelling along familiar trails; therefore, it is not difficult to conceive Colter's state of mind at this point. He would have needed steel wires for nerves not to have acquired an overpowering conviction that that locality was no place for a lonely trapper to be loitering far from his base of supplies.

Consequently, Colter's understandable urge to return to Manuel's Fort, would seem to be the most logical explanation why he did not describe to Clark phenomena that he either did not see or pause to examine. This haste would account for the outlet of the lake being placed too far to the east, as it is unlikely that Colter ever had more than a distant view of the almost imperceptible conversion of the lake waters into a river. There is only slight evidence on the map that he was aware of how the nearly stagnant waters of Yellowstone River are transformed into a raging, frothy torrent by two roaring leaps into the depths of the canyon. The dotted line crosses the stub end of a mountain chain, and suggests that at least part of his route in this area has been retraced by the modern road as it goes over Dunraven Pass behind Mount Washburn. Colter's trail descends a short stream that may have been Tower Creek, and then continues along the rim of the lower canyon. Thus he could not have been ignorant of the fact that the river races for miles between the variegated yellows and browns of the precipitate canyon walls. The Indians often used a ford not far below Tower Falls, and it is presumed that Colter also crossed at this point.

The legend "Hot Spring Brimestone" is written against the mountains that parallel the Yellowstone River and are the source of the Gallatin River. The use of the word "Brimestone" with its Biblical connotations strongly suggests that Colter may have seen the spectacular terraces at Mammoth Springs on the Gallatin River; but the trail, according to the map, definitely does not cross the divide. Nevertheless, there are many interesting springs still active along the Yellowstone in this vicinity, as well as extensive travertine formations, remnants of earlier thermal activity, to have justified the caption. The possibility also exists that the "Brimestone" description was inserted on the strength of Indian information, as the terraces were not taboo as a topic of conversation.

There are other reasons for surmising that Colter may have been traveling with Indians at this stage of his journey. His knowledge of the country was such that he must have known he was on the Yellowstone, and that the easiest way to return to the trading post was simply to follow down the river; nonetheless, the chart clearly indicates that Colter abandoned the direct and easy route to ascend the Lamar River and then Soda Butte Creek. Clark's map makes no mention of these streams, although it shows the trail later on descending one of the main branches of the Clark's Fork. The Bannock Trail came in from the north and crossed the Yellowstone at the ford below Tower Falls. It then went up the Lamar River and Soda Butte Creek, crossed the divide, and then followed the Clark's Fork downstream to its junction with the Yellowstone River. The only practicable way to go through this region was via this well-traveled Indian trail, used by the Bannocks and by other Pacific slope tribes such as the Nez Percé and Shoshone, on their way to making their annual buffalo hunts in the valley of the Yellowstone. These tribes chose this difficult mountain trail in order to keep away from the Blackfeet whose territory lay to the north of the Yellowstone. The fact that Colter chose this route on this leg of his trip suggests that it was late spring, and that most of the snow had gone off the lower mountains.

The modern Cooke City Road follows in a general way the old Bannock trail from the crossing of the Yellowstone until it leaves the upper Clark's Fork to cross Cooke Pass onto Rock Creek. The rugged complexity of the country is apparent to those who make the most casual study of a relief map, let alone to those who have had the good fortune to drive over the highway, one of the most beautiful in the United States. Thus the pleasure of traveling in relative security with an Indian hunting party, seems the most plausible reason for Colter having once again and unnecessarily entered an unfamiliar mountainous section.

The omission of such important streams as the Lamar River and Soda Butte Creek on Clark's 1814 map fits in with the lack of other pertinent data of which Colter could not have been ignorant. The key to this enigma may be that Clark found it impossible to spend as much time discussing such matters with Colter as he desired. The striking difference in detail and accuracy between the two maps prepared on the information obtained from Drouillard, graphically demonstrate how much more comprehensive the section entitled "Colter's Route" would have been, if Clark had been able to question Colter thoroughly about his trip with the Drouillard and master maps in front of them.

Clark would hardly have depicted the rough country between the ford of the Yellowstone and Sunlight Basin as a waterless plain if he had been able to exhaust Colter's geographic memories. Clark's very practical interest in conspicuous landmarks and beaver streams would have dictated his portraying the twin peaks that dominate the entire region, if he had had any intimation of the important part they played in Colter's orientation on the last section of unknown trail. Once the thin silhouettes of the two peaks had been positively identified, Colter must have hurried along the trail through the patches of heavy timber into the lush green mountain parks and finally across the naked vastness of the hills exposed to the glare of the yellow rimrocks. When he arrived at Dead Indian Hill, some unknown influence caused Colter to make an odd decision.

There are no arrows on the 1814 map indicating the *direction* John Colter traveled on his route. In this discussion, it has been assumed that he followed the normal channels of travel in the manner most consistent with his known reasons for making the trip. From the Sunlight Basin, Colter's logical course would have been to follow the Bannock trail down to the Yellowstone and the fort, as he well knew.

However, he chose to return to the Stinking Water. No matter how one assumes Colter traveled, there is no question of his having gone twice over the section between Dead Indian Hill and the Stinking Water.

Several explanations suggest themselves for this illogical detour, but the most plausible reason may have been a chance meeting with a trapping party from the fort. Colter's craving for companionship after so many anxious, lonely weeks, and the greater safety afforded by traveling in a group, represent cogent reasons for altering his plans. In addition, by joining the party he could have done some trapping for his own account before the season ended. Such activities had been impossible during the time he was carrying all of his belongings on his back.

Whatever the cause, the trail definitely goes back to the Stinking Water and then descends that stream almost to the junction with the Big Horn, just above the entrance to the lower canyon. The trip from Colter's Hell, down the Stinking Water, up Gap Creek (which could only be today's Sage Creek), to Pryor's Gap on the top of Pryor Mountains, was not nearly as difficult as the 1814 map would indicate. The misplaced mountain range and magnified scale of part of Colter's route, as incorporated into Clark's map, are most confusing on this segment of the trail. However, since a well-known Indian trail went up Sage Creek, then through Pryor's Gap, and thence down Pryor Creek to the Yellowstone, there can be no question but that Colter, already familiar with the region, would have traveled in the same manner.

The dotted line of Colter's trail stops on the headwaters of Pryor's Fork, and it is a reasonable assumption that from there he lost no time in returning to Manuel's Fort. Many of the company may have tacitly given Colter up for dead, months before he entered the newly erected log palisade that encircled the cabins of the trading post. The trappers' code frowned on displays of emotion without the catalytic action of alcohol; therefore, unless Lisa brought out the whisky barrel for the occasion, Colter's welcome was probably as quiet and prosaic as his accomplishment outstanding.

Chapter Six

Blackfeet

After Colter and the other emissaries to the Indians had departed, those remaining at Manuel's Fort devoted their attention to completing the trading post. The *engagés* spent the short winter days clearing brush and cutting timber for the log houses, and the stockade that was to be erected after the spring thaw. The first small cabin was quickly finished, as the men soon discovered how far the paralyzing winds from the north could penetrate their leather and woolen clothing, and that even the most vigorous axe-swinging had only a temporary warming effect. During the periods when the air was heavy and alive with cold and the snow audibly protested all pressure, the men would not stray far from the blazing brush fires that created more illusion than actual warmth.

Inevitably the weather was the principal topic of conversation as the men churned the melting snow around the fire into a sordid blot of dark mud on the surrounding whiteness. However, the perverse cottonwood, with its jagged heavy bark and frequently misshapen trunks that complicated its use as building material, may have prompted almost as much bitter comment. The apparent freedom of the hunters also might have caused some resentment among the *engagés*, restricted to their monotonous hard labors, until the sobering thought occurred of the dangers to which those men were constantly exposed in their incessant search for game. Part of the hunters' job was to locate desirable beaver dams for the spring trapping season. Beaver were plentiful near the fort, particularly on the Big Horn and its tributaries.

The restless Manuel Lisa can readily be visualized, rushing from supervising the building operations to arranging the trade goods, interviewing the hunters and keeping the trails converging upon the fort under constant observation. Sometime during the winter or spring months the Crows began arriving, to erect their graceful lodges along the river banks and preparing to barter their skins and robes. The log structures and their crude wooden furnishings may have aroused more than idle curiosity, particularly among the older and more mature men who could not fail to notice the sturdy permanence of the fort's installations. The Absaroka had had only limited experience with white traders, and there were undoubtedly many novelties in the resplendent display of blankets, needles, knives, guns, powder, lead and vermilion, that soon brought out the last of the squaws' prized skins and robes which had required years to prepare.

In later years the Crows were noted as one of the few tribes that did not crave whisky. One can only wonder if one of their first trading sessions at Manuel's Fort did not degenerate into such a bacchanal that the tribe became thoroughly disgusted with the effects of alcohol, and the wisdom gained from the experience prevailed for several generations. There is no reason to believe that Lisa would have had any scruples about using liquor to increase the trading profits, as it was standard procedure among almost all fur traders. We know that whisky was available at the Fort, since Etienne Brant stole some for his own consumption.[1] On the same occasion he also took some breech cloths and moccasin awls, which were reputed to be particularly appealing to the squaws.

Apparently Lisa's affairs had taken a decided turn for the better by the time this theft occurred, because Brant was only slapped and called a "*coquin*" by the fiery leader whose temper frequently got out of control. Nonetheless, excitement was scarce at the trading post and the slapping of Brant was the subject of lively conversations among the *engagés* for many weeks. Ultimately, Lisa debited Brant's account $162.00 to pay for the missing goods. We may presume that the malcontent Bouché lost no opportunity to make certain that the affair did not reflect any credit upon Lisa.

Bouché behaved himself reasonably well during this period, although there was not the slightest evidence of a change of heart. On one occasion he made a completely futile threat to take his rifle and quit Lisa's employ. The head of the expedition would have aided this impulsive action, had there been any chance that Bouché would really have gone away and not hung around the fort to foment trouble as well as steal everything that was not under lock and key. The sly, conniving Bouché was far from idle in his own interest, as in some completely inexplicable manner he obtained a rifle for which he forced Lisa to exchange a silver watch worth forty-five dollars.[2]

When Bouché returned to St. Louis with Lisa, in the summer of 1808, he had two packs of furs of his own and notes or due bills on Lisa totaling ninety dollars. Aside from the possession of these assets being contrary to his contract of employment, none of the furs could have been procured by his own inexperienced hands, as he steadfastly played his obstreperous and non-cooperative role during the entire spring trapping season. Bouché had been assigned to assist Benito Vasquez, Lisa's second in command, but he stubbornly refused to lay his traps where he was ordered, or to aid Benito in any manner. Since Bouché was reputed never to have caught a beaver in any of his traps, there must be another explanation for his having been so successful in accumulating worldly goods. The consideration with which Lisa transported to St. Louis the personal property of his worthless *engagé* the following summer suggests that in some manner Bouché may have succeeded in blackmailing the trader.

The exact time of John Colter's return to the Fort is not known, but the late spring, after the dirty, dusty patches of snow had disappeared from the gulches, would appear to have been the logical time. The chances are that the small garrison had just about given up hope of seeing Colter again, when he strode into the Fort with his momentous news. After the welcome of the hunters and *engagés*, Lisa, the businessman, probably lost no time in taking Colter aside to obtain a factual and detailed report on the number of tribes willing to come to the fort for trade, their potential stocks of furs, and how soon they could be expected to pitch their buffalo skin tipis along the river banks. Only after Lisa had made careful mental notes of the information about the Indians and the location of the good beaver streams, was there time for much talk about the region where fire and boiling water gushed from the earth and pure sulphur lay upon the ground.

Colter most likely returned to the Fort to find all of the *engagés* in a turmoil. As the weather had gradually become warmer, and the beaver skins less desirable, the thoughts of the men had more often dwelt upon the pleasures of returning home. The ugly, encroaching, and destructive flood waters of the two rivers, in their convulsive breaking loose from the ice that had bound them all winter, had spread dark muddy filth upon the land but had also cleared the channels for the keel boat's return to St. Louis. While the drowned buffalo floated past, victims of their senseless gregarious instinct, and their bloated carcasses sullied the fresh, spring air, Bouché put into effect his most subtle and diabolical plan. Selecting the more gullible *engagés*, he slyly imparted to them the startling news that he was leaving Lisa's employ because his gun powder was so weak that it would hardly flash. This disturbing information evidently upset the men, for Bouché had chosen the proper psychological moment to plant the seeds of his poisonous rumor. In time, cooler heads remembered that Lisa, an experienced trader, was most unlikely to economize on such an important item, an economy that would have jeopardized all of their lives, including his own.

The storeroom had gradually filled with fat, heavy bales of furs, obtained from the Indians by barter, or from the nearby streams. The overpowering stench of green hides did not encourage any long periods of gloating contemplation by the leader, who now realized his first year's operations would show a profit if the furs could be transported safely to St. Louis. Lisa was anxious to leave by the time the cottonwoods had attained their full leaf and the grass on the hilltops had begun to shrivel and brown. His departure actually took place in July, by which time the water in the Yellowstone would have been getting low and the sand bars more plentiful.

There can be but little doubt but that Edward Rose was the cause of the delayed departure. As previously stated, Rose had found the ways and customs of the Crows to his liking, and had thrown himself wholeheartedly into the life of the tribe. They praised his ability to run a buffalo or the Blackfeet, and the more gifts he dispersed, the more amazed they became that a white man could be so competent in their special accomplishments. Rose, in the very beginning of his stay had taken careful note of the esteem with which the Crows held the individual who actually distributed the presents. Subsequent events proved that the beneficiaries had observed the reaction of Lisa's agent to flattery. Rose was so susceptible to the crafty homage of his hosts that by the time summer arrived he had given away all of the barter goods for his personal pleasure and aggrandizement, but without obtaining any skins for Lisa's storeroom.[3]

Countless books have been written and millions of words spoken regarding the shameless manner in which the white men despoiled the Indians of their resources, but little mention has been made of the fact that the tables were sometimes turned. The Crows early perfected their technique, of which Rose was the first-known victim, and several other men, who should have known better, including Jim Beckworth,[4] turned over their worldly possessions under the intoxicating influence of Absaroka propaganda.

Rose finally returned empty-handed to Manuel's Fort in July, on the day that Lisa was prepared to leave. The two men met in the "counting house," and quickly began to quarrel because Lisa could not believe Rose's fantastic explanation of why he had brought back no furs. Sharp, bitter words soon did not suffice Rose, now insane with rage, and he began to attack Lisa. John Potts intervened in time to save Lisa from being killed by his opponent's onslaught, only to find himself unable to cope with the fury of the berserk man. Potts took a very severe beating at Rose's hands until several other men joined the battle and succeeded in subduing Rose. Displaying a trait which may have been the weakness in his character which created so many misunderstandings, Lisa had walked out of the "counting house," leaving his rescuer alone to fight a valiant but losing battle.

Captain Holmes stated that Lisa walked straight from the struggle in the fort to board his keel boat. The crew had already taken their places, so only a brief time was needed to complete the formalities and cast off the lines.

Rose, seeing the boat beginning to swing out into the current, broke away from the men who had been holding him, and seizing a lighted pipe, fired the fuse of the swivel gun that had been mounted in the fort. The gun was well-aimed, as the shot hit the cargo box on the boat, but, in some miraculous manner, did not touch anyone of the crew. The members of the expedition, whose monotonous existence had created a craving for novelty, were destined to enjoy a ludicrous, but fitting, climax to the whole eventful day. Just as Rose fired the swivel gun, a nameless, but long-legged man had sauntered by, and was exactly in front of the muzzle when the shot was fired. The canister of shot passed harmlessly between his legs, but so completely undermined his composure that he leaped into the air and then fell to the ground shouting that he was dead.

While the innocent passerby was loudly summoning all hands to view his lifeless corpse, the men in the counting house managed to prevent Rose from recharging the swivel gun for a second shot at the boat, which by now was being borne rapidly away by the main current.

Rose, shunned by nearly everyone, loitered around the now nearly deserted trading post for several days, attempting to procure more trading goods with but very little success. He soon tired of this occupation, and as Bouché was on the boat with Lisa, he was deprived of the companionship of at least one man who would have applauded his murderous intentions. The chilly atmosphere of the fort soon convinced Rose that he had always wanted to be an Indian, and that he could do nothing better than return to his newly found people, the Crows. Taking up his few possessions he marched over the hills to spend many months of unrecorded life as an Absaroka.

By the time the keel boat bearing Lisa arrived in St. Louis, on August 5, 1808, the hunters and trappers still at the fort had completed their summer refitting and were well advanced in their preparation for the fall beaver hunt. The status of John Colter with the expedition is not known, but it is likely that when he was not specifically directed to perform definite tasks for the company, he could trap and hunt for his own account. However, it is probable that he was more of a hunter and guide than a "free trapper," as the term was generally understood in the fur trade. Some of the companies made a practice of outfitting experienced mountain men, with the understanding that they, in return for financial assistance, would sell them all of their catch. John Potts, Colter's friend, may have been a "free trapper," since he rented two horses from Lisa on July 7, to be returned in

December after the fall hunt. Ten large beaver skins was the rental agreed upon for each horse, and the contract further provided a penalty of 60 piastres per animal if it was stolen.[5] From the agreement alone, it would have been difficult for Potts to have avoided paying the forfeit if either horse had died of natural causes.

The Blackfeet, when first encountered by Lisa's men, had given a courteous reception. Lisa, therefore, began to put into operation, his carefully reasoned plan of profiting by the proximity of Manuel's Fort to the territory of the Blackfeet, and the plentiful beaver above the Three Forks of the Missouri. Colter, now rested from his long, but successful, journey, had been selected as the ambassador to the Blackfeet.

Setting out from the fort, Colter went up the Yellowstone River, following Indian and game trails that led through the gap in the mountains now known as Bozeman's Pass onto the Gallatin River. These had been used by Captain Clark and his party two years before. Since Colter was not a member of that group it is quite natural that he should have joined up with the party of Flat Heads and Crows he encountered along the way. The Indians could spare him the exertion of choosing the best route through strange country until he began again to recognize familiar landmarks. Old friends among the Crows, and possibly former acquaintances in the band of Flat Heads, persuaded him to stay with them as long as possible.

The hunting expedition proceeded leisurely down the Gallatin River, until it was about one day's journey from Three Forks. Then hundreds of Blackfeet suddenly attacked. The details of this battle were given to James personally by Colter on the battle field proper. James reported the affair years later as follows: "On the next day we passed a battle field of the Indians, where the skulls and bones were lying around on the ground in vast numbers. The battle which had caused this terrible slaughter, took place in 1808, the year but one before, between the Black Feet to the number of fifteen hundred on the one side, and the Flat Heads and Crows, numbering together about eight hundred on the other. Colter was in the battle on the side of the latter, and was wounded in the leg, and thus disabled from standing. He crawled to a small thicket and there loaded and fired while sitting on the ground. The battle was desperately fought on both sides, but victory remained with the weaker party. The Black Feet engaged at first about five hundred Flat Heads, whom they attacked in great fury. The noise, shouts and firing brought a reinforcement of Crows to the Flat Heads, who were fighting with great spirit and defending the ground manfully. The Black Feet, who are the Arabs of this region, were at length repulsed, but retired in perfect order and could hardly be said to have been defeated. The Flat-Heads are a noble race of men, brave, generous and hospitable. They might be called the Spartans of Oregon. Lewis and Clark had received much kindness from them in their expedition to the Columbia, which waters their country; and at the time of this well fought battle, Colter was leading them to Manuel's Fort to trade with the Americans, when the Black Feet fell upon them in such numbers as seemingly to make their destruction certain. Their desperate courage saved them from a general massacre." [6]

Thomas James supported his friends with the same vigor and abandon with which he attacked his enemies. John Colter was both his friend and creditor; therefore, it is understandable that he may have added a few hundred Indians to the account in memory of his former companion, when years later, he related the adventures of his youth. Indian fighters were never inclined to shorten the odds, but in this instance, some elaboration may have been appropriate since the battle was to assume an importance far beyond the mere fact that traditional Indian enemies had met in a bitter struggle for prestige and hunting grounds.

The Blackfeet saw Colter, a white man, fighting side by side with their detested enemies the Crows; they also suffered the effects of his deadly shooting. They did not pause to consider that Colter had no choice but to fight for his own life and that of his friends, but rather construed it as proof that the Americans were allied with their implacable foe, the Absaroka. During the half century that followed, the Blackfeet attacked all Americans they encountered, and took an appalling number of American lives by vicious, remorseless fighting on every possible occasion that presented itself, or could be created.

For nearly a century the enmity of the Blackfeet for all Americans was attributed to Captain Meriwether Lewis's encounter on the Marias River, when two members of the tribe were killed. However, those individuals intimately connected with the fur trade on the Upper Missouri were well aware of the fact that the dubious distinction of causing this hostility belonged to John Colter, rather than to Captain Lewis. The James account substantiates in detail an earlier report to exactly the same effect, which lay buried and unnoticed for many years in the most obvious of all hiding places, government records available to all. On October 29, 1819, Major Thomas Biddle made a detailed report on conditions along the Missouri River to Col. Henry Atkinson, from Camp Missouri. This subsequently became a matter of public record.

Major Biddle described the misfortune by which Colter earned the animosity of all the Blackfeet as follows: "It is an act of justice due to the memory of the late Captain Lewis, to state that the Black Feet Indians (in whose vicinity Lisa now lives) were so convinced of the propriety of his conduct in the rencounter between him and a party of their people, in which two of them were killed, that they did not consider it a cause of war or hostility on their part; this is proved, in as much as the first party of Lisa's men that were met by the Black Feet were treated civilly. This circumstance induced Lisa to despatch one of his men (Coulter) to the forks of the Missouri to endeavor to find the Black Feet nation, and bring them to his establishment to trade. The messenger unfortunately fell in with a party of the Crow nation, with whom he stayed several days. While with them they were attacked by their enemies the Black Feet. Coulter, in self defence, took part with the Crows. He distinguished himself very much in the combat; and the Black Feet were defeated, having plainly observed a white man fighting in the ranks of their enemy. Coulter returned to the trading house." [7]

Colter was wounded in this, his first known serious fight with the Indians, and presumably had to remain within the confines of the log palisades of the fort until his leg healed. Brackenridge described this battle in such a way as to give the impression that it had occurred while Colter was making his famous trip. Early students of the

123

period, unaware of the James narrative, had placed the scene of the battle in the Teton Basin, the only place where Colter's route encroached upon what was normally regarded as Blackfeet territory. This would have been a sound deduction, were it not that the circumstantial evidence of James is amply corroborated by the Biddle letter. On the basis of available information, the battlefield can only be placed on the lower Gallatin River.

After the wound had closed, but probably before the scar tissue had quit itching, Colter set out again to hunt the plentiful beaver on the three rivers that combine to form the Missouri. Authorities refer to his having been on at least one uneventful trapping expedition in that region, before he and John Potts were surprised in their canoes on the Jefferson River by the Blackfeet. Several famous authors, including Washington Irving, have failed to improve upon the first printed account by John Bradbury of the tragic death of Potts and the miraculous escape of Colter. Bradbury's classic description which has withstood all competition for more than a hundred years reads as follows:

"Soon after he separated from Dixon, and trapped in company with a hunter named Potts; and aware of the hostility of the Blackfeet Indians, one of whom had been killed by Lewis, they set their traps at night, and took them up early in the morning, remaining concealed during the day. They were examining their traps early one morning, in a creek about six miles from that branch of the Missouri called Jefferson's Fork, and were ascending in a canoe, when they suddenly heard a great noise, resembling the trampling of animals; but they could not ascertain the fact, as the high perpendicular banks on each side of the river impeded their view. Colter immediately pronounced it to be occasioned by Indians, and advised an instant retreat, but was accused of cowardice by Potts, who insisted that the noise was caused by buffalo, and they proceeded on. In a few minutes afterwards their doubts were removed, by a party of Indians making their appearance on both sides of the creek, to the amount of five or six hundred, who beckoned them to come ashore. As retreat was now impossible, Colter turned the head of the canoe to the shore; and at the moment of its touching, an Indian seized the rifle belonging to Potts; but Colter, who is a remarkably strong man, immediately retook it, and handed it to Potts, who remained in the canoe, and on receiving it pushed off into the river. He had scarcely quitted the shore when an arrow was shot at him, and he cried out, 'Colter, I am wounded.' Colter remonstrated with him on the folly of attempting to escape, and urged him to come ashore. Instead of complying, he instantly levelled his rifle at an Indian, and shot him dead on the spot. This conduct, situated as he was, may appear to have been an act of madness; but it was doubtless the effect of sudden, but sound reasoning; for if taken alive, he must have expected to be tortured to death, according to their custom. He was instantly pierced with arrows so numerous, that, to use the language of Colter, 'he was made a riddle of.' They now seized Colter, stripped him entirely naked, and began to consult on the manner in which he should be put to death. They were first inclined to set him up as a mark to shoot at; but the chief interfered, and seizing him by the shoulder, asked him if he could run fast? Colter, who had been some time amongst the Kee-kat-sa, or Crow Indians, had in a considerably degree acquired the Blackfoot language, and was also well acquainted with Indian customs, he knew that he had now to run for his life, with the dreadful odds of five or six hundred against him, and those armed Indians; therefore cunningly replied that he was a very bad runner, although he was considered by the hunters as remarkably swift. The chief now commanded the party to remain stationary, and led Colter out on the prairie three or four hundred yards, and released him, bidding him to save himself if he could. At that instant the horrid war whoop, sounded in the ears of poor Colter, who, urged with the hope of preserving life, ran with a speed at which he was himself surprised. He proceeded towards the Jefferson Fork, having to traverse a plain six miles in breadth, abounding with the prickly pear, on which he was every instant treading with his naked feet. He ran nearly half way across the plain before he ventured to look over his shoulder, when he perceived that the Indians were very much scattered, and that he had gained ground to a considerable distance from the main body; but one Indian, who carried a spear, was much before all the rest, and not more than a hundred yards from him. A faint gleam of hope now cheered the heart of Colter; he derived confidence from the belief that escape was within the bounds of possibility, but that confidence was nearly being fatal to him, for he exerted himself to such a degree, that the blood gushed from his nostrils, and soon almost covered the fore part of his body. He had now arrived within a mile of the river, when he distinctly heard the appalling sound of footsteps behind him, and every instant expected to feel the spear of his pursuer. Again he turned his head, and saw the savage not twenty yards from him. Determined if possible to avoid the expected blow, he suddenly stopped, turned round, and spread out his arms. The Indian, surprised by the suddenness of the action, and perhaps at the bloody appearance of Colter, also attempted to stop, but exhausted with running, he fell whilst endeavouring to throw his spear, which stuck in the ground, and broke in his hand. Colter instantly snatched up the pointed part, with which he pinned him to the earth, and then continued his flight. The foremost of the Indians, on arriving at the place, stopped till others came up to join them, when they set up a hideous yell. Every moment of this time was improved by Colter, who, although fainting and exhausted, succeeded in gaining the skirting of the cotton wood trees, on the borders of the fork, through which he ran, and plunged into the river. Fortunately for him, a little below this place there was an island, against the upper point of which a raft of drift timber had lodged, he dived under the raft, and after several efforts, got his head above water amongst the trunks of trees, covered over with smaller wood to the depth of several feet. Scarcely had he secured himself, when the Indians arrived on the river, screeching and yelling, as Colter expressed it, 'like so many devils.' They were frequently on the raft during the day, and were seen through the chinks by Colter, who was congratulating himself on his escape, until the idea arose that they might set the raft on fire. In horrible suspense he remained until night, when hearing no more of the Indians, he dived from under the raft, and swam silently down the river to a considerable distance, when he landed, and travelled all night. Although happy in having escaped from the Indians, his situation was still dreadful: he was completely naked, under a burning sun: the soles of his feet were entirely filled with the thorns of the prickly pear; he was hungry, and had no means of killing game, although he saw abundance around him, and was at least seven days journey from Lisa's Fort, on the Bighorn branch of the Roche Jaune River. These were circumstances under which almost any man but an American hunter would have despaired. He arrived at the fort in seven days, having subsisted on a root much esteemed by the Indians of the Missouri, now known by naturalists as *Psoralea esculenta*." [8]

Responsibility for the hostility of the Blackfeet is attributed by inference to Captain Lewis, in Bradbury's account. Since the story was reprinted many times, it is very possible the widespread impression that the incident on the Marias River brought about the fifty years of warfare with that tribe, arose largely from that story. On the other hand, the Biddle letter unequivocally ascribed the death of Potts, and Colter's escape, as a direct sequel to the battle between the Blackfeet, Crows and Flat Heads, in the following terse passage: "In traversing the same country a short time after, in company with another man, a party of the Blackfeet attempted to stop them, without, however, evincing any hostile intention; a rencounter ensued, in which the companion of Coulter and two Indians were killed, and Coulter made his escape. The next time the whites were met by Blackfeet, the latter attacked without any parley. Thus originated the hostility which has prevented American traders penetrating the Fur country of the Missouri." [9]

Some time later, John Colter led a party from Manuel's Fort on the Yellowstone to the Three Forks of the Missouri, and in so doing retraced the route by which he had escaped. Thomas James was a member of that party, and the firsthand information he received from Colter about that event must have made a profound impression upon him, judging from the vivid and colorful description in his narrative. The version given by James does not have the literary merit of Bradbury's work, but it is an enthusiastic memorial to a personal friend. The following description by James is more realistic and logical than the Bradbury account, except for the hardly plausible statement about Colter's having hidden in a beaver lodge.

127

"He [Colter] had gone with a companion named Potts to the Jefferson river, which is the most western of the three Forks, and runs near the base of the mountains. They were both proceeding up the river in search of beaver, each in his own canoe, when a war party of about eight hundred Black-Feet Indians suddenly appeared on the east bank of the river. The Chiefs ordered them to come ashore, and apprehending robbery only, and knowing the utter hopelessness of flight, and having dropped his traps over the side of the canoe from the Indians, into the water, which was here quite shallow, he hastened to obey their mandate. On reaching the shore, he was seized, disarmed and stripped entirely naked. Potts was still in his canoe in the middle of the stream, where he remained stationary, watching the result. Colter requested him to come ashore, which he refused to do, saying he might as well lose his life at once, as be stripped and robbed in the manner Colter had been. An Indian immediately fired and shot him about the hip; he dropped down in the canoe, but instantly rose with his rifle in his hands. 'Are you hurt,' said Colter. 'Yes, said he, too much hurt to escape; if you can get away do so. I will kill at least one of them.' He leveled his rifle and shot an Indian dead. In an instant, at least a hundred bullets pierced his body and as many savages rushed into the stream and pulled the canoe, containing his riddled corpse, ashore. They dragged the body up onto the bank, and with their hatchets and knives cut and hacked it all to pieces, and limb from limb. The entrails, heart, lungs &c., they threw into Colter's face. The relations of the killed Indian were furious with rage and struggled, with tomahawk in hand, to reach Colter, while others held them back. He was every moment expecting the death blow or the fatal shot that should lay him beside his companion. A council was hastily held over him and his fate quickly determined upon. He expected to die by tomahawk, slow, lingering and horrible. But they had magnanimously determined to give him a chance, though a slight one, for his life. After the council, a Chief pointed to the prairie and motioned him away with his hand, saying in the Crow language, 'go—go away.' He supposed they intended to shoot him as soon as he was out of the crowd and presented a fair mark to their guns. He started in a walk, and an old Indian with impatient signs and exclamations, told him to go faster, and as he still kept a walk, the same Indian manifested his wishes by still more violent gestures and adjurations. When he had gone a distance of eighty or a hundred yards from the army of his enemies, he saw the younger Indians throwing off their blankets, leggings, and other incumbrances, as if for a race. Now he knew their object. He was to run a race, of which the prize was to be his own life and scalp. Off he started with the speed of the wind. The war-whoop and yell immediately arose behind him; and looking back, he saw a large company of young warriors, with spears, in rapid pursuit. He ran with all the strength that nature, excited to the utmost, could give; fear and hope lent a supernatural vigor to his limbs and the rapidity of his flight astonished himself. The Madison Fork lay directly before him, five miles from his starting place. He had run half the distance when his strength began to fail and the blood to gush from his nostrils. At every leap the red stream spurted before him, and his limbs were growing rapidly weaker and weaker. He stopped and looked back; he had far outstripped all his pursuers and could get off if strength would only hold out. One solitary Indian, far ahead of the others, was rapidly approaching, with a spear in his right hand, and a blanket streaming behind from his left hand and shoulder. Despairing of escape, Colter awaited his pursuer and called to him in the Crow language, to save his life. The savage did not seem to hear him, but letting go his blanket, and seizing his spear with both hands, he rushed at Colter, naked and defenceless as he stood before him and made a desperate lunge to transfix him. Colter seized the spear, near the head, with his right hand, and exerting his whole strength, aided by the weight of the falling Indian, who had lost his balance in the fury of the onset, he broke off the iron head or blade which remained in his hand, while the savage fell to the ground and lay prostrate and disarmed before him. Now was his turn to beg for his life, which he did in the Crow language, and held up his hands imploringly, but Colter was not in a mood to remember the golden rule, and pinned his adversary through the body to the earth by one stab with the spear head. He quickly drew the weapon from the body of the now dying Indian, and seizing his blanket as lawful spoil, he again set out with renewed strength, feeling, he said to me, as if he had not run a mile. A shout and yell arose from the pursuing army in his rear as from a legion of devils, and he saw the prairie behind him covered with Indians in full and rapid chase. Before him, if anywhere, was life and safety; behind him certain death; and running as never man before sped the foot, except, perhaps, at the Olympic Games, he reached his goal, the Madison river and the end of his five mile heat. Dashing through the willows on the bank he plunged into the stream and saw close beside him a beaver house, standing like a coal-pile about ten feet above the surface of the water, which was here of about the same depth. This presented to him a refuge from his ferocious enemies of which he immediately availed himself. Diving under the water he arose into the beaver house, where he found a dry and comfortable resting place on the upper floor or story of this singular structure. The Indians soon came up, and in their search for him they stood upon the roof of his house of refuge, which he expected every moment to hear them breaking open. He also feared that they would set it on fire. After a diligent search on that side of the river, they crossed over, and in about two hours returned again to his temporary habitation in which he was enjoying bodily rest, though with much anxious foreboding. The beaver houses are divided into two stories and will generally accommodate several men in a dry and comfortable lodging. In this asylum Colter kept fast till night. The cries of his terrible enemies had gradually died away, and all was still around him, when he ventured out of his hiding place, by the same opening under the water by which he entered and which admits the beavers to their building. He swam the river and hastened towards the mountain gap or ravine, about thirty miles above on the river, through which our company passed in the snow with so much difficulty. Fearing that the Indians might have guarded this pass, which was the only outlet from the valley, and to avoid the danger of a surprise, Colter ascended the almost perpendicular mountain before him, the tops and sides of which a great way down, were covered with perpetual snow. He clambered up this fearful ascent about four miles below the gap, holding on by the rocks, shrubs and branches of trees, and by morning had reached the top. He lay there concealed all that day, and at night proceeded on in the descent of the mountain, which he accomplished by dawn. He now hastened on in the open plain towards Manuel's Fort on the Big Horn, about three hundred miles ahead in the northeast. He travelled day and night, stopping only for necessary repose, and eating roots and the bark of trees, for eleven days. He reached the Fort, nearly exhausted by hunger, fatigue and excitement. His only clothing was the Indian's blanket, whom he had killed in the race, and his only weapon, the same Indian's spear which he brought to the Fort as a trophy. His beard was long, his face and whole body were thin and emaciated by hunger, and his limbs and feet swollen and sore. The company at the Fort did not recognize him in this dismal plight until he made himself known. Colter now with me passed over the scene of his capture and wonderful escape, and described his emotions during the whole adventure with great minuteness. Not the least of his exploits was the scaling of the mountain, which seemed to me impassible even by the mountain goat. As I looked at its rugged and perpendicular sides I wondered how he ever reached the top—a feat probably never performed before by mortal man. The whole affair is a fine example of the quick and ready thoughtfulness and presence of mind in a desperate situation, and the power of endurance, which characterise the western pioneer.[10]

Everyone who has experienced the chilling drop in temperature in the Rocky Mountain region that coincides with the setting of the sun, particularly during the fall months, will have realized the importance of the Indian blanket Colter acquired during his flight. That covering would have shielded him from the numbing exposure of the early morning as he made his way in the darkness along the protective sides of the hills. However, he was too large a man to have squeezed into a normal-sized beaver lodge, and this feature may have been added by James for effect.

The exhausted man who finally arrived at Manuel's Fort, was not long in recovering his strength. The tremendous endurance that carried Colter through such an ordeal undoubtedly assisted his recovery. Shortly afterward he proved conclusively that his courage was a worthy companion to his stamina.

James relates that, during the winter that followed, Colter set out alone to retrieve the traps he had dropped into the Jefferson River. Beaver traps had an entirely disproportionate value to the trapper in the mountains, but there were not many men who would have considered them so indispensable as to retrace alone those painful fleeing footsteps. The attempt to recover the traps was completely unsuccessful as James relates:

"Colter told us the particulars of a second adventure which I will give to the reader. In the winter when he had recovered from the fatigues of his long race and journey, he wished to recover the traps which he had dropped into the Jefferson Fork on the first appearance of the Indians who captured him. He supposed the Indians were all quiet in winter quarters, and retraced his steps to the Gallatin Fork. He had just passed the mountain gap, and encamped on the bank of the river for the night and kindled a fire to cook his supper of buffalo meat when he heard the crackling of leaves and branches behind him in the direction of the river. He could see nothing, it being quite dark, but quickly heard the cocking of guns and instantly leaped over the fire. Several shots followed and bullets whistled around him, knocking the coals off his fire over the ground. Again he fled for life, and the second time, ascended the perpendicular mountain which he had gone up in his former flight fearing now as then, that the pass might be guarded by Indians. He reached the top before morning and resting for the day descended the next night, and then made his way with all possible speed, to the Fort. He said that at the time, he promised God Almighty that he would never return to this region again if he were only permitted to escape once more with his life. He did escape once more, and was now again in the same country, courting the same dangers, which he had so often braved, and that seemed to have for him a kind of fascination. Such men, and there are thousands of such, can only live in a state of excitement and constant action. Perils and danger are their natural element and their familiarity with them and indifference to their fate, are well illustrated in these adventures of Colter." [11]

Colter's three encounters with the Blackfeet apparently all took place during the summer, fall and winter of 1808, thus making that the most eventful year of his life. The information which enables us to place the three meetings with the Blackfeet was obtained several hundred miles to the north. On September 13, 1809, Alexander Henry arrived at Fort Vermilion on the Saskatchewan River to take charge of a new territory for the Northwest Company. Awaiting his arrival with the Brigade bearing the new supplies, were three hundred tents of Painted Feather's people, and the Cold Band, from two different Blackfeet tribes. Both parties of Blackfeet informed Henry they had very little to trade as they had just returned from fruitless war expeditions on the Upper Missouri and had failed to find any of their traditional Indian adversaries, or their newly selected enemies, the Americans.

Since the Blackfeet rarely hunted beaver, and the wolf skins they did acquire were not regarded as desirable merchandise by the Northwest Company, Alexander Henry did not consider them as worthwhile customers. The previous year the Slave Indians, as Henry called the Blackfeet, had brought in valuable pelts, and we are fortunate in having his exact but cold-blooded comments on the subject, as follows: "The trade with the Slaves is of very little consequence to us. They kill scarcely any good furs; a beaver of their own hunt is seldom found among them; their principal trade is wolves, of which of late years we take none, while our H. B. [Hudson Bay] neighbours continue to pay well for them. At present our neighbours trade with about two thirds of the Black Feet, and I would willingly give up the whole of them. Last year, it is true, we got some beaver from them; but this was the spoils of war, they having fallen upon a party of Americans on the Missourie, stripped them of every thing, and brought off a quantity of skins." [12]

This description exactly fits the encounter in which Potts lost his life and Colter made his remarkable escape. The Blackfeet discreetly said nothing about Potts' death, and their pride prohibited any mention of Colter's having escaped from all of them. Henry was not sufficiently interested in the affair of the previous summer to obtain further details, although he did discuss the same subject on a different date in his journal. The quoted excerpt may not have been the exact words used by Henry in his verbose jottings down of his everyday activities since they were edited by Elliott Coues; however, that editor's standing is so high among historical writers that unquestionably the quotation reflects Henry's feelings.

Years of lonely life in isolated trading posts, constant association with Indians incessantly begging for enough liquor for brutal bloody debauches, and a complete immersion in involved machinations to best the competing trading company, could leave the most sensitive and humane man callous to reports of the sufferings and misfortunes of others. In monotonous detail Henry reported in his journal the senseless bloodlettings and ruthless murders he witnessed among his savage customers, and he painted each picture with the acid of his profound contempt never absent from the brush. The habit of viewing all human activities through the analytical prism of a profit and loss statement is by no means modern, but only the African slave dealers in the last two centuries could surpass the fur trade for heartless commercial exploitation. Therefore, it is not surprising that Alexander Henry implied regret that the Blackfeet were unsuccessful in the summer of 1809 in obtaining additional beaver skins from John Colter and other American trappers.

Chapter Seven

1810 — Three Forks

The Big Horn Mountains to the south and the Absaroka loom-ing black against the setting sun became the most attractive hunting grounds for the trappers of Manuel's Fort after Colter had related the treatment he had received at the hands of the Blackfeet. The latter were unable to seize beaver skins in the spring and summer of 1809, because no Americans apparently dared to trap that year on the Upper Missouri.

The leather- and blanket-clad men, with their rifles and traps com-prising most of their equipment, traveled many miles along both slopes of the Big Horn and the eastern side of the Absaroka Moun-tains. Their method of exploring was peculiarly that of trappers; the parties ascended one stream as far as beaver were plentiful, then fol-lowed down the next adjacent until it joined the main stream. This zigzag survey undoubtedly included the steaming and spouting mar-vels of Colter's Hell on the Stinking Water. Colter would have been a strange man indeed, if he did not lead at least one party of trappers to the sights at both ends of the Stinking Water canyon. Considerable personal satisfaction would have resulted from his proving to those skeptics, unconvinced despite Drouillard's corroborative testimony, that his tall stories had a solid basis of fact. The relative nearness to Manuel's Fort of Colter's Hell, situated at the gateway of excellent beaver country, makes it virtually a foregone conclusion that many trappers, other than Colter and Drouillard, journeyed there; and this is substantiated by Lisa's statement, as quoted by Brackenridge, that "his men" had seen the sulphur lying on the ground about two hun-dred miles from the post.[1]

When the last bale of skins had been compressed in the wooden press and bound with wet strips of raw hide that shrunk as they dried, the trappers had little to do besides wait for the expedition from St. Louis. Perhaps the unknown person in charge of Fort Raymond was impatient for news from home. Whatever the reason, a number of men took the year's catch down to the Mandan villages and there waited for the supply boats and new recruits. This would have been a welcome diversion for the men like Colter, to whom the villages along the Missouri represented the nearest resemblance to a town they had seen in years. The extent of Colter's stay among the Mandans in their earthen lodges is not known. The huts were large enough for several families and their horses, and were protected by log palisades. The housekeeping of the plains Indians was based on their ability to move away when the stench of the trash, removed only as far as they could toss it, became too strong. Considering the potency of a few greasy bones exposed to the sun, it is hardly plausible that Colter and his friends sought the protection of the cavelike lodges during the dog-days of August, unless the Sioux were actually attacking.

Irrespective of whether his period of waiting was a vacation or an ordeal, John Colter was known to have been at the Hidatsa villages in September, 1809.[2] The expedition that came up the river in that year was radically different from that of 1807. Lisa's daring gamble had proved to be such a success that the principal fur traders in St. Louis had joined with him to form a new company, known as the St. Louis Missouri Fur Trading Company. There have been a number of theories advanced as to why so many experienced traders became partners of the new company.

The most common assumption has been that Lisa was virtually bankrupt and needed additional capital.

This is not consistent with the fact that such men as Benjamin Wilkinson and the Chouteaus would have watched the agonies of a Lisa in financial difficulties with the ghoulish anticipation of starved hyenas. The presence of partners like William Clark, Pierre Menard, and Reuben Lewis, who represented his brother, Meriwether Lewis, fits perfectly with the belief that Lisa in order to avoid ruinous competition was forced to admit the large number of shareholders, an act which caused him to lose control of the company and ultimately brought about its dissolution.

The new expedition, consisting of at least 172 men, 9 barges, and a canoe,[3] differed greatly from the small force that had set out two years before. This party was subject to military discipline under the command of Pierre Chouteau, as the company had contracted to take the Mandan chief, Shehaka, to his people. Ensign Pryor had failed to return the chief the previous year, so the United States government was willing to pay $10,000 to the fur company for Shehaka's safe delivery.

Lisa, as so frequently happened, had a lawsuit, so he could not leave until June, or after the fleet had already started up the river. Despite the military discipline, there were a number of desertions and insubordination was very common, particularly among the friends of Thomas James, our principal source of information about this trip. The size of the party served as protection against the piratical Teton Sioux. Nonetheless, morale was very low among the raw American recruits commanded by James. These men cared little for strict discipline in any form, and had a violent antipathy to the brand employed by Manuel Lisa. Notwithstanding the internal dissensions, the Arikaras were safely passed and the subsidy of $10,000 properly earned by depositing Chief Shehaka safely among his people, who, however, refused to believe his stories of life in the United States.

Several miles above the Gros Ventre villages, the expedition constructed Fort Lisa. The fifteen-foot log palisade was no sooner erected to protect the square blockhouse,[4] than the partners began interpreting the contracts of the troublesome recruits to the best interests of the company. Fine print, the bane of the modern contract, was not a factor, but rather the broad and loose terminology of these documents, which permitted many different interpretations. James and his friends rebelled against the company's point of view that guns, traps and equipment should not be furnished free, but rather debited to their accounts at trading post prices. For several weeks the recalcitrant men camped away from the fort, but they could obtain food only by bartering with the Indians. This was an expensive procedure, since the necessary trade goods had to be bought from the fort at exorbitant prices, thereby creating large debts that would be charged against their catch of beaver skins the following spring.

John Colter stepped into this picture in the role of a good samaritan, as James describes in detail: "On arriving at the Gros-Ventre village we had found a hunter and trapper named Colter, who had been one of Lewis & Clark's men, and had returned thus far with them in 1806. Of him I purchased a set of beaver traps for $120, a pound and a half of powder for $6, and a gun for $40." [5] Colter took a note for $140 from James dated October 7, 1809, and witnessed by W. R. Miller, one of James's companions.

This incident reveals a good deal about Colter's lack of business acumen, as the sum of $140 represented a sizeable portion of his earnings with the expedition. Several years before, he had joined the partnership of Dixon and Hancock after only a few days acquaintanceship; now on this occasion he invested a large part of his capital with an almost complete stranger. His eyes were excellent for spotting game and Indians, but had none of the glassy characteristic often attributed to bankers. Colter never collected the note during his lifetime, but his estate did make an out-of-court settlement for $176.[6]

The James narrative was suppressed for many years because of its vitriolic accusations against several of the principal fur traders in St. Louis. However, James gains stature for revealing the details of a transaction which, in the last analysis, was a serious reflection upon no one but himself. The common reaction would have been to deride and malign the trusting friend and creditor whose representatives had forced a settlement. James consistently expresses generous admiration for Colter throughout his book.

There was a stubborn sense of fairness in James that caused him to describe in detail the various acts of insubordination to which he was a party during the trip up the river. The result is that James's own words justify the treatment accorded him and his friends as mutineers by the partners. Nonetheless, he concluded his comments on the transaction with Colter with the following bitter remarks about Manuel Lisa: "Seeing me thus equipped, Liza, the most active, the meanest and most rascally of the whole, offered me new and good traps, a gun and ammunition. I told him he appeared willing enough to help when help was not needed, and after I was provided at my own expense." [7]

Colter, as an old employee of the company, hardly would have been expected to assist an outright rebel unless he also did not see eye to eye with the management's policy. Colter's natural desire to make a little money on the side in a private trade may have been intensified by the fact he had probably just settled accounts for the year's operations. The high-handed and invariably greedy bookkeeping practices employed by the fur companies caused more than one man to commit rash and intemperate deeds in the heat of anger.

The acquisition of the new equipment prompted James to join with his two friends, Miller and McDaniels, for an independent trapping venture up the river. After they had journeyed only a few days by canoe, the cold weather and floating ice forced them to abandon their imprudent plans for trapping on the Upper Missouri, and to build a rudimentary log hut. James celebrated Christmas day by freezing his feet; whereupon, his so-called friends left him virtually helpless on the pretext of trading their few beaver skins at the fort. The two deserters were subsequently reported to have been killed by the Arikaras.

Two French Canadians, bearing messages to Manuel's Fort on the Yellowstone, rescued James from his starving plight. James relates all of the gruesome hardships they encountered while traveling across the plains in the bitter February weather; not the least of which was the sensation in his feet, encased in buffalo skin moccasins, of the blood gurgling and bubbling in this casing at every step. After going without food for five days, the party in desperation was preparing to kill one of their horses when a buffalo herd was discovered. The supper of buffalo meat did not end their sufferings because all of the men gorged themselves and were sick for days afterwards.

While recuperating at Manuel's Fort from his various ailments, James brought himself up-to-date regarding the rest of the expedition. He found that most of his old crew mates, and also John Colter, had already spent several months in the trading post. Colter's return was probably by boat, and could hardly have been more unpleasant.

Much to James's surprise, Col. Pierre Menard was in command because the previous fall Lisa had decided to return to St. Louis. Judging from his book, James spent a good part of his time during his stay at the fort in unearthing new reasons for criticizing Manuel Lisa.

Late in the winter of 1810, probably in March, a party of thirty-two French and Americans left Manuel's Fort. Under the guidance of John Colter, the expedition which included Thomas James took the trail that went up the Yellowstone River. The expedition was bound for the Three Forks of the Missouri, where a trading post was to be constructed. The company planned to trap the plentiful beaver in the nearby streams despite the warring Blackfeet, trusting to the protection of the Fort and the numerical strength of the party. The fateful expedition left under auspicious conditions, with the sun shining brightly; but before the day was over the dazzling reflection from the snow had claimed Brown as the first victim. The poor man, with his eyeballs throbbing as if they would burst, begged his friend James to shoot him in order to end his misery. James, of course, steadfastly refused, and kept watch all night to prevent the sufferer from taking matters into his own hands. James led Brown by the hand along the trail for two days before his aching eyeballs were again able to support light.

There was some compensation in Brown's plight, since he was spared, on the second day, the sight of the freshly mutilated bodies of two Snake Indians, lying in the ruins of what had been their lodge. The experienced hunters, like Colter, regarded the badly hacked remains as conclusive evidence that the Gros Ventre were in the immediate vicinity. This tribe, the most vicious of all those known by the comprehensive term Blackfeet, was in an ugly mood that year. The traders on the Saskatchewan River had refused to accept anything in trade from them except beaver skins, which they did not want to trap themselves. The resentment of the tribe at their inability to trade, and the projected invasion of their hunting grounds, boded ill for any trapper who encountered one of their wide-ranging war parties. They were conspicuous among all of the neighboring tribes for their generous supply of plain and fancy meanness, which usually manifested itself in senseless mutilations.[8]

About eight or ten days later, as the party began to go through a gap in the mountains that may have been Bozeman's Pass, snow began to fall. James gives the following account, quite in keeping with the Colter legend:

"—where it commenced snowing most violently and so continued all night. The morning showed us the heads and backs of our horses just visible above the snow which had crushed down all our tents. We proceeded on with the greatest difficulty. As we entered the ravine or opening of the mountain the snow greatly increased in depth being in places from fifty to sixty feet on the ground, a third of which had fallen and drifted in that night. The wind had heaped it up in many places to a prodigious height. The strongest horses took the front to make a road for us, but soon gave out and the ablest bodied men took their places as pioneers. A horse occasionally stepped out of the beaten track and sunk entirely out of sight in the snow. By night we had made four miles for that day's travel." [9]

The new snow would have altered the landscape somewhat, even if such colossal quantities did not fall as James stated, and perhaps this was the reason why Colter was unable to find the trail immediately after the party reached the Gallatin River. Whatever the cause, Colter only succeeded in finding the proper route, after four men, including James, had crossed the river and proceeded on down the left bank. Picking up the trail the main party descended on the right-hand side of the stream.

The sun came out in full force after the storm, and the white blanket covering the land perfectly reflected the glaring light. Snow-blindness soon afflicted the members of the expedition so badly that they were unable to sight their guns and kill any game. They became so desperate that three dogs and two horses were eaten before some hunters recovered enough to hunt again. One noon while the blindness was at its agonizing worst, thirty Snake Indians passed through the camp without causing any damage. Brown was less affected than the others and could see well enough to count the savages as they filed past the helpless company. The Indians knew how to prevent snow blindness by blackening their faces under the eyes with charred wood.

The fact that the Blackfeet Indians did not fall upon the helpless party at that critical time, should be considered as one of Colter's narrow escapes from death.

John Colter's mind must have been in a turmoil during this stage of the trip. The butchered Snakes, fatigue from the struggle with the heavy snow, submission to the aching impotence of snow-blindness, and, with returning sight, the memories evoked by the otherwise pleasant valley of the Gallatin River, could only have made him suspect that there were Blackfeet hiding behind every rock, tree or bush along the trail.

The experienced men in the expedition kept a constant watch for "Indian Sign"—buffalo herds quietly grazing miles away suddenly starting to run, cowering stray dogs slinking away after scenting the white men, a stray horse with beaded bridle joining the herd, or fresh pony tracks in the mud or snow. The new recruits could only speculate in amazement at the constant examination of the horizon for smoke or horsemen, and at the study of all objects found along the trail including discarded moccasins, camp equipment, or horse droppings; for all of these signs and hundreds more would indicate the presence of Indians to men like Colter.

While the party descended the Gallatin Valley, Colter pointed out to James and others the cliff he had scaled in the night and the battlefield where he had assisted the Crows and Flatheads in their defeat of the Blackfeet. The recitation of his experiences in that region let Colter give vent to his nervousness, and served to keep all members of the expedition on the alert. However, everyone was apprehensive as they advanced into the hunting grounds of the Blackfeet and tension became high, judging from the following comments by James: "As we passed over the ground where Colter ran his race, and listened to his story, an undefinable fear crept over all. We felt awe-struck by the nameless and numerous dangers that evidently beset us on every side. Even Cheek's courage sunk and his hitherto buoyant and cheerful spirit was depressed at hearing of the perils of the place. He spoke despondingly and his mind was uneasy, restless and fearful. 'I am afraid,' said he, 'and I acknowledge it. I never felt fear before but now I feel it.' A melancholy that seemed like a presentiment of his own fate, possessed him, and to us he was serious almost to sadness, until he met his death a few days afterwards from the same Blackfeet from whom Colter escaped." [10]

James Cheek, a close friend of Thomas James, was of the type that seemed to prefer fighting to most any other occupation, and was, therefore, not one to get nervous over trifles. Discounting, as usual, James's love of telling a melodramatic story, the incident well illustrates the state of mind of the party members.

Subsequent events proved that the company had good reason to fear an ambush; for the Blackfeet were aroused for more reasons than simply the invasion of their territory. The previous summer, the Piegans, another branch of the Blackfeet, had lost sixteen warriors in a humiliating defeat before the newly acquired guns of the Flat Heads. In retaliation for this disaster they had attempted to prevent both the Hudson Bay Company and the Northwest Company, which had supplied the Flat Heads, from trading with their enemies. The trading companies finally succeeded in thwarting this vengeful plan by clever maneuvering of their brigades. Whereupon, the Piegans decided to cross the Missouri and attack the Crows and Americans. In this way, the Piegans hoped to appease their grief in a more satisfying fashion than the usual custom of the mourning relatives cutting off some of their finger joints. The Bloods, a third division of the Blackfeet, were also on their way south, but they were stirred by incentives no more unusual than a lust for the liquor that beaver skins would buy and their boundless love of fighting.

On April 3, 1810, the party reached the Three Forks of the Missouri, formed by the junction of the Gallatin, Madison and Jefferson rivers, [11] near the site of Colter's first escape from the Blackfeet. The erection of a log stockade culminated Lisa's plan to establish the principal trading post of the company in the midst of the excellent beaver country on the Upper Missouri.

The hard labor of cutting trees to build the stockade served to relieve the nervous tension, and the expedition's morale rose with the log palisades. The construction work went so well that within a few days enough of the fort had been completed to afford adequate protection for a small garrison. Therefore, on the ninth of April, Col.

143

Menard was able to despatch a party of eighteen men to trap on the Jefferson River, and a group of four men, including James, was allowed to start down the Missouri. The latter party was permitted to depart solely because there were no indications of Indians in the vicinity.

John Colter, undoubtedly served as both guide and hunter for the party that went up the Jefferson River. His knowledge of the country may have been the reason for the excellent progress made, since they had travelled about forty miles by April 12. On that day, about half the men, including Colter and Michael Immel, were out taking up their traps or setting them in new locations, while those in camp were occupied with their meagre housekeeping chores and the drying of beaver skins. Three of the men in camp, Cheek, Hull, and Ayers, looked up from their work to see some thirty or forty Gros Ventres charging across the prairie from the south. While the Indians, both on foot and horseback, were converging upon the camp, Valle and two other Frenchmen ran up and urged the others to catch their horses and flee. Valle and his men immediately followed their own advice, whereupon the mounted Indians promptly started to follow them. The fleeing horsemen clearly observed Cheek and Hull calmly making preparations to defend themselves, while Ayers had become so panicky that he could neither catch his horse tethered nearby nor hold a gun in his own defense, but ran around quite futilely deploring his fate. The retreating Frenchmen distinctly heard the reports of Cheek's rifle and pistols, and then the roar of Indian muskets which terminated the valiant resistance of Cheek and the fear that gripped Ayers.

Michael Immel and a companion returned to the camp site just at dusk, but were unable to find the tents. Unaware of what had happened, Immel casually strolled around looking for some indication as to where the tents had been moved. An unusual noise attracted him to the river bank, where he saw an Indian woman forcing her way through the brush on the opposite bank, on her way to get water in a brass kettle that looked very much like his own. Sighting immediately thereafter a white man bound to a tree whom he could not identify, Immel realized what had occurred and took flight as quietly as possible. Immel and his companion found the scalped body of Cheek near their former tent site before they set off in the darkness for the safety of the fort. Several days later the body of Ayers was found in the river, but that of Hull was never located.

The arrival of Francois Valle and his two men in the middle of the night gave the garrison of the fort the first report on the tragedy. Early the following morning, Colter and several more men came in to supply additional details and the useful information that there were no Indians near the stockade. The party of four that had been trapping down the Missouri had been summoned back to the fort by the time Immel and his companion had reported their appalling discoveries.[12]

James commented that all those who reached the protection of the log walls had had, in their own opinions, narrow escapes, but that John Colter probably considered his as an ordinary occurrence due to his greater experience. After all the survivors had returned to the fort, a party, comprising the majority of the men, was organized to visit the scene of the battle and pursue the Gros Ventre. The expedition buried Cheek and Ayers, and then discovered the body of a Gros Ventre "carefully concealed under leaves and earth, surrounded by logs." The dead Indian had been shot twice in the head, apparently by Cheek, who had obstinately refused to flee on the grounds that his time to die had arrived. Blood along the trail of the fleeing Indians convinced the pursuers that another Gros Ventre had been seriously wounded. Despite a careful search no trace was ever found of Hull, or of two other trappers, Rucker and Fleehart, who had had their camp about two miles upstream. Since the bodies of the three men were never located, it was generally believed that the Gros Ventre had taken them along in their flight so that the excruciating pain of their deaths by torture could be protracted over a period of several days.[13]

Months later, Alexander Henry reported the purchase of beaver skins on the Saskatchewan that had been obtained by the Gros Ventre on the Jefferson River. Henry stated that some of the pelts had been marked "Valley and Jnumell." [14] The detailed James narrative confirms Coues's guess that the skins were stolen by the Gros Ventre on this occasion. During the year that had intervened since his earlier comments on the depredations of the Blackfeet, Henry himself had seen their eagerness to do violence, and his remarks thereafter no longer reflected a glacial disdain for the fate of the rival traders. In fact he purchased the only known captive of the Gros Ventre that survived, a mongrel dog. Henry paid a fathom of tobacco and a scalper for the animal, half Newfoundland and the balance mostly hound, because he was touched by the dog's manifest delight in being with white men again.

The expedition commanded by Col. Menard followed the trail of the Gros Ventre for two days and succeeded in recovering forty-four beaver traps and three horses. Some hotheads were anxious to plunge into the mountains after the Gros Ventre even though the trail was lost on the second day, but Col. Menard ordered them all to return to the fort. For several days the entire garrison stayed on the alert night and day, while the Colonel fervently hoped that the Blackfeet would attack the stockade. However, the Gros Ventre used barricades themselves and understood their value, so they refused to make a costly frontal attack on the log palisades. Hunger and the powerful urge for beaver skins soon induced the more venturesome trappers to make short trips from the stockade during the night in order to hunt in the early morning hours.

No Indians were seen for miles around and the men gradually became more bold, only to encounter danger from another quarter. The grizzly bears had quite recovered from the slight inroads made upon their ranks by the Lewis and Clark expedition and were again merrily chasing the hunters. This new group of trappers soon learned the savagery of the grizzly when aroused, and of the large number of bullet wounds its incredibly powerful body could sustain before it lost its power to kill with one swipe of a paw.

During this period of furtive hunting when the entire garrison was on edge in anticipation of an attack that never came, John Colter made an important decision. The events of the preceding weeks had forced him to conclude that as far as he personally was concerned the Blackfeet were very "bad Medicine" and that he had exhausted all the luck to which he was legitimately entitled in his several miraculous escapes from death at their hands.

James always tried to tell a good story, and it seems likely that a certain amount of histrionics was incorporated into his description of Colter's action as follows:

"A few days afterward, when Cheek was killed and Colter had another narrow escape, he came into the Fort, and said he had promised his Maker to leave the country, and 'now' said he, throwing down his hat on the ground, 'if God will only forgive me this time and let me off I *will* leave the country day after to-morrow—and be d——d if I ever come into it again.' He left accordingly, in company with young Bryant of Philadelphia, whose father was a merchant of that city, and one other whose name I forget. They were attacked by the Blackfeet just beyond the mountains, but escaped by hiding in a thicket, where the Indians were afraid to follow them, and at night they proceeded towards the Big Horn, lying concealed in the daytime." [15]

On April 21, 1810, or the eve of Colter's departure, Colonel Pierre Menard took up his seldom used quill and wrote his famed report to his brother-in-law, Pierre Chouteau, of the desperate state of affairs in the expedition at that time.[16]

Menard's report to Pierre Chouteau, his friend and business partner, was composed largely in the impersonal language of one business man recounting to an associate the disagreeable cause for so many red ink entries in the record of the year's operations. The fact that there had been a substantial loss of blood and life, plus the continuing jeopardy of the fort's garrison, accounts for the fleeting glimpses of emotion that crept into the report. Menard wrote another and far more difficult letter that same night.

Colter's unforeseen decision to leave the following morning forced Menard to write a hurried letter to his young and beautiful wife at Kaskaskia. Weeks of preparation might have rendered Menard's task less trying, for he was trying to avoid alarming his wife with a gloomy report on what had happened or might occur, and express at the same time the tender personal thoughts of a devoted husband who had been separated from his family for many months. Menard succeeded admirably well in supplying the data about health and associates, with

147

just enough of the story about the disasters to convince his wife that he was not withholding anything from her, except for one slip of the pen. Menard, while scratching out his letter, wrote the word prospects, and then added "du vent," a commercial expression meaning sales prospects. This lapse on the part of her distraught husband should have given Mrs. Menard a true insight as to how disturbed he had really been on April 21, 1810. In fact, it must have had a great deal to do with the keeping of the letter with other important correspondence that ultimately arrived in custody of the Illinois Historical Society. The letter in translation reads as follows:

"Three Forks of the
Missouri, April 21, 1810

Dear Doll

I am taking advantage of the fact that John Colter leaves for St. Louis tomorrow morning to inform you that I am always in perfect health although at the moment I am the image of a skeleton since I do not have an ounce of fat, but I never felt better. I cannot tell you anything new at this time for the prospects (of sale) that I have at the moment are not as bright as they were eight days ago. The country is rich in beaver, but the incursion of the Blackfeet discourages so much our hunters. Two days after they had begun their hunt about 10 leagues from here the Blackfeet attacked and plundered them. In this defeat we have found only two of the whites who were killed, three others are missing and from their possessions we have found we believe that they are either dead or prisoners. It would be much better if they were dead rather than prisoners. Whatever they are, we returned yesterday from their pursuit. I have always before my eyes the barbarity of the Blackfeet—they mutilated with their knives the two they had killed. We reciprocated on one of theirs who had been killed by James Cheaque before he himself was killed. Our greatest sorrow is that we did not encounter the party in order to revenge the outrages of the Blackfeet monsters.—

Kiss our dear child for me and tell him to expect me in July. Between the 5th and 10th of June, I should leave here to descend. Remember me to Mr. Langlais and his family, also to Mr. Pepe St. Gemes, and a word to all of my other friends, Jane and her family and Brindamaure and believe me for life your affectionate P. M.

If I had known in advance that some one was leaving I would have written to all my friends."

148

William Bryant, one of those who accompanied Colter to St. Louis, actually delivered the letters to Chouteau.

While Colter and his two companions were making their cautious way up the Gallatin River, a new expedition of fourteen trappers and sixteen Frenchmen made its way back to the battle site on the Jefferson River. In order to avoid further serious losses each trapper was allotted only three traps, and all had strict orders not to break up into the usual small trapping groups. In a gesture of defiance before they left the fort, the men had lowered the American flag and run up the scalp lock of the Indian that Cheek had killed. Because the Blackfeet had not accepted the challenge, Colonel Menard had issued orders that the trapping party should bend all efforts toward capturing a member of the tribe, treat him kindly, and then send him back to his people with a message of goodwill. However, the harassed leader obviously realized that this scheme had little chance of success, since he was also studying the possibility of arming the Snakes and Flat Heads in the hope they would ally themselves with the whites and exterminate the Blackfeet.

Everyone realized that the company either had to inflict a serious defeat upon the Blackfeet or leave the country. This sober conviction, symbolized by the raising of the scalp lock, and the desire to take some advantage of the last days of the trapping season may have impelled the men to leave the protection of the stockade. George Drouillard of Lewis and Clark fame, who must have been one of the guides, at this point allowed his Shawnee blood to override the white and subordinate his judgment, and made the rash remark, "I am too much of an Indian to be caught by Indians." [17] Disobeying the order of the Colonel that there should be no hunting in small groups, Drouillard set off to hunt alone. The first two excursions were so highly successful that he laughed at those who cautioned him to be careful. Later, after Drouillard had gone off for the third time, the company advancing up the Jefferson came upon the bodies of Drouillard, his horse, and two Shawnee Indians who had also disobeyed the order. The marks on the ground and the horribly mutilated and decapitated corpse of Drouillard clearly indicated he had made a courageous stand with his rifle, pistol, knife and tomahawk, and that it had been a costly victory for the Indians. Months later the Bloods informed Alexander Henry that two of their men had been killed by the officer, or trader, from whom they looted "fine cotton shirts, beaver traps, hats, knives, dirks, handkerchiefs, Russia sheeting tents, and a number of banknotes, some signed New Jersey and Trenton Banking Company." [18]

Once again the men returned to the fort after burying their dead. The Blackfeet kept the stockade under constant surveillance and when the hunters did succeed in escaping their vigilance, the ever-belligerent grizzlies restricted the search for game. Soon the morale of the garrison was as low as the practically non-existent food supply, and the majority of the men became convinced that Colter and his companions had established an excellent precedent.

The death of Drouillard, and the ignominy of being cooped up in a small stockade by invisible Indians and noisy bears, completely changed the company's plans. Colonel Andrew Henry, Menard's lieutenant, was selected to lead a small group of men further west, across the Rockies and beyond the hunting grounds of the Blackfeet. Colonel Menard led the bulk of the company in the retreat back to the Yellowstone River. Here it was discovered that the Hidatsa had located and looted their cache. This loss of supplies was to handicap seriously the desperate attempt by Henry to salvage something from the disastrous year's operations. Henry's party, which could not have numbered many more than nine, said farewell to the main party on the Yellowstone and returned to the fort.

For an unknown period of time Henry stayed in the trading post, preparing for the trip across the Rocky Mountains. Whether Henry's men burned the trading post as they departed, or the Blackfeet fired it in celebration of their victory, is not known. Henry led his men onto the tributaries of the Snake River, apparently crossing the divide somewhere near the headwaters of the Yellowstone. On what is now known as Henry's Fork of the Snake River, a small trading post was erected. The intrepid band was no longer plagued with Blackfeet and grizzlies, but the deep snow drove away almost all the game and the entire company nearly succumbed to starvation. The venture was abandoned the following summer and the men scattered in different directions. Some eventually made their way to the Spanish settlements to the south, and others were encountered months later on the Missouri with little desire to discuss their discoveries. One member, Archibald Pelton, was rescued in December, 1811, from his demented solitary wanderings, by the expedition of William Hunt, bound for the mouth of the Columbia River.

The literature of the fur trade is replete with tantalizing but all too brief descriptions of the ordeals these men endured, and the extent of their explorations. It is to be hoped that eventually the faint outline now available will be filled in by the discovery in some attic of journals or papers of participants.

The balance of the men, led by Colonel Menard, remained at Manuel's Fort only long enough to repair a keel boat. Little time was required to load the thirty bales of furs that represented the pitiful return for a year's operation of the large and expensive expedition. The party made excellent time, arriving in St. Louis during August, but their feat was dwarfed by that of John Colter and his companions.

John Bradbury reported that Colter arrived in St. Louis in May, 1810, having required only thirty days to make the trip from the headwaters of the Missouri.[20] From this fact it is obvious that Colter stayed at Manuel's Fort only long enough to settle his accounts and build a canoe. His precipitate departure from the Three Forks might be construed as proof that he had lost his nerve; however, had this been the case, Colter would have surely refused to leave the protection of the fort until a large party was ready to descend the river. Only a courageous man would have dared attempt running a gauntlet nearly two thousand miles long through the territory of the Arikara, Sioux, Pawnee, and other tribes with similar piratical habits. There were few Indians along the Missouri at that time who could resist the temptation to rob a small party, and no one knew this better than John Colter.

Chapter Eight

Retirement in Missouri

After six years in the mountains, John Colter must have felt he was returning to a veritable metropolis. The houses and stone walls of St. Louis in 1810 extended for a mile-and-a-half along the bank of the Mississippi. Travelers from down the river were impressed by the town's imposing appearance from the water, and usually concluded that they were nearing a city rather than a town of fourteen hundred inhabitants. The old Spanish fort, which served both as jail and court-house, stood on the second bench above the river and was familiar, but the tiers of homes and buildings beside it and on the level below had thickened and become more extended. This growth had followed the raising of the American flag, and was an inevitable conse-quence of a situation near the junction of two mighty, far-reaching rivers.

After disembarking from their canoe, Colter and his two com-panions would have needed little time to discover that the view from the river was deceiving. True, the town had grown; but it had still only about a dozen business establishments, including a printing press. These enterprises, however, were operated with a bustling efficiency that left no doubt St. Louisans were aware their town was destined to become one of the most important cities on the Mississippi. Even then it was the center of the thriving fur trade, a position it had attained while still an outpost of the Spanish government. During the fifty years of settlement the weather had softened the raw angularity of the public buildings, while vines and trees had veiled the glaring newness of the hastily constructed private dwellings. This feeling of established permanency was in keeping with the fact that the frontier, in its slow advance up the river, had overtaken St. Louis just a few years before and had then progressed less than two days' travel up the Missouri.

The arrival of leather-clad men with long, unkempt hair and matted beards was anything but a novelty in a community catering to the fur trade. In fact it was such a commonplace affair that no mention of the arrival of Colter and his companions was made in the weekly newspaper, despite their momentous news about the disastrous battles with the Blackfeet and the severe financial losses of the company; news which in one way or another concerned every resident of the town. This omission seems incredible, until the file of the newspaper over a period of several years has been analyzed. The editor consistently ignored all local happenings except for some gory and scandalous murders and the doings of the socially *élite*, and filled up the spaces between advertisement of a wide variety of topics with what the modern newsmen term "canned copy" from the east. The editor quite obviously did not realize that vital history was being made before his eyes by his friends and neighbors, and only reluctantly published any account of occurrences west of the cultural centers on the Atlantic coast.[1]

Although the local newspaper man preferred to concentrate on stuffy classical and cosmopolitan abstractions, the leading citizens must have grilled and cross-examined the three trappers the moment they arrived until their fund of information and conjecture about the fate of their mutual friends and the future of the expedition had been exhausted. Notwithstanding their interest, the merchants would not have stayed too long the desire of the trappers to acquire some new, clean clothing. The by-products of the trapper's trade on a warm summer day would have been distinctly unpleasant. The trappers had probably bathed out of sight of the town and donned their best beaded leather garments before they came in; but a few scornful glances from well-dressed townswomen as they fastidiously maneuvered their voluminous skirts away from any contact with grimy clothing that had been the height of fashion in the Indian villages, would have told the trappers their garb was not even regarded as picturesque, except at a considerable distance.

John Colter, a member of a respectable Virginia family, probably had an acute attack of that overpowering urge which impels a man after months in the open to rush to the nearest bath-house and put on fresh store-bought clothing.

The three trappers would have been most unusual if they did not feel just as conspicuous the moment they stepped out of doors in their new suits and stiff hats. The unwonted breezes playing on newly-sheared necks and jowls seemed as peculiar to the mountain men, as their appearance, with half of their faces dead white and the other seared to a dark brown.

Another cause of uneasiness would have been the impending settlement of accounts with the fur company. Colter's own choice of negotiator for that purpose could only have been William Clark, as an old friend and experienced mountain man. Unfortunately Clark, who had been appointed a general of the militia and Indian Agent, was visiting in Virginia and would not return for two months. Actually, Colter may have had to settle his accounts with a virtual stranger, as Manuel Lisa had left that spring for a trip up the Missouri, and in all probability the two men had already met and determined the details of Colter's credit balance. Lisa would have been brought up to date on the sad state of affairs on the Three Forks of the Missouri.

Only one meaningless entry in Colter's account with the company and two promissory notes signed at Fort Raymond in 1809 have been found; thus the amount of the final payment for all of his years and efforts in the employ of the company is unknown.[2] Nonetheless, it is logical that he could not have been paid more than a few hundred dollars at best, in view of the unprofitable operations, and the fact that Colter had left before the end of the spring trapping season. Between his bad investments and the several times the Blackfeet had looted everything he owned, Colter had little equipment to cash in with the company store.

Colter was to receive some more bad news at the same time and from an entirely unexpected direction. Meriwether Lewis had died the year before under mysterious circumstances while traveling the Natchez Trace on his way to Washington. Long before Lewis had been appointed governor of the Territory of Louisiana he had been subject to spells of melancholia, and this condition had become pronounced after some discrepancies in his territorial accounts had been questioned. These facts prompted several of his close friends, like Thomas Jefferson and Clark, to conclude that Lewis had committed suicide. Investigations made many years later disclosed a number of facts that suggest he was murdered for his money. The reluctance of the natives to talk about the affair long after the event adds credence to the theory that Lewis was killed in cold blood by a tavern keeper.[3]

After his death it was discovered that Lewis had had good reasons for worrying, as he left his own financial affairs so badly involved that his estate subsequently became insolvent. While still in St. Louis, John Colter found it necessary to sue the Lewis estate and obtained a judgment in the amount of $377.60.[4] Colter never collected a penny of this claim which must have represented a substantial part of the capital with which he had planned to retire from the mountains. The sum of $377.60 probably represented the balance due Colter of his wages from the Lewis and Clark expedition after he had been outfitted at the Mandan Villages, as well as the proceeds of his private trapping activities. In addition, Congress had voted a bonus to all members of the expedition, and these funds would logically have been placed in the custody of Lewis, pending Colter's return.

Colter may have been given some relief from his financial problems and the difficulties of conforming again with the half forgotten *mores* of the settlements by the probing questions of John Bradbury, the English naturalist.[5] Bradbury had spent several months in St. Louis getting acquainted with the partners of the St. Louis Missouri Fur Company. The story of the escape from the Blackfeet may have been related to Bradbury by one of the resident partners, but only the curiosity of a naturalist would have elicited some of the details of that flight, which Colter alone could have supplied. The question naturally arises as to why Bradbury, with his great interest in all natural phenomena, did not report other experiences of Colter which were of equal appeal and covered subjects more his immediate concern. Bradbury's book gives no clue whether time did not permit his obtaining further confidences from Colter, or that other experiences would have led him too far afield from the theme of his own narrative. The avidity with which Bradbury hunted for new plants, even amid threatening Indians, makes it hard to believe that he received any information about the existence of such curiosities as geysers, and supports the belief that he was unable to gain Colter's complete confidence.

The fact that Bradbury with his foreign ways did not succeed in getting Colter to talk freely is not strange, when it is considered that General Clark, after his return probably in July, evidently did not meet with complete success either. Colter had every reason to trust Clark, but from the omission of some details on the map of the route, it is evident that Colter hesitated to tell the entire story to his former commander. Unfortunately, Clark was no longer compelled by military orders to keep a detailed journal; therefore, that portion of his map called "Colter's Route," is the principal record we have of a story which must have amazed the former explorer despite his years of similar experience. There can be no doubt in the mind of anyone who has read the original journals of the Lewis and Clark expedition that Colter was subjected to a searching cross examination about his own activities after parting in 1806, about the battles with the Blackfeet, and particularly the geography of the new country he had explored.

Town life never had appealed to Colter, and after the initial celebration, the expenses of staying in a tavern must have seemed very heavy, especially to a man whose capital had been badly depleted. Confirmation of the final blow to his hopes of financial security could only have taken place during August, at which time, Thomas James arrived in St. Louis with Colonel Menard's party. Colter must have been informed by James personally that the note for $140 signed the previous fall could not be paid at that time, since the two men parted as friends. Colter was later listed as a potential witness [6] for James in the suit the latter brought against the company. The case never came to trial because all of the witnesses, except Colter, were up the river when the subpoenas were issued.

The conversation between the two former trappers possibly took place somewhere on the Missouri River, rather than in St. Louis. According to a tradition that still persists around Dundee, Missouri, Colter came back up the Missouri in his search for some good trapping country in which to settle down. Beaver were plentiful at that time on both the Big and Little Boeuf Creeks, and the trapping possibilities, coupled with good farm land, apparently represented Colter's reasons for selecting that locality.

All members of the Lewis and Clark expedition were rewarded by Congress with a land grant as well as a bonus. Colter did not settle on his grant of 320 acres, since the Land Office in Washington states it was taken up in 1829 by a man named John G. Comegys.[7] Therefore, the presumption is that Colter sold his grant to a speculator.

There is no entry in Colter's name for the land on which he settled just a few miles north of Charette at the mouth of Big Boeuf Creek. The site of his farm is near present-day Dundee,[8] in Labadie Township, Franklin County, Missouri. In Colter's time the village of Charette was situated very near the Marthasville of to-day, but the Missouri during one of its spring rampages has washed away the land on which it stood. Charette, located some sixty miles from the mouth of the Missouri, had thirty families, and the entire district was settling up rapidly. Further up the river, there were few settlements other than trading posts. The settlers always had to keep their rifles handy, as game formed an important part of their food supply and the danger of Indian raids had not been entirely eliminated.

The district had also attracted another outstanding man, but of a different period of exploration. Daniel Boone lived in Charette for one or two years and was undoubtedly known to Colter. The two men obviously liked the region for much the same reasons, since Boone despite his eighty-odd years caught nearly sixty beaver on a trapping trip in the spring of 1811.[9]

The location of Colter's property cannot be determined with exactitude, but it was probably near the Sullens Spring, a short distance above the junction of the Little Boeuf with the Big Boeuf, on the south bank of the Missouri. John Sullens is known to have been Colter's neighbor, and although the land entry on the Sullens's land was only made in 1818, it does serve, in conjunction with other known facts, definitely to establish the general locality.

The years of living in leather tipis and drafty trading posts must have engendered a desire in Colter to acquire a home of his own—

a desire which had become more intense every time he spent a night in a snowdrift with only a blanket for protection. And the picture he had evolved of contented retirement in the settlements could not have been complete without including a devoted helpmate.

Unfortunately, no details of Colter's courtship are available, and we do not know whether he had carried memories of the girl with him during his years in the mountains, or if a brief acquaintance with her represented the decisive argument for settling near Sullens Spring. Our positive knowledge of this important phase of his life is limited to the bare fact that sometime between May, 1810, and March, 1811, John Colter married a girl by the name of Sally. No record of the marriage has been found and her complete maiden name is not known. Colter's wife also used the name "Loucy" since this is the name under which she placed her mark on a receipt.

Well-substantiated tradition exists around Dundee that the Colters had a son named Hiram and that some of his descendants still live in the region. The same informants state that two years after Colter's death his widow married a man by the name of James Brown. There are today people bearing the names of Colter and Brown living near Dundee, who claim relationship with John Colter of the Lewis and Clark expedition.

The extent of the family's pride in the accomplishments of their ancestor is revealed by their tradition that Colter retired from the mountains with a collection of Indian scalps numbering no less than one hundred and one. Some descendant was truly inspired when he passed on the legend to the younger generation that Colter's Indian victims were always left in a distinctive sitting position, so that the savages would know it was unwise to attack John Colter. The effect of a good fire and an appreciative audience upon a gifted storyteller is well known, and so no offense is intended by recalling that Colter positively killed only one Indian. This victim was killed in self-defense while Colter was fleeing from the Blackfeet, and there was hardly time on that occasion to place the body in a sitting position.[10]

John Bradbury, who described so well the escape from the Blackfeet, has also given us the last available description of John Colter. General William Clark had told Bradbury of seeing the skeleton of a fish over forty feet long on the upper Missouri and suggested that Colter would be able to supply the precise information necessary to locate the gigantic fossil. Bradbury had been invited to accompany the William Hunt expedition up the Missouri. Hunt's party reached Charette on March 17, 1811,[11] and Bradbury immediately sought out Daniel Boone. After a pleasant chat with the venerable pioneer, just returned from a trapping trip, Bradbury set out along the bank of the Missouri in pursuit of the boats which had continued upstream. The Charette River, about a mile from the town, was in flood, so Bradbury had to swim the stream and walk for nearly three hours before overtaking the party encamped at the mouth of Boeuf Creek.

The camp was near the home of John Sullens, and Bradbury immediately began inquiring as to the whereabouts of John Colter. Sullens stated that Colter lived about a mile away and that he would send his son to announce the arrival of the expedition. The following morning, shortly after daybreak, Colter came into the camp but was unable to give Bradbury the information he wanted about the skeleton. Hunt had enlisted the services of several experienced mountain men after considerable difficulty. Nonetheless, he eagerly took advantage of Colter's extensive geographic knowledge and plied him with questions.

On behalf of John Jacob Astor, Hunt was making an overland trip to the mouth of the Columbia River, where it was planned that the schooner *Tonquin* would meet the party. Colter's stories of Blackfeet ferocity undoubtedly had a good deal to do with the decision Hunt subsequently made to leave the Missouri at the Arikara Villages, purchase horses, and cross the Rockies south of the area visited by Lewis and Clark.

Colter was well qualified to counsel avoidance of the Blackfeet at all costs, but from personal experience he might not have been able to recommend an alternate route better than the Yellowstone River. For this reason Hunt fully appreciated his good fortune in acquiring the services of Edward Robinson, John Hoback, and Jacob Rizner,[12] whom the party met on the Missouri just above the mouth of the Rapid River. These men had been with Andrew Henry on the Snake

River and had returned over the Rockies by a route that exactly answered Hunt's problem.

The fur traders rarely disclosed what they paid their men unless a law suit resulted from the transaction. However, it would appear that at least one of the trio was easily persuaded to enlist in the expedition. Robinson had spent the greater part of his sixty-six years of life as a trapper, and was fully aware of the dangers since he always wore a handkerchief over his head to conceal the scar acquired years before when an Indian had scalped him. The fascination of the trappers' life, rather than wages, represents the only valid reason why any man would turn back into the mountains after having undergone the hardships that beset Henry's small party.

Colter must have felt the old force of that attraction for the exciting and untrammeled existence of the mountain man, for he spent the entire morning with the expedition, sharing his experience and debating whether or not he should accept Hunt's offer of a position. By noon he reached his decision, and bidding farewell to Hunt's expedition, started back down stream. The recently established home and new bride had won; and Colter had again demonstrated his high sense of responsibility.

From Amos Richardson, a friend and neighbor, we have a rather picturesque description of the general feeling Colter may have had as he followed the trail toward his cabin. Richardson, a relative of Daniel Richardson who subsequently became the executor of Colter's estate, had also trapped on the upper river. Richardson accompanied Hunt up to the Arikara Villages and was one of those selected to bring Bradbury back to St. Louis. Richardson whiled away the time as they floated down the Missouri by telling Bradbury of his experiences with the Indians and why he wanted to stay in the settlements. The chief cause of Richardson's desire to quit trapping was an arrowhead imbedded in his shoulder, which he had acquired during an encounter with the Indians. Yet only a few weeks after the return to St. Louis, Bradbury, who was planning a trip up the Arkansas River, was surprised by Richardson applying for a position on that expedition. Bradbury quotes Richardson's graphic explanation for changing his mind as follows: "I find so much deceit and selfishness amongst white men, that I am already tired of them. The arrowhead which is not yet extracted pains me when I chop wood, whiskey I can't drink, and bread and salt I don't care about: I will go again amongst the Indians." [13]

The year 1811 is one of the best known in the early history of the fur trade because two unusually competent writers accompanied the main expeditions up the river that spring. As previously mentioned, John Bradbury went with William Hunt's party to the Arikara Villages; whereas Henry Brackenridge was the guest of Manuel Lisa's expedition. Both Bradbury and Brackenridge described their experiences in detail and had the unusual ability of reporting entirely alien customs without incorporating too many of their own preconceived opinions. Brackenridge wrote with a warmth and understanding of human behavior that does not appear in Bradbury's cool scientific reports.

Although Brackenridge has given us so much information about Colter and the times in which he lived, the two men did not meet on this occasion. The boat bearing Brackenridge passed by Charette without stopping for even a friendly chat, due to Lisa's anxiety to overtake Hunt's party. The trader's natural desire to keep an eye on the activities of his competitor was only partly the cause of Lisa's haste. His party was so small, after the disasters of the previous year, that he felt it imperative to join forces with Hunt while passing through the Sioux country. Hunt had already had dealings with Lisa, and mistrusted his desire to combine the two parties. The most exciting race up the river ever reported was the result.

The passings of the occasional keel boat and the commonplace wooden canoes on the river represented the principal outside distraction for the settlers. There was so much to be done in building a home and clearing the bottom land of trees and brush that time could be spared only rarely for a trip to a nearby village for supplies. Important business transactions alone warranted a journey to St. Louis. John Colter evidently made such a trip in 1812, as he signed a promissory note for $45.00, apparently in favor of William Clark, February 24, 1812. [14] How long he stayed there and whether he had the opportunity to increase the geographic knowledge of his old commander is not known.

He would have been acting out of character, however, if he had stayed in St. Louis longer than absolutely necessary.

The clearing of the land had to go on, long after the first temporary shelters had been converted into comfortable residences. The men, stung by the meagre returns from the first plantings among the stumps of newly felled trees, intensified their attacks upon the surrounding forest and the luxuriant strength of the weeds just liberated from the stunting shadows. When the air was full of the heavy smoke from smoldering green wood, the need for fresh meat encouraged the men to leave the clearings by the river and explore the back country. There were few who could have taken up their rifles with more pleasure than John Colter. In fact it would have been strange if Colter did not promote many deals involving the exchange of game for toil on his farm with an axe and hoe.

Settling on the Missouri could not have represented too radical a change for Colter, since hunting and trapping continually provided pleasant escapes from the difficulties of growing corn, burning out stumps and tending livestock with few restraining fences. The pleasures and responsibilities of the new home must have altered the feelings with which he watched the slow progress up the river of the fur brigades in the succeeding springs. The unexpected fascination of watching his son, Hiram, progress from complete helplessness to the over-confidence of the curious toddler, undoubtedly curtailed many of Colter's hunting trips.

The contrasts of the succeeding seasons were probably the most exciting disturbances in the even tempo of Colter's life until the year 1813. The humid blanket of summer heat had scarcely become a memory that year before Colter began to feel tired and discouraged. By the time a few raw cloudy days had indicated the nearness of winter, Colter discovered that his skin and the whites of his eyes had turned yellow. This discoloration and constantly itching skin indicated that he had the dreaded jaundice. The cumulative effects of Colter's exertions in the mountains and the impossibility of correcting his diet all combined to aggravate the disease, with the result that Colter died of jaundice in November, 1813.[15]

Colter was buried in the graveyard on the top of what is now called Tunnel Hill, according to trustworthy old-time residents around Dundee. This promontory, the most outstanding landmark on that part of the Missouri River, lies between the Little and Big Boeuf Creeks, and overlooks Sullens Spring, as well as the site of Colter's farm. The name, Tunnel Hill, is derived from the fact that the Missouri Pacific dug a tunnel through the hill, directly under the graves, when its lines were first extended westward in 1850.[16]

At the time of his death, John Colter was perhaps better off financially than most of his neighbors. The proceeds from the liquidation of his estate totaled $442.73½, but the net was reduced to $233.76¾, after his debts had been paid in full. The sale bill of his personal property reveals with appalling clarity the austerity of life on the frontier.

Sale Bill

	$	c
Hartley Sappington—one pot and pothooks	4	00
John Simpson—one Dutch oven	3	87
James Higgins—one weeding hoe	1	43½
Zachariah Surlans—one plow irons	8	
Wm. Greenstreet—one dish and five puter plates	8	37½
John Morrow—two tie pans	2	25
James Higgins—one puter bason	3	50
William Greenstreet—one puter bason	3	50
John Woollums—one puter bason	1	62½
Enoch Greenstreete—one coffey pot	1	62½
John Woollums—one little spining wheel	7	12½
Hartley Sappington—glass tumbler	0	85
Samuel Cantley—one bottle	0	37½
Mosias Maupin—one bottle	0	50
James Higgins—Knives, forks and spoons	2	12½
James Higgins—for tin cups	1	85
Wm. Greenstreet—one piggan	0	68
Wm. Greenstreet—four chairs	2	60
Michal Early—one feather bed	22	00
John Morrow—one feather bed	17	00
James Higgins—one pane of cotton cards	10	37½
Benjamin Heathley—one book	0	64
Mosias Maupin—one book	1	75
Samuel Cantley—one book	0	86

James Higgins—one flat iron	2	75
Hartley Sappington—one mare	42	75
William Davis—one colt	16	50
William Davis—one heffer	7	26½
James Higgins—one cow and calf	9	00
John Sullins—article is completely obliterated	5	62½
NAME and article also completely obliterated	2	00
	124	44½

December 10, 1813

Daniel Richardson
Administrator." [17]

Any man preoccupied with his place in history would have made certain that he left ample information about his career behind in the form of letters, journals, or even an autobiography. The lack of personal records and the reticence with which he talked to the few people he encountered capable of writing an account of his experiences, indicate that Colter would not have been too perturbed had he realized that nearly a century would elapse before his contribution to western exploration was appreciated. In fact, John Colter almost became one of the forgotten men of history, during the years his mortal remains lay in an unmarked grave on Tunnel Hill.

Misfortune dogged Colter throughout his life and robbed him of the just rewards he had earned. This perverse pattern carried on even after his death to culminate in one final irony. In 1926, the Missouri Pacific began putting in double tracks, and their engineers decided to make a cut through Tunnel Hill rather than enlarge the existing tunnel. Giant steamshovels, operated by men ignorant of the forgotten graves above the tunnel, worked night and day loading dirt into railroad cars to be utilized as fill on several nearby parts of the line. Before the local people were aware of what was happening, the shovels had devoured the whole graveyard, and the remains of the early settlers buried there had become part of the track bed of the Missouri Pacific.

This contribution to the development of the West made it impossible even to mark Colter's last resting place with a simple monument, commemorating his name. Perhaps it is more fitting that the memory of John Colter, discoverer of Yellowstone Park and Colter's Hell, should be perpetuated by the stories of the mountain men who understand the significance of his deeds, rather than by a cold, mute, piece of carved stone.

Notes

CHAPTER ONE

None.

CHAPTER TWO

(1) *Original Journals of the Lewis and Clark Expedition 1804–1806.* Edited by Reuben Gold Thwaites, New York, 1904. (hereafter called *Original Journals*) Vol. VII, p. 360.

(2) *Three Years Among the Indians and Mexicans.* By Thomas James. Edited by W. B. Douglas, St. Louis, 1916 (hereafter called *James's Three Years Among the Indians*) p. 58.

(3) Vinton, Stallo, *John Colter: Discoverer of Yellowstone Park.* New York, 1926. (hereafter called *Vinton's John Colter*) p. 27.

(4) *James's Three Years Among the Indians.* p. 278.

(5) See Chapter Eight for the inventory of the sale of Colter's possessions.

(6) *Original Journals.* Vol. VII, p. 360.

(7) Wisconsin State Historical *Collections.* (hereafter called *Wisconsin Collections*) Vol. XXII.

(8) *James's Three Years Among the Indians.* pp. 57–58.

(9) Letter dated June 19, 1803, Washington, from Meriwether Lewis to William Clark, quoted *Original Journals.* Vol. VII, p. 227.

(10) *History of the Expedition Under the Command of Lewis and Clark.* Edited by Elliott Coues. New York, 1893. (hereafter called *Coues' Lewis & Clark*) Vol. I, p. LXX–LXXIII.

(11) *Original Journals.* Vol. I, p. 10.

(12) *Persimmon Hill. A Narrative of Old St. Louis and the Far West.* By William Clark Kennerly as told to Elizabeth Russel. Norman, Oklahoma, 1948, p. 141.

(13) *Original Journals.* Vol. I., p. 10.

(14) Ibid. Vol. VII. Whitehouse Journal. p. 36.

(15) Ibid. Vol. I, Part II. pp. 128–145.

(16) *A Journal of the Voyages and Travels of a Corps of Discovery.* Sergeant Gass. Pittsburgh, 1807. p. 38 and p. 43.

(17) *Wisconsin Collections.* Vol. XXII, p. 126. and p. 136. *Original Journals.* Vol. I. Part II, p. 162.

(18) *Original Journals.* Vol. I, Part II, p. 162. Sergeant Ordway's Journal in *Wisconsin Collections.* Vol. XXII, p. 136.

(19) Fort Mandan was located about 60 miles above modern Bismarck, North Dakota. The site of the original fort had washed into the river before 1833. See *North Dakota Historical Quarterly.* Vol. II, October 1927, pp. 5 to 22.

(20) *Les Bourgeois de la Compagnie du Nord-ouest,* L. R. Masson. Quebec, 1889–1890. *The Manuscript Journals of Alexander Henry and of David Thompson.* Edited by Elliott Coues. New York, 1897.

(21) Ordway's Journal in *Wisconsin Collections.* Vol. XXII, p. 234. *Original Journals.* Vol. II, Part I. p. 171.

(22) *Original Journals.* Vol. III. Part I. pp. 32, 33–42.

(23) Ibid. Vol. III. Part I. pp. 60, 61.

(24) Ibid. Vol. III. Part I. pp. 87–89.

(25) Ibid. Vol. III. Part I. p. 90.

(26) *Coues' Lewis & Clark.* Vol. II. pp. 616, 617. Note 48.

(27) *Original Journals.* Vol. III. Part II. p. 221. *A Journal of the Voyages and Travels of a Corps of Discovery.* By Sergeant Gass. Pittsburgh, 1807. p. 163.

(28) Ibid. Vol. III. Part II. p. 229.

(29) Ibid. Vol. IV. Part II. pp. 257, 258.

(30) Ibid. Vol. IV. Part II. pp. 258–261.

(31) Ibid. Vol. IV. Part II. pp. 364–366.

(32) Ibid. Vol. V. Part I. p. 107.

(33) Ibid. Vol. V. Part I. pp. 144, 146.

(34) Ibid. Vol. V. Part I. pp. 145, 146.

(35) Sergeant Ordway in *Wisconsin Collections.* Vol. XXII. pp. 377–380.

(36) Ibid. Vol. XXII. p. 381.

(37) Ibid. Vol. XXII. p. 385, 386. *Original Journals.* Vol. V. Part I. pp. 229, 233, 234.

(38) *Original Journals.* Vol. V. Part I. p. 237. *Wisconsin Collections.* Vol. XXII. p. 386.

(39) *Original Journals.* Vol. V. Part I. p. 242.

CHAPTER THREE

(1) *Wisconsin Collections.* Vol. XXII. pp. 388, 389.

(2) *A Journal of the Voyages and Travels of a Corps of Discovery.* By Sergeant Gass. Pittsburgh, 1807.

(3) *Wisconsin Collections.* Vol. XXII. p. 389.

(4) *History of the Expedition under the Command of Captains Lewis and Clark.* By Paul Allen. Philadelphia, 1814. Hereafter called *Allen's Lewis and Clark.* p. 408.

(5) *Wisconsin Collections.* Vol. XXII. p. 390. *Original Journals.* Vol. V. p. 342.

(6) *Original Journals.* Vol. VII. Part II. p. 360.

(7) Ibid. Vol. VII. Part II, p. 362. Letter from William Clark to his brother Major Edmund Clark.

(8) *James's Three Years Among the Indians.* p. 279.

(9) The Journal of Francois Antoine Larocque from the Assiniboine River to the Yellowstone, 1805, in *Sources of Northwest History*, No. 20, State University of Montana. Edited by Ruth Hazlitt. The *Manuscript Journals of Alexander Henry and of David Thompson.* Edited by Elliott Coues, 1897. *Les Bourgeois de la Compagnie du Nord-ouest.* L. R. Masson, 1889–1890. *Journal of Larocque: From the Assiniboine to the Yellowstone, 1805.* Edited with notes by L. J. Burgess, Ottawa, Govt. Printing Bureau, 1910.

(10) *A Topographical Description of the State of Ohio, Indiana Territory and Louisiana—By a late officer in the U. S. Army.* (Col. Jervis Cutler). Charles Williams, Boston, 1812. (hereafter called *Charles Le Raye Journal*). See also, South Dakota Historical Society *Collections.* Vol. IV, pp. 150–180.

(11) *Charles Le Raye Journal.* p. 191.

(12) Robert Lowie. *The Crow Indian.* Frank B. Linderman. *American, the Life Story of a Great Indian. Plenty Coups, Chief of the Crows.* New York, 1930.

(13) W. A. Allen. *The Sheep Eaters,* New York, 1913. Lt. Gen. P. H. Sheridan. *Report of an Exploration of Parts of Wyoming, Idaho and Montana in August and September 1882.* Washington, Government Printing Office, 1882. pp. 11–12.

(14) *The Personal Narrative of James O. Pattie of Kentucky.* Edited by Timothy Flint. Cincinnati. 1833. *Pattie's Personal Narrative 1824–1830.* Edited by Reuben Gold Thwaites, 1905. *The Personal Narrative of James O. Pattie.* Edited by M. M. Quaife, 1930. *James's Three Years Among the Indians.*

(15) George E. Hyde, *Red Cloud's Folk: A History of the Oglala Sioux Indians.* Norman, Oklahoma, 1937. p. 27, note 4.

(16) The comments on the beaver are based upon *The American Beaver and His Works,* by Lewis H. Morgan, Philadelphia, 1868; *The Trapper's Guide,* by S. Newhouse, New York, 1869; various Encyclopedias, and the personal observations of a not too avid trout fisherman.

(17) Ruxton, George Frederick, *Life in the Far West.* Reprinted, *In the Old West.* Edited by Horace Kephart. New York, 1915, p. 298.

(18) Bancroft, Hubert Howe, *History of Nevada, Colorado, and Wyoming.* p. 675.

(19) Historical Sketch of Upper Clark's Fork of the Yellowstone and Its Tributaries Within the State of Wyoming. *Wyoming Annals,* July 1940, p. 221. Also a personal letter to the author from J. K. Rollinson.

(20) *Wisconsin Collections.* Vol. V. Part II. pp. 315–317.

CHAPTER FOUR

(1) Missouri Historical Society *Collections.* 1911. Vol. III. Number 8 (hereafter called *Missouri Collections*) "Manuel Lisa," By Walter B. Douglas, p. 251.

(2) Ibid. Numbers 3 and 4. pp. 238–268, and 367–406.

(3) Ibid. Number 3. p. 246.

(4) *The Expeditions of Zebulon Montgomery Pike*. Edited by Elliott Coues. New York. 1895. (hereafter called *Coues' Pike*)

(5) Judge Walter B. Douglas listed the definitely known members in his article on Manuel Lisa, *Missouri Collections*, Vol. III, p. 250, as: Manuel Lisa, George Drouillard, Benito Vasquez, Etienne Brant, Joseph Brazeau, Francois Bouché, Jean Baptiste Bouché, Francois Solas dit Sansquartier, ——— Cousin, Jean Baptiste Champlain, fils, Pierre Deseve, Antoine Dubrevil, Joseph Laderoute dit Casse, Jean La Fargue, Jean Baptiste Lusignan, John McPherson, Jean Baptiste Mayette, Calliste Montardy, Jean Muriz, Daniel Murray, ——— Poitras, John Potts, Charles Sanquinet, fils, Peter Wiser and Antoine Bissonet. Judge Douglas was of the opinion that Amos Richardson may also have been a member.

(6) Brackenridge, H. M. *Views of Louisiana Together with a Journal of a Voyage up the Missouri River in 1811*. Pittsburgh, 1814. p. 90. (hereafter called *Brackenridge's Views of Louisiana*). *Missouri Collections*. Vol. III, p. 254, note 39.

(7) Original document in the collection of the Missouri Historical Society, Jefferson Memorial Building, St. Louis.

(8) Trial records in possession of the Missouri Historical Society.

(9) *Missouri Collections*. Vol. III, p. 251.

(10) Ibid. p. 251.

(11) *Brackenridge's Views of Louisiana*, p. 90.

(12) Masson, L. R., *Les Bourgeois de la Compagnie du Nord-ouest*; and *Manuscript Journals of Alexander Henry and of David Thompson*. Edited by Elliott Coues. (hereafter called *Coues' Manuscript Journals of Alexander Henry*.) New York, 1897.

(13) *Brackenridge's Views of Louisiana*, p. 91.

(14) Ibid. p. 91.

(15) Ibid. p. 91.

(16) The map is in the possession of the Library of Congress, Washington, D. C.

(17) *Missouri Collections*. Vol. III, p. 255.

(18) *Sources of the History of Oregon*. Vol. I. "The Correspondence & Journals of Captain Nathaniel J. Wyeth," 1831–6. Edited by F. G. Young, 1899, p. 210.

(19) Holmes, Capt. R. "The Five Scalps." *Weekly Reveille*. St. Louis. July 17, 1848.

CHAPTER FIVE

(1) *Brackenridge's Views of Louisiana*. p. 91.

(2) *Allen's Lewis & Clark*. Frontispiece.

(3) *Original Journals*. Vol. V. See Charts.

(4) Letter in possession of American Philosophical Society, Philadelphia, Pa., from Thomas Jefferson, Poplar Forest, to Abbe M. Correa de Serra, dated April 26, 1816.

(5) Letter in Hassler papers, New York Public Library, New York City, from John Vaughan, Philadelphia, to Dr. F. R. Hassler, Schenectady, dated October 13, 1810, sending a copy of letter addressed to Vaughan from Nicholas Biddle.

(6) Letter in Hassler papers, New York Public Library.

(7) *Coues' Lewis & Clark*, pp. lxxxvi–lxxxvii.

(8) This map is owned by the Missouri Historical Society, St. Louis, Mo.

(9) *Brackenridge's Views of Louisiana*, p. 91.

(10) The Journal of Francois Antoine Larocque. In *Sources of Northwest History*, No. 20. p. 21.

(11) Due to the kindness of Lt. Col. and Mrs. George T. Beck we have a summary of the controversy that has caused considerable discussion in Cody, Wyoming, as to whether the name of the mountain is spelled Heart or Hart. The adherents to the latter method of spelling are also divided into two camps. One party, led by the old timers, insist the mountain was named for a fur trapper called Hart, and the other group main-

tain that the name was that of one of the army officers who took part in the pursuit of Chief Joseph of the Nez Percé tribe.

The advocates of the Heart spelling, however, point to the name of the misplaced mountain of that name on the 1814 printed map. They also cite several other sources to the effect that the Indian name translated into English for the mountain is Heart. The most interesting example is found in *Finn Burnett, Frontiersman,* by Robert Beebe David, Glendale, California, 1937, p. 356, which reads as follows: "It is a high mountain. It is so high that it is called Givina-Cari-To-Yo-Be, which in the Indian tongue means Mountain-where-the-birds-stay. The white man's name for that peak was Heart Mountain." Burnett was quoting the Shoshone who had guided him on a trip from Fort Washakie to Bozeman, Montana, and return in 1878, when settlers were just beginning to locate in the Big Horn Basin.

Indian names with few exceptions have survived to the present day in the Big Horn Basin. This fact plus Burnett's testimony and the circumstance of Clark's usually having spelled the name Heart on his maps seem to eliminate all reasonable doubts but that the correct spelling is Heart Mountain.

(12) *Professional Papers No. 53, U. S. Geological Survey: Geology and Water Resources of the Big Horn Basin, Wyoming.* Cassius A. Fisher. 1906. p. 61.

(13) Bancroft, Hubert Howe. *History of Nevada, Colorado and Wyoming.* San Francisco, 1890, p. 676, note 8.

(14) *Life, Letters and Travels of Father Pierre-Jean De Smet.* By H. M. Chittenden & A. T. Richardson. New York, 1905, Vol. II, p. 660.

(15) *Brackenridge's Views of Louisiana.* p. 67.

(16) Irving, Washington. *The Rocky Mountains.* Philadelphia, 1837, Vol. I. p. 223.

(17) Victor, Mrs. Frances Fuller. *The River of the West.* Hartford, 1870, pp. 75–79.

(18) Letter from Mr. J. K. Rollinson, to the author, dated Nov. 20, 1944,

reads in part: "In the years prior to the government Shoshone Reclamation Project . . . there was a spring of water highly impregnated with sulphur and magnesium located on the extreme north end of the ranch then known as the Buffalo Meadows, which lay at the junction of the Forks of the Stinking Water River. There were also a half-a-dozen little 'puffer' or semi geyser spouts . . . these small sulpho-sodium geysers which steamed up all the time and bubbled up mud and minerals. Then exactly at the very foot of Cedar Mountain close to these incipient geysers there was a forty foot cut bank or cave-in, and from the bottom of this came a considerable flow of asphaltum, which travelled by gravity about eighty feet before it disappeared for a few feet (about 30 feet) where it again appeared in one of the hot Sulpho-Magnesia Springs. While the temperature was (in my time) never hot enough to boil, still the gasses came up and gave the spring the bubbling appearance. . . . I suppose the temperature was about 90 degrees and with the foam and gas from the subterranial passage, it gave the complete effect of a boiling tar spring. This spring and all others on the side of Cedar Mountain were inundated by the impounding of the flood waters."

(19) Note on Clark's map drawn on the basis of Drouillard's information.

(20) Jones, William A. *Report Upon the Reconnaissance of North Western Wyoming Including Yellowstone National Park Made in Summer of 1873.* Washington: Government Printing Office, 1875, p. 295.

(21) Strahorn, Robert E. *The Hand-Book of Wyoming and Guide to the Black Hills and Big Horn Region—for the Citizen Emigrant and Tourist.* Cheyenne, 1877, pp. 10–11.

(22) *South Western Historical Quarterly.* Vol. XVII, (July) p. 64.

(23) Irving, Washington. *The Adventures of Captain Bonneville,* Philadelphia, 1837, p. 136.

(24) *Coues' Pike.* pp. 479, 481, 729.

(25) *Overland to the Pacific: Zebulon Pike's Arkansas Journal.* Edited by Stephen Harding Hart and Archer Butler Hulbert. Denver, 1932, p. 142.

(26) *Coues' Pike.* pp. 523–524.
(27) *Original Journals.* Vol. V. p. 320.
(28) *Nouvelles Annales des Voyages, de la Geographie et de l'Histoire.* par Mm. **J. B.** Eyrles et Malte-Brun. Paris, Libraire de Gide Fils, Tomes X et XII, 1821. The map is also reproduced in *The Discovery of the Oregon Trail,* edited by Philip Ashton Rollins, 1935, p. 270.
(29) *James's Three Years Among the Indians.* pp. 52–53.
(30) *Vinton's John Colter.* pp. 61–62.

CHAPTER SIX

(1) Documents in the Collection of the Missouri Historical Society.
(2) Manuel Lisa's appeal in the May term, 1811, of the judgment Bouché had previously obtained for $322.50. Lisa papers in the Missouri Historical Society.
(3) Holmes, Capt. R. "The Five Scalps," *Weekly Reveille,* St. Louis. July 17, 1848.
(4) Bonner, T. D. *The Life and Adventures of James P. Beckwourth.* New York, 1856. *James P. Beckwourth* by T. D. Bonner; Edited by Bernard De Voto. 1931.
(5) Receipt among Lisa papers owned by Missouri Historical Society.
(6) *James's Three Years Among the Indians,* pp. 52–53.
(7) United States Senate *Documents.* Vol. I. 16th Congress, First Session. p. 47.
(8) Bradbury, John. *Travels in the Interior of America.* London, 1817, (hereafter called *Bradbury's Travels*). pp. 18–21.
(9) United States Senate *Documents.* Vol. I. 16th Congress. First Session. p. 47.
(10) *James's Three Years Among the Indians.* pp. 58–62.
(11) Ibid. pp. 64–65.
(12) *The Manuscript Journals of Alexander Henry and of David Thompson.* Edited by Elliott Coues, New York, 1897. (hereafter called *Coues' Manuscript Journals of Alexander Henry.*) Vol. II. pp. 540–541.

CHAPTER SEVEN

(1) *Brackenridge's Views of Louisiana.* p. 67.
(2) *James's Three Years Among the Indians.* pp. 34, 35.
(3) Letter from Lisa to General Clark, from the Osage River, dated June 24, 1809, quoted in *James's Three Years Among the Indians.* p. 16, footnote 8.
(4) *Bradbury's Travels.* p. 143. Bradbury saw the fort in 1811.
(5) *James's Three Years Among the Indians.* pp. 34–35.
(6) Mumey, Nolie. *The Teton Mountains.* Denver, 1947. p. 51.
(7) *James's Three Years Among the Indians.* p. 35.
(8) *Coues' Manuscript Journals of Alexander Henry.* pp. 539–737, *passim.*
(9) *James's Three Years Among the Indians.* pp. 49–50.
(10) Ibid. pp. 63–64.
(11) Ibid. p. 66.
(12) Ibid. pp. 66–72.
(13) Ibid. pp. 72–78.
(14) *Coues' Manuscript Journals of Alexander Henry.* pp. 734–6.
(15) *James's Three Years Among the Indians.* pp. 65–6.
(16) Chittenden, Hiram Martin. *The American Fur Trade of the Far West.* Introduction and notes by Stallo Vinton. 1935. Vol. II. pp. 878–883.
(17) *James's Three Years Among the Indians.* p. 80.
(18) *Coues' Manuscript Journals of Alexander Henry.* p. 736.
(19) *James's Three Years Among the Indians.* p. 78. Cox, Ross. *Adventures on the Columbia.* Vol. I. p. 91. *Franchere's Narrative of a Voyage to the Northwest Coast, 1811–1814,* reprint of J. J. Huntington's English translation, New York, 1854, p. 271. *The Discovery of the Oregon Trail, Robert Stuart's Narratives.* Edited by Philip Ashton Rollins.
(20) *Bradbury's Travels.* p. 17.

CHAPTER EIGHT

(1) Missouri Historical Society, Jefferson Memorial Building, St. Louis. Newspaper file.

(2) Missouri Historical Society, Colter papers. Mumey, Dr. Nolie. *The Teton Mountains*, Denver, 1947, pp. 42 & 45 shows facsimiles of the notes and statement of J. Colter's indebtedness to Auguste Chouteau for $36.50, Dec. 31, 1809, in favor of J. Bte Repay including interest. The later indebtedness totalled $46.18.

(3) *Coues' Lewis & Clark*. pp. xliii-lvii.

(4) *James's Three Years Among the Indians*. p. 279.

(5) *Bradbury's Travels*. pp. 17–21.

(6) *James's Three Years Among the Indians*. pp. 92–93.

(7) *Vinton's John Colter*. p. 105.

(8) "Bits of Franklin County History, Giving the Life and Adventures of John Colter." Dr. E. B. Trail. *Washington Citizen*, March 16, 1928. Dr. Trail, a dentist, practising in Berger, Mo., spent years tracing down local legends about John Colter in Labadie Township, where descendants of Colter's son, Hiram, still live. In addition Dr. Trail located various court records including the Bill of Sale of Colter's personal effects, which points up the loss sustained by some similarly conscientious person not having done the same thing a century earlier.

(9) *Bradbury's Travels*. pp. 16–17.

(10) Trail's article.

(11) *Bradbury's Travels*. pp. 17–21.

(12) Ibid. pp. 77–8. Irving, Washington, *Astoria, or Anecdotes of an Enterprise beyond the Rocky Mountains*, Philadelphia, 1836.

(13) *Bradbury's Travels*. pp. 190–191.

(14) Mumey, Nolie. *The Teton Mountains*. p. 47.

(15) James's *Three Years Among the Indians*. p. 66. Trail's article. Mumey, Nolie. *The Teton Mountains*. p. 54. Voucher 5 refers to an amicable settlement of John Colter's debt of $22.50, through the administrator of his estate Don Richardson due to W. V. Strewe & Co. The judgement was confessed on November 22, 1813, and the interest amounted to $2.81¼ by the time the obligation was paid, Dec. 16, 1814. Thus Colter must have died on or before Nov. 22, 1813.

(16) Trail's article.

(17) Extract of sale bill dated December 10, 1813, made from records of the Probate Court, City of St. Louis, originally located by Dr. Trail. The figures quoted are precisely as quoted by the Probate Court. The careful reader will note that the totals are incorrect.

Bibliography

Allen, W. A. *The Sheep Eaters*. New York, 1913.

Bancroft, Hubert Howe. *History of Nevada, Colorado and Wyoming*. San Francisco, 1890.

Bonner, T. D. *The Life and Adventures of James P. Beckwourth*. New York, 1856.

Brackenridge, H. M. *Views of Louisiana Together with a Journal of a Voyage up the Missouri River in 1811*. Pittsburgh, 1814.

Bradbury, John. *Travels in the Interior of America in the Years 1809, 1810, and 1811*. Liverpool, 1817.

Burgess, L. J. *Journal of Larocque: From the Assiniboine to the Yellowstone 1805*. Ottawa, 1910.

Chittenden, Hiram Martin. *The American Fur Trade of the Far West*. Edited by Stallo Vinton. New York, 1935.

Chittenden, H. M. & Richardson, A. T., *Life, Letters and Travels of Father Pierre-Jean De Smet*. New York, 1905.

Chittenden, Hiram Martin. *The Yellowstone National Park*. Fourth Edition. Cincinnati, 1903.

Coues, Elliott. *History of the Expedition under the Command of Lewis and Clark*. New York, 1893.

Coues, Elliott. *The Expeditions of Zebulon Montgomery Pike*. New York, 1895.

Coues, Elliott. *The Manuscript Journals of Alexander Henry and of David Thompson*. New York, 1897.

Coutant, C. G. *The History of Wyoming*. Laramie, Wyoming, 1899.

Cutler, Col. Jervis. *Topographical Description of the State of Ohio, Indiana Territory and Louisiana*. Boston, 1812.

David, Robert Beebe. *Finn Burnett Frontiersman*. Glendale, California, 1937.

Eyries, J. B. et Malte-Brun. *Nouvelles Annales des Voyages, de la Geographie et de l'Histoire*. Paris, 1821.

Fisher, Cassius. *Professional Papers No. 53. U. S. Geological Survey*. 1906.

Flint, Timothy. *The Personal Narrative of James O. Pattie of Kentucky*. Cincinnati, 1833.

Gass, Sergeant Patrick. *A Journal of the Voyages and Travels of a Corps of Discovery*. Pittsburgh, 1807.

Hart, Stephen Harding & Hulbert, Archer Butler. *Zebulon Pike's Arkansas Journal*. Denver, 1932.

Hebard, Grace Raymond. *Sacajawea*. Glendale, California, 1933.

Hazlitt, Ruth. The Journal of Francois Antoine Larocque from the Assiniboine River to the Yellowstone, 1805, in *Sources of Northwest History No. 20*. State University of Montana.

Hodge, Frederick Webb. *Handbook of American Indians*. Washington, 1907.

Hyde, George E. *Red Cloud's Folk—A History of the Oglala Sioux Indians*. Norman, 1937.

Irving, Washington. *Astoria, or Anecdotes of an Enterprise beyond the Rocky Mountains*. 2 Vols. Philadelphia, 1836.

Irving, Washington. *The Adventures of Captain Bonneville*. Philadelphia, 1837.

Irving, Washington. *The Rocky Mountains*. Philadelphia, 1836.

James, Thomas. *Three Years Among the Indians and Mexicans*. St. Louis, 1916.

Jones, William A. *Report upon the Reconnaissance of Northwestern Wyoming*. Washington, 1875.

Kennerly, William Clark. *Persimmon Hill*. As told to Elizabeth Russell. Norman, 1948.

Linderman, Frank B. *American. The Life Story of a Great Indian*. New York, 1930.

Lindsay, Charles. *The Big Horn Basin*. Lincoln, Nebraska, 1930.

Lowie, Robert. *The Crow Indian*.

Masson, L. R. *Les Bourgeois de la Compagnie du Nord-ouest*. 2 Vols. Quebec, 1889–1890.

Missouri Historical Society Collections. Vol. III. 1911.

Morgan, Lewis H. *The American Beaver*. Philadelphia, 1868.

Mumey, Dr. Nolie. *The Teton Mountains*. Denver, 1947.

Pike, Major Z. M. *An Account of Expeditions to the Sources of the Mississippi and through the Western Parts of Louisiana*. Philadelphia, 1810.

Quaife, M. M. *The Personal Narrative of James O. Pattie*. Chicago, 1930.

Raynolds, Bvt. Brig. Gen. W. F. *Report on the Exploration of the Yellowstone River*. Washington, 1868.

Rollins, Philip Ashton. *The Discovery of the Oregon Trail*. New York, 1935.

Ruxton, George Frederick. *In the Old West*. Edited by Horace Kephart. New York, 1915.

Sheridan, Lt. Gen. P. W. *Report of an Exploration of Parts of Wyoming, Idaho and Montana in August and September 1882*. Washington, 1882.

South Dakota Historical Society Collections. Vol. IV. Edited by Doane Robinson.

South Western Historical Quarterly. Vol. XVII.

Strahorn, Robert E. *The Hand-book of Wyoming and Guide to the Black Hills and Big Horn Region*. Cheyenne, 1877.

Thwaites, Reuben Gold. *Journal of a Voyage up the River Missouri*, by H. M. Brackenridge. Cleveland, 1904.

Thwaites, Reuben Gold. *Original Journals of the Lewis and Clark Expedition 1804–1806*. New York, 1904.

Thwaites, Reuben Gold. *Pattie's Personal Narrative 1824–1830*. Cleveland, 1905.

Victor, Mrs. Frances Fuller. *The River of the West*. Hartford, 1870.

Vinton, Stallo. *John Colter*. New York, 1926.

Wheeler, Olin D. *The Trail of Lewis and Clark*. New York, 1904.

Wisconsin State Historical Society Collections. Vols. XXII & V.

Wyoming Annals. Laramie, Wyoming.

Young, F. G. *Sources of the History of Oregon*. Vol. I. The Correspondence & Journals of Captain Nathaniel J. Wyeth. 1899.

Index

Absaroka (Indians), *see* Crow
Absaroka Mountains, 54, 85, 92, 135
American Philosophical Society, 79, 81
Arapahoe, 21, 89
Arapooish, 100
Arikara, 65–67, 137, 139
Arkansas River, 60, 101
Assiniboine (Indians), 68
Assiniboine River, 41, 67
Astor, John Jacob, 159
Astorians, 103, 159–161
Atkinson, Col. Henry, 123
Ayers, ——, 144–145

Bancroft, Hubert Howe, 52
Bannock (Indians), 71, 104, 112
Bannock Trail, 112
Basil, Andy, 21
Basin, Wyoming, 21
Beard, William, 105–106
Beaver (habits of), 44–51
Beckworth, Jim, 119
Biddle Lake, 103, 108
Biddle, Nicholas, 36–37, 60, 78–79
Biddle, Major Thomas, 123, 127
Big Boeuf Creek, 157
Big Horn Basin, 83–84, 87–91, 97
Big Horn Mountains, 41, 71, 80–81, 88–89, 97, 103, 135
Big Horn River, 41, 49, 69–71, 82–84, 89, 92–93, 99–100, 102, 113, 131, 147
Billings, Montana, 54
Bissonet, Antoine, 63
Bitter Root Mountains, 24, 29–30
Bitter Root River, 31
Blackfeet Indians, 32, 40, 68, 71, 103–104, 107, 112, 121, 135, 142, 148–150, 159
Bloods (Indians), 143
Blue Bead quarry, 86
Blue Bead River, 86

Boiling Spa, 90–91
Boiling Tar Spring, 95
Bolye, ——, 17
Boone, Daniel, 157, 159
Bouché, Jean Baptiste, 62–63, 65, 69–71, 116–118
Bozeman's Pass, 31, 121, 141
Brackenridge, H. M., 61, 66–68, 82, 92–93, 107, 124, 135, 160
Bradbury, John, 82, 124–127, 151, 155–156, 158–161
Brant, Etienne, 116
Bratten, ——, 29
Bridger Mountains, 83
Brown, ——, 140–141
Brown, James, 158
Bryant, William, 147
Buffalo Bill Dam, 88, 95
Burroughs, E. C., 10

Cameahwait, 23
Camp Missouri, 123
Campbell, Robert, 100
Canyon City, Colorado, 101
Cedar Mountain, 88–96
Charbonneau, Toussaint, 21, 38
Charette, Missouri, 157, 159
Cheek, James, 142, 145, 148
Chetish Mountains, 41
Cheyenne (Indians), 71, 89
Chouteau, Pierre, 60, 66–67, 136–137, 147
Clark, William, 12, 15, 21–24, 26, 30, 34–38, 69, 75, 79 (maps), 81–87, 97–100, 103, 105, 110, 113, 136, 154–156, 158, 161
Clark's Fork of the Yellowstone, 54, 112
Clark's River, 31
Clearwater, 25
Coalter, Micajah, 12

177

Rosebud River, 89
Royal Gorge of the Arkansas, 101
Rucker, ——, 145

Sacajawea, 21, 23, 26, 31, 38
Sage Creek, 89, 114
St. Charles, Missouri, 18, 63
St. Louis, Missouri, 16–17, 38, 61, 152
St. Louis Missouri Fur Trading Company, 136–138, 155
St. Mary's River, 31
Salmon River, 23
Salt Cave, 97
Salt Fork, 88, 97–98
Santa Fe, New Mexico, 61, 98, 102
Saskatchewan River, 133, 140, 145
Saugrain, Dr., 17
Serra, Abbé Correa da, 76
Shannon, George, 18, 19, 26
Sheep Eater (Indians), 43, 109
Shehaka, 67, 137
Shell Creek Canyon, 84
Shields, John, 16, 17, 20
Shoshone Dam, 88, 95
Shoshone (Indians), 21, 23, 43, 71, 96, 104, 109, 112, 140–141, 149
Shoshone Lake, 107
Shoshone River, 83, 87–93
Sioux, Bois Brulé, 42
Sioux, Oglala, 71, 89
Sioux, Teton, 20, 33, 64, 137
Slave (Indians), 133
Snake River, 25, 103, 105, 107, 150
Soda Butte Creek, 112–113
South Fork, Stinking Water, 96–98, 108
South Pass, 104
Spanish Settlements, 97, 105
Staunton, Virginia, 12–13
Stinking Water River, 83, 87–97, 108, 114, 135
Stuart, Robert, 104
Stuart's Draft, 12
Sullens' Spring, 157–158, 163

Sullens, John, 157, 159
Sunlight Basin, 54, 81, 85–88, 113

Teton Basin, 105–107
Teton Mountains, 104–108
Teton Pass, 104–107
Tetonia, Wyoming, 106
Three Forks of the Missouri, 23, 31, 107, 121, 124, 143, 148
Togwotee Pass, 103
Tongue River, 41, 89
Tower Creek, 111
Trail, Dr. E. B., 172
Tulloch's Fork, 89
Tunnel Hill, 163
Twisted Hair, 29
Two Ocean Pass, 106–107

Valle, Francois, 144
Vasquez, Benito, 60, 68, 117
Vaughan, John, 79–80
Vinton, Stallo, 12

Wahclellah (Indians), 28
Wapiti Range, 81
Washakie, Chief, 21
Whitehouse, Joseph, 18
Wilkinson, Benjamin, 136
Wilkinson, General James, 61, 101
Willard, ——, 22, 26
Wind River, 97, 101, 103
Wind River Range, 102, 103
Wiser, Peter, 17, 59
Wolf Mountains, 41
Woody, Tazewell, 108
Wyeth, Nathaniel, 71, 73

Yellowstone Lake, 81, 109–110
Yellowstone Park, 88, 92, 107–112
Yellowstone River, 31, 33, 40–44, 49, 52, 68, 71, 82–84, 89, 92, 101, 110–112, 114, 118, 121, 140, 150
York, 21, 26